new edition

Living History 2

A Complete Course for Junior Certificate

M.E. Collins :: Gráinne Henry :: Stephen Tonge

THE EDUCATIONAL COMPANY OF IRELAND

Contents Part 3

Foreword

This volume of Living History covers the third year of the Junior Certificate history syllabus. The topics for this year are dealt with in a fresh and challenging way, using language that is carefully chosen to make the information and concepts accessible to students.

Interesting and colourful illustrations are included to help students understand the story that is unfolding in the text. Some of these are original sources; many others are specially prepared by our own artists and mapmakers. Detailed captions accompany these illustrations to help students extract the maximum information from them.

Questions, similar to those on the Junior Certificate papers, are inserted at regular intervals throughout the chapters. These are carefully designed to help the student extract relevant information from the text and to prepare for the examinations.

Within each section, there are also many questions based on sources, both written and visual. These allow students to practise the skills of the historian. Areas for further research are also suggested, and to facilitate this lists of relevant websites are included in each section. Finally, each section concludes with a short note on what students need to know from each section to answer questions on the Junior Certificate papers.

M.E. Collins
March 2004

Part 3

New Edition Living History

M.E. Collins :: Gráinne Henry :: Stephen Tonge

THE EDUCATIONAL COMPANY OF IRELAND

Section 1

International Relations

Introduction

There are four **topics** to the International Relations Section of the syllabus:

A: War and Peace in Europe, 1920–45
B: The Rise of the Superpowers
C: Moves to European Unity
D: India – A Study in Asian Nationalism

If you are doing Higher Level, you must study A **and one of** B or C or D (i.e. two topics).
If you are doing Ordinary Level, you must study A **or** B **or** C **or** D (i.e. one topic).

Topic 1A

War and Peace in Europe, 1920–45

Chapter 1 The Consequences of World War I

The Great War

When the Napoleonic wars ended in 1815 (twenty years after the French Revolution), Europe settled down and remained fairly peaceful over the next hundred years. However, this was to change dramatically in August 1914, when World War I, the bloodiest war Europe had seen yet, broke out. The six biggest countries in Europe grouped themselves into two opposing factions:

The Allies	The Central Powers
■ Britain	■ Germany
■ France	■ Austria-Hungary
■ Russia	■ Turkish (Ottoman) Empire
■ Italy (joined in 1915)	
■ The US (joined in 1917)	

Millions of men fought in trenches like these in the First World War. Conditions for the soldiers were very bad. In winter the trenches were often flooded and there were rats everywhere. The land between enemy trenches was known as 'no man's land'. The soldiers suffered dreadful casualties as they ran through 'no man's land' to attack enemy trenches.

When the war first started, people thought it would be over by Christmas. However, the Great War, as it came to be called, lasted over four years. The fighting was constant and the loss of human life was huge. Russia suffered terrible casualties and food shortages, and surrendered to Germany in early 1918. In 1917 the US had joined with the Allies, and this gave them the advantage they needed to defeat the Central Powers. World War I finally ended on 11 November 1918.

Over eight million men were dead and millions more were wounded. The impact of this war was felt by everyone in Europe, and it left a legacy of deep bitterness and resentment between opposing countries.

A changed Europe

When the war ended, Europe was forever changed. Many of the old monarchies no longer existed:

- The German Emperor William II was forced to give up his throne and flee to Holland. Germany now became a republic.
- The Austrian Empire collapsed and several new countries appeared in its place.
- Emperor Nicholas II was overthrown in Russia in 1917. Later that year the communists seized power.

The 'Big Three' in Paris in 1919. The British prime minister David Lloyd George is on the left. In the centre is the French prime minister Georges Clemenceau, and on the right is the American president Woodrow Wilson. Wilson was the first serving US president to visit Europe.

The Allies hold a peace conference

Early in 1919, the victorious Allied leaders met in Paris to work out a plan for peace. The war had caused great suffering to people in Europe, and the Allied leaders hoped to prevent another one like it. They wanted to draw up a peace treaty that would ensure peace forever.

However, the defeated Central Powers were not included in the discussions. They were forced to accept the terms imposed on them by the Allied countries. This proved to be the greatest weakness of the peace treaty and created resentments that eventually led to World War II twenty years later.

The Treaty of Versailles

Each of the Allied leaders had a different view as to how Germany should be treated. President Woodrow Wilson believed that in order to ensure lasting peace, the Germans should not be treated too harshly. However, Britain and France had suffered terrible losses as a result of the war, and the people of these countries put pressure on their leaders to punish the Germans.

The Allied leaders drew up the Treaty of Versailles. Under it:

- Germany lost land to France, Poland, Denmark and Belgium (see map opposite). In all, Germany lost one-eighth of its territory and 10 per cent of its population.
- Germany's army was restricted in size to 100,000 men. It was not allowed to possess an air force, tanks or submarines. The navy was limited to only a few battleships.

The Treaty of Versailles forced Germany to disarm. This photograph shows German tanks being smashed as part of these terms.

In Russia, the Emperor was called the **Tsar**. In Germany and Austria, the Emperor was called the **Kaiser**.

Germany was not allowed to place troops in an area of Germany bordering France called the Rhineland (see map).

- The Allies blamed Germany for starting the war. Article 231 of the Treaty, known as the 'war guilt clause', stated:

  'The Allied…Governments affirm and Germany accepts the responsibility of Germany and her allies for causing all the loss and damage which the Allied…Governments… have been subjected to as a consequence of the war imposed upon them by the aggression of Germany and her allies.'

- Because of this the Germans were to pay **reparations** (compensation) for the damage caused by the war. The bill for reparations was £6.6 billion. (Today that would be about €1,200 billion.)

North Sea
DENMARK
Baltic Sea
EAST PRUSSIA
to Poland
POLAND
NETHERLANDS
GERMANY
to Poland
BELGIUM
to Belgium
RHINELAND
LUX.
CZECHOSLOVAKIA
to France
FRANCE
AUSTRIA
SWITZERLAND

Land lost by Germany
Demilitarised zone / Rhineland
Under League of Nations control

Land lost by Germany under the Treaty of Versailles

The German reaction to the Treaty

- The German people greatly disliked the Treaty of Versailles.
- They felt the 'guilt clause' was unfair, as they did not believe that they had started the war.
- They resented that land had been taken from Germany.
- Trying to pay the huge bill for reparations badly damaged their economy.

This German cartoon shows what Germans thought of the Treaty. **Who do you think the three men in black are? Who do you think the other man represents? Explain the point the cartoonist is making.**

This hatred of the Treaty of Versailles was later used by Adolf Hitler as a way to gain support in Germany for his policies. Hitler used his power to begin World War II in 1939.

Why Italy was dissatisfied

Although Italy was one of the victorious Allied countries, the Italians were not satisfied with the outcome of the peace conference. In 1915 they had entered the war on the side of Britain and France, who had promised them territory in the Austrian Empire.

But the Allies went back on these promises. They felt that it was unfair to give Italy land in places where most people were not Italians. The Italian leaders stormed out and Italians were very resentful. An Italian leader, Benito Mussolini, later used this resentment to gain support.

Woodrow Wilson's plan for a League of Nations

To prevent another war, the American president Woodrow Wilson proposed setting up an international organisation. He called it the **League of Nations**. Wilson hoped it would:

- act as a neutral place where countries could discuss their quarrels without going to war
- protect smaller, weaker countries from attack by bigger neighbours. This was known as 'collective security', i.e. all the members of the League would act together to protect any member that was the victim of an aggressive attack.

Because the other countries at the peace conference had borrowed money from America to pay for the war, they let Wilson have his way and agreed to set up a League of Nations.

The failure of the League of Nations

Unfortunately, the League did not succeed in the way Wilson had hoped. Some reasons for this failure included:

- **No America:** Although the League was Wilson's idea, most Americans did not want to be involved in European quarrels. (This was known as '**isolationism**'.) As a result, Wilson's party lost the 1920 election and America stayed out of the League.
- **No Germany or Russia:** Germany and Russia were not invited to join the League when it began. They joined later, but always regarded it as a League of their enemies.
- **No army:** The League had no army of its own to keep the peace. That meant it had to rely on the big countries like Britain and France to take action. But they were only interested in their own problems and ignored the League when it suited them.

Questions

1. Describe how World War I changed (a) Germany and (b) Russia.
2. Name the three most important leaders at the peace conference in Paris and say which country each man represented.
3. Mention two decisions reached about Germany at the peace conference.
4. Give two reasons why the Germans were very unhappy with the Treaty of Versailles.
5. What had Wilson hoped the League of Nations would achieve?
6. Give two reasons why the League of Nations was a failure.

Communism in Russia

Look

In 1917 Russia was using a different calendar to the rest of Europe. As a result, Russia was 13 days behind the West. That is why the 'February Revolution' actually took place in March and the 'October Revolution' took place in November!

The February Revolution

Up to 1917, **Tsar Nicholas II** ruled Russia. He gave the Russian people little say in how their country was governed. In 1914 the Tsar joined Britain and France in the war against Germany. But his government was very inefficient. Russian soldiers were short of guns and ammunition and millions of them died. At home, people went hungry because the government could not organise supplies of food.

People blamed the Tsar for their suffering. In February 1917, they rose against him and he was forced to give up his throne. The monarchy was replaced by a **Provisional Government** and Russia became a republic.

Lenin leads the October Revolution

The Provisional Government made a disastrous mistake by continuing the war. Food remained scarce and the new government was soon very unpopular.

A small political party called the **Bolsheviks** began to gain support. Led by **Vladimir Lenin**, they promised to end the war and restore food supplies. They believed in the communist ideas of Karl Marx, who wanted a society where the wealth of the country was shared equally among the citizens. There would be no rich and poor. Many Russian workers began to support the Bolsheviks.

In October 1917 the Bolsheviks overthrew the Provisional Government and renamed themselves the **Communist Party**. This event became known as the **October Revolution**. Lenin took Russia out of the war in early 1918.

Vladimir Lenin (1870–1924) speaking to a crowd in Moscow. In October 1917 he took power in Russia. **What kind of state did he set up?**

The policies of the communists

When Lenin and his followers came to power, they began to set up the world's first communist state. All wealth was to be shared equally by the people, so the government took over all banks, railways, shops, houses and all private property. All of these now belonged to the state.

The communists announced that Russia was an atheistic state (i.e. they thought there was no God). They persecuted Christians, Muslims and Jews who believed in God. The communists claimed that councils of workers called 'soviets' ruled Russia. They renamed Russia 'The Union of Soviet Socialist Republics' ('Soviet Union' or 'USSR' for short). In reality, however, the Communist Party controlled the soviets and workers had no say in the running of the country.

Lenin's party did not believe in democracy – only one party, the Communist Party, was allowed. People were not allowed to criticise the government, and the secret police spied on everyone. People who disagreed with the communists were arrested. Hundreds of thousands were executed. But many Russians supported Lenin because they hoped the communists would make life better for the ordinary people, who had been very poor under the Tsars.

Josef Stalin (1879–1953) was from Georgia in the south of the USSR. He was appointed General Secretary of the Communist Party in 1922. After Lenin's death, he became the ruler of Russia.

Stalin modernises the Soviet Union

Lenin died in 1924 and **Josef Stalin** became the dictator of the Soviet Union. He wanted to make it a modern industrial country. Look at the box below to see the main decisions that he took:

Agriculture

Farms were taken from the peasants and joined together into huge state-owned **collective farms**. Stalin believed this would make Soviet farming more efficient.

Industry

Stalin industrialised the Soviet Union through a number of **Five-Year Plans**. These set targets that industry had to meet after five years. The first plan began in 1928. In ten years, the plans dramatically changed Soviet industry, as these figures show:

Production in millions of tonnes

	1928	1932	1937
Coal	36.1	65.6	138.6
Oil	11.9	22.7	29.1
Steel	4.1	6.0	18.1

Modernisation but at a terrible price

Stalin did modernise the Soviet Union but at a terrible human cost.

- Workers lived in fear of not reaching the targets set for them by the government. Those who failed to reach their targets were jailed or fined, and thousands died from overwork.
- Wealthy peasants called **kulaks** opposed Stalin's policies. They were rounded up, shot or sent to labour camps to work as slaves.
- In the Ukraine, Stalin deliberately caused a famine because people there opposed his policies. Millions starved to death.
- In the 1930s, the secret police, the **NKVD,** arrested anyone who criticised Stalin's policies. They were executed or sent to slave labour camps called **gulags**. In these camps millions of people died from starvation, disease, cold or overwork.

Look

Historians differ about how many deaths Stalin caused in the USSR. Some think it was ten million. Others claim it was up to twenty million.

Communism spreads across Europe

Today we know about the misery that Lenin's and Stalin's harsh policies caused to millions of Russians. But in the 1920s and 1930s, these facts were hidden from most people. All they heard was the propaganda coming from the Communist Party, which said that in the Soviet Union there were good working conditions with free health and education services for all workers.

This impressed many poor people around Europe. After World War I unemployment was high, workers lived in squalid slums and were often hungry. They thought life might be better under a communist government. They joined their local communist parties, which grew quickly after Lenin took power.

Communists around Europe wanted to copy Lenin. They plotted to overthrow their own governments and replace them with Soviet-style communism. When World War I ended, communists unsuccessfully tried to seize power in Germany and Hungary. There were communists-led strikes and riots in Britain, France and Italy.

A Soviet propaganda poster. What image off life in the Soviet Union did it want to portray?

Fear of communism and distrust of democracy

Communism terrified many people.

- Businessmen feared that they would lose their factories and wealth.
- Farmers worried that they would lose their land.
- Christians feared they would be persecuted.
- Some were shocked at the undemocratic and brutal nature of communism.

Many of these people also distrusted democracy. They did not think democratic governments would be able to stop a communist takeover. They began to feel that only a strong leader could prevent it. This opinion was especially strong in Italy and Germany.

Fascism – a new political idea

The fear of communism led to the growth of a new political idea called **fascism**. It began in Italy. Here are some of the characteristics of fascism:

Anti-communist	Anti-democratic	Nationalist	Racist
Fascists promised to protect property owners and businessmen from a communist takeover. This appealed to people in countries like Italy and Germany where the Communist Party was strong.	Fascists warned that in a democracy, it was possible for communists to win an election. A strong ruler was needed to prevent this from happening.	Fascists claimed that they would make their country strong and powerful. In both Germany and Italy they built strong armies and planned wars.	Fascists encouraged people to believe that their race was superior to others. This led to harsh treatment of minority groups. In Germany, Hitler hated Jewish people and this was to lead to terrible persecution of Jews.

Questions

1. Why was the Tsar overthrown in February 1917?
2. Who seized power in Russia in the October Revolution of 1917?
3. Describe two policies introduced by Lenin and the communists.
4. How did Stalin modernise Russia?
5. How did Stalin treat the people who opposed him?
6. Why was communism popular in Europe in the 1920s and 1930s?
7. What kind of people were frightened of communism? Explain why.
8. List and explain two characteristics of fascism.

Review the chapter

1 **Source Question**

Study the two extracts below and answer the questions that follow.

A The French prime minister, Georges Clemenceau, gives the French position towards Germany at the Paris peace conference:

> *'I said yesterday that I entirely agreed with Mr David Lloyd George and President Wilson on how Germany should be treated; we cannot take unfair advantage of our victory; we must deal fairly with peoples for fear of provoking a surge of national feeling...President Wilson warns us against giving the Germans a sense of injustice. Agreed, but what we regard as just here in this room will not necessarily be accepted as such by the Germans...Every effort must be made to be just towards the Germans; but when it comes to persuading them that we are just to them, that is another matter. We can, I believe, save the world from German aggression; but the German spirit is not going to change so fast.'*

B Adolf Hitler, later leader of Germany and instigator of World War II, on the Versailles Treaty:

> *'Peace treaties whose demands are a scourge to nations often strike the first roll of drums for the uprising to come…We had to form a front against this treaty, so that later, when the harsh reality of this treacherous treaty would be revealed in its naked hate, the recollection of our attitude at that time would win us confidence.'*

(i) Name the two leaders that Clemenceau 'entirely agreed with'.
(ii) Why did Clemenceau wish to 'deal fairly' with the Germans?
(iii) What does he think the Germans might not agree with?
(iv) Did Hitler like the Treaty? Pick out the words in Extract B that support your answer.
(v) From Extract B, what advantage did Hitler hope to gain as an enemy of the Treaty?
(vi) From your study of history, give two reasons why the Germans were unhappy with the Treaty of Versailles. *(Based on the Junior Certificate, 1998)*

2 Picture Source

Study the picture and answer the following questions:

(i) Who is sitting in the chair?
(ii) This cartoon is very critical of him. Do you agree? Give two pieces of evidence from the picture to support your answer.
(iii) Do you think this cartoon is making a fair point? Explain your answer.

3 Write a paragraph on two of the following:

- The main terms of the Versailles Treaty
- Why the Treaty was unpopular in Germany
- The weaknesses of the League of Nations
- How the communists ruled Russia between 1917 and 1939
- What the fascists believed

4 Research Topic

Find out more about one of the following:

- The main battles during World War I
- Conditions for the ordinary troops in the trenches
- The overthrow of the Tsar in 1917
- Vladimir Lenin

Chapter 2 Italy Under Fascism, 1922–43

Benito Mussolini (1883–1945) was a very intelligent but arrogant man. He made himself the dictator of Italy and ruled it for twenty-three years. His ambition was to make Italy a great power. This led to a disastrous alliance with Germany.

Benito Mussolini, the founder of fascism

Italy was the first country where a fascist dictator came to power. He was **Benito Mussolini**. He was born in 1883. His father was a blacksmith and his mother was a teacher. He became a well-known journalist and at first was a follower of socialism. He was appointed editor of the socialist newspaper *Avanti*. This was a very popular newspaper in Italy.

Mussolini joined the Italian army to fight for the Allies in World War I. He was injured in 1917 and left the army.

Difficult times after World War I

After the war, life was very difficult. Most Italians were disappointed by the amount of land that Italy received at the end of World War I. The economy was in trouble too. Prices rose quickly and there was a lot of unemployment. There were many strikes and riots.

Businessmen became worried as the Communist Party attracted many followers. They feared that a communist revolution like the one that had happened in Russia might happen in Italy.

The start of the Fascist Party

In 1919, Mussolini set up a new party called the **Fascio di Combattimento**. Like the communists, the fascists did not believe in democracy. Instead they believed there should be one ruling party. This was called a **dictatorship**, because all the power would be in the hands of the leader of the ruling party, the dictator. However, fascism differed from communism in that the fascists did not believe in confiscating people's businesses or land.

Mussolini's party promised to improve the economy, end strikes and fight the spread of communism. Mussolini also campaigned against the treatment that Italy had received in the Paris peace conference. His followers dressed in a uniform of black shirts and they became known as **Blackshirts** or **fascists**.

Because the fascists opposed communism, wealthy businessmen gave them money. Blackshirts attacked strikers, fought with communists and broke up their meetings. Between 1919 and 1922 street fights between communists and Blackshirts were common. Over 300 people were killed.

Although the fascists often started these fights, Mussolini used them to claim that the democratic governments were too weak to keep order. He argued that only a fascist government, which of course would be led by him, could restore order.

Mussolini and the 'March on Rome'

In October 1922, Mussolini declared that the fascists would march on Rome and seize power. The prime minister asked the king, **Victor Emmanuel III**, to use the army to stop the fascists. The king refused and the prime minister resigned in protest. The king then appointed Mussolini as prime minister. Mussolini never marched to Rome himself, he took the train!

A fascist propaganda poster showing the March on Rome. **What image of that event does it want to give? Do you think that it is a truthful image? Explain your answer.**

Mussolini becomes a dictator

Mussolini became prime minister in a democratic way, but once in power he began to destroy democracy and establish a dictatorship. He gave the Blackshirts jobs in the police. As a result, Mussolini's followers could attack their enemies and not worry about being arrested. A leading socialist, **Giacomo Matteotti**, protested. Soon after, fascists murdered him.

Mussolini first banned the Communist Party and then all of the other parties. By 1926 only the Fascist Party remained. Mussolini was now the dictator of Italy.

How the fascist dictatorship worked

Mussolini called himself **'Il Duce',** which means 'the leader'. He ruled through propaganda and fear.

- **Propaganda:** The fascists controlled newspapers, radio and films. Only comments and pictures favourable to Mussolini could appear. He used propaganda to tell the Italians that he was a superman who would lead them to greatness.

Two propaganda posters from fascist Italy. **What message did they give Italians about their leader and about life under fascism?**

- **Fear:** No one was allowed to criticise Mussolini. A secret police, the **OVRA,** kept an eye on everyone. They beat up people they suspected of being anti-fascist. Between 1927 and 1940, ten people were executed for opposing Mussolini. Four thousand of his political opponents were imprisoned.
- **Youth policy:** Mussolini wanted all young people to be fascists. Teachers had to take an oath of loyalty to the fascist government. Schools taught children to be loyal to Il Duce. From the age of eight, children had to belong to the **Balilla**. This was the fascist youth movement.

A young member of the Balilla, the Italian fascist youth organisation, receives his rifle as part of Mussolini's policy of militarising the nation. Mussolini looks on from the platform.

Questions

1 Give a short account of Mussolini's life to the end of World War I.
2 What problems did Italy face after World War I?
3 What was the name of the party that Mussolini founded?
4 What nickname did Mussolini's followers have and how did they get it?
5 Why were many businessmen prepared to support Mussolini's party?
6 How was Mussolini appointed prime minister?
7 How did Mussolini establish a dictatorship in Italy?
8 As dictator, what was Mussolini called?
9 Explain how Mussolini ruled Italy.
10 What was the Balilla?

Mussolini and the Catholic Church

Although Mussolini's government was brutal and dishonest, he was very popular at first. One of the reasons for this was that Mussolini improved relations between the Catholic Church and the Italian government.

Nearly all Italians were Catholics and the pope lived in Rome. But in the 1860s, the pope had quarrelled with the Italian government when it took over Church-owned property.

In 1929, Pope Pius XI and Mussolini settled the quarrel over land. Their agreement was called the **Lateran Treaty**. As a result of the Treaty:

Look

Mussolini destroyed the power of the Mafia in Italy. Many of the gangsters emigrated to the US.

- An independent Vatican State ruled by the pope was set up.
- Compensation was paid to the Church for the land it lost.
- Catholicism became the official religion of Italy.

This agreement brought Mussolini great praise internationally.

Mussolini signing the Lateran Treaty

Mussolini's foreign policy

Mussolini wished to make Italy great again like it had been at the time of the Roman Empire. He built up the Italian army.

In the 1920s and early 1930s, Mussolini supported the League of Nations and was friendly with Britain and France. When Hitler came to power in Germany, Mussolini at first joined Britain and France in opposing him. In 1934, he sent Italian troops to the Austrian border to stop Hitler invading that country.

Note

The League of Nations had no army of its own. The only way it could punish a country that broke its rules was to forbid the other members to trade with it. That was known as **'imposing sanctions'**.

The invasion of Abyssinia

But Mussolini still wanted to conquer an empire for Italy. In 1935, he got his chance. He ordered his army to invade **Abyssinia** (Ethiopia). This was an independent African country and a member of the League of Nations. The Italian army used poison gas and behaved with great brutality.

The Abyssinians appealed to the League of Nations for help. The League condemned the Italians and imposed sanctions on Italy. Britain and France reluctantly supported this decision but Hitler continued to trade with Mussolini.

This propaganda picture celebrates Hitler's visit to Italy and the alliance between the two fascist dictators. **What impression was it intended to make on the people who saw it?**

A disastrous mistake!

Mussolini was angered by the policy of Britain and France. He changed sides. In December 1936 he made an alliance with Hitler called the **Rome-Berlin Axis**. This alliance was further strengthened with **'The Pact of Steel'** in 1939. The alliance with Hitler was a serious error, which would lead to Mussolini's removal from power and his eventual execution.

Italy and World War II

In 1939, when World War II started, Italy stayed neutral. It was not ready for war. In 1940, just as the Germans defeated France, Mussolini joined in on Hitler's side.

The Italian armies were not very successful. In 1940 when they invaded Greece they were defeated and had to be rescued by German forces. In North Africa, the British army also defeated them and Hitler had to send his best general, **Rommel**, to help them.

Mussolini is removed from power

In 1943, the Allied armies (British and American) defeated the Germans and Italians in North Africa. In Italy, the alliance with Germany had never been popular, so when the Allies invaded Italy, the king sacked Mussolini. The new government surrendered to the Allies and declared war on Germany. Mussolini was arrested.

In a daring raid, the Germans rescued Mussolini. They made him ruler of German-controlled Northern Italy.

By April 1945 it was clear the Germans had lost. Mussolini attempted to flee to Switzerland but was captured by anti-fascist Italians. He was shot and his body was hung upside down in Milan. Mussolini's death marked the end of fascism in Italy.

Questions

1. Name the pope who signed the Lateran Treaty with Mussolini.
2. What was agreed under the Treaty?
3. What ancient empire did Mussolini admire and how did that influence him?
4. Name the country that Italy invaded in 1935.
5. How did Mussolini view Hitler when he first came to power?
6. Why did Mussolini change his policy and join with Hitler in 1936? Name the alliance they formed.
7. Briefly describe what happened to Mussolini during World War II.

Review the chapter

1. Read the following extract from a speech by Mussolini defending the Italian invasion of Abyssinia (Ethiopia) in 1935:

> *'It is not only an army that strives toward its objectives but a whole people of 44 million souls against whom an attempt is being made to accomplish the blackest of injustices; that of depriving us of some small place in the sun.*
>
> *When in 1915 Italy exposed itself to the risks of war and joined its destiny with that of the Allies, how much praise there was for our courage and how many promises were made! But after the common victory to which Italy had made the supreme contribution of 670,000 dead, 400,000 mutilated, and a million wounded, around the hateful peace table Italy received but a few crumbs from the rich colonial booty gathered by others…*
>
> *In the League of Nations there is talk of sanctions instead of recognition of our rights. Until there is proof to the contrary, I shall refuse to believe that the real and generous people of France can support sanctions against Italy…Similarly, I refuse to believe that the real people of Great Britain, who have never had disagreements with Italy, are prepared to run the risk of hurling Europe along the road to catastrophe for the sake of defending an African country universally branded as a country without the slightest shadow of civilisation.*
>
> *But let it be said once more and in the most categorical manner – and at this moment I make before you a sacred pledge – that we shall do all that is possible to prevent this conflict of a colonial character from assuming the nature of a European conflict.'*

(i) What in Mussolini's view was the 'blackest of injustices'?
(ii) How many Italians died in World War I? Did Mussolini feel Italy was well rewarded for that sacrifice?
(iii) What does Mussolini think is the attitude of the 'real... people of France... and Great Britain'?
(iv) What African country do you think Mussolini is referring to in the extract?
(v) What 'sacred pledge' does Mussolini make?
(vi) Give two examples of propaganda from this extract. Explain why you selected them.

2 Are the following statements true or false? If false, write down the correct statement.
(i) Italians were happy with the results of the Paris peace conference.
(ii) Many Italians were worried by the spread of communism.
(iii) Mussolini's followers wore red shirts.
(iv) Mussolini's followers never used violence when dealing with political opponents.
(v) As a result of the March on Rome, Mussolini was appointed prime minister of Italy.

3 Write a paragraph on two of the following:
(i) How Mussolini established a dictatorship in Italy.
(ii) How Mussolini became an ally of Hitler.
(iii) Italy and World War II.

Chapter 3

Germany and Hitler, 1919–39

Adolf Hitler became the dictator of Germany in 1933 and ruled it until 1945. He was responsible for the bloodiest war the world has ever seen and the deliberate destruction of a race of people, the Jews of Europe. In this chapter, we will see how he came to power.

The Weimar Republic

In November 1918, Germany surrendered to the Allies after four bloody years of war. The Emperor, **Kaiser William II**, fled to Holland, and Germany became a republic. The constitution for the new republic was drawn up in the town of **Weimar**. For that reason this period of German history is known as the **Weimar Republic**.

The Weimar Republic was very democratic. All men and women could vote for its parliament – **the Reichstag**. The Reichstag made the laws, approved taxes and elected the government. The people also elected the president, who stayed in office for seven years. If there was an emergency, he had the power to rule **by decree** (laws did not have to be approved by the Reichstag).

Many powerful groups in Germany did not like the new republic. They included businessmen, army officers and judges. They looked back to the good old days, when the Kaiser ruled and they had more power.

What Germans thought of the Treaty of Versailles

The Weimar Republic got off to a bad start when its leaders had to sign the Treaty of Versailles. Germans hated the Treaty because they thought it was so unfair to Germany. Some Germans believed that the politicians who signed it had betrayed the brave soldiers who had never been defeated. This is called the **'stab in the back' theory**. It was nonsense but many Germans believed it.

Problems in Germany after the war

The German economy was badly damaged by defeat in the war. Many people were out of work and they were hungry and cold. Some of them became communists. In 1919, there were several communist-led revolts around Germany, though none of them was successful. Riots between communists and their opponents were common.

This cartoon shows what Germans thought of the peace settlement in 1919. **Who are the three 'angels'? What are they standing on?**

In 1921, the Allies demanded that the Germans pay £6.6 billion in reparations. The Weimar government tried to pay but in 1923 this caused huge inflation. Prices went up very fast. Inflation destroyed the savings of many Germans. They blamed the Weimar government and this event seriously weakened German people's support for democracy.

Hitler with some of his comrades during World War I. He is on the right of the picture at the back. Although a brave soldier, he never rose above the rank of corporal.

Hitler's Early Years

During the crisis caused by the inflation, a little-known Austrian called Adolf Hitler came to prominence. He led a rebellion in Munich against the government. It failed and he was imprisoned.

Adolf Hitler was born on 20 April 1889 at **Braunau am Inn** in Austria. His father was a customs official. At eighteen, he went to Vienna to become an artist.

Before World War I, Vienna had a large Jewish population. Many Viennese were **anti-Semitic**. This means that they disliked Jewish people. Some historians believe that it was in Vienna that Hitler developed his own anti-Semitism.

Hitler welcomed the outbreak of war in 1914 and joined the German army. He was a courageous soldier and was wounded twice. He won the Iron Cross, First Class for bravery. It was very unusual for an ordinary soldier like Hitler to get this award. It was normally given to officers.

Like many other soldiers, Hitler was surprised when he heard that Germany had surrendered. He did not believe that the German army had been defeated. He thought that the army had been 'stabbed in the back' by democratic politicians. Along with most Germans, he strongly opposed the Treaty of Versailles.

Note

Anti-Semitism = Hating Jewish people simply because they belong to the Jewish race.

The creation of the Nazi party

When the war was over, Hitler returned to Munich where he remained in the army. He was sent to spy on a new political party called the **German Worker's Party**. He liked its ideas and joined it. Quickly he became the **führer**, or leader of the party. He changed its name to the **National Socialist German Worker's Party**. It was soon nicknamed the Nazi Party. The Nazis wanted to restore Germany to its former greatness, and overthrow the Treaty of Versailles. They believed that the Weimar government was too weak to achieve these aims.

Hitler discovered he had a gift for public speaking. At meetings he won supporters for the Nazis and their ideas.

Hitler's private armies: the SA and the SS

Like Mussolini, Hitler formed his own private army. Led by **Ernst Röhm**, it was called the SA. They were nicknamed the **Brownshirts** because of the colour of their uniforms. They were very violent. They protected Nazi meetings and fought with communists.

Hitler also set up a smaller group called the SS to act as his personal bodyguards. They were the elite of the party and **Heinrich Himmler** was their leader.

Note

SA stood for Sturm Abteilung or Stormtroopers. SS stood for Schutzstaffel or Protection Squad.

The Munich Putsch and *Mein Kampf*

In November 1923, inflation was out of control and the government was very unpopular. Hitler took the opportunity to stage a putsch (revolt) in Munich. It was easily defeated and Hitler was sent to jail.

While he was in prison Hitler wrote a book called ***Mein Kampf*** (My Struggle). In this book, he put forward his main beliefs:

- The German race was made up of superior, racially pure people, whom Hitler called 'Aryans'. Hitler said they were the 'master race'. Anyone who didn't fit into this category, particularly Jewish people, were treated as inferiors.
- Austria and other German-speaking areas in Europe should be united with Germany. He called this idea ***Anschluss***.
- Hitler planned to conquer Eastern Europe and Russia to provide more land and resources for the German 'master race'. This was called *lebensraum* (living space).
- Hitler wanted to ignore the terms of the hated Versailles Treaty and rebuild a powerful German army.

Hitler with the other leaders of the Munich Putsch. The judge at his trial sympathised with Hitler. The sentence he received was very short – five years in jail. He only served one year.

Look

The swastika, a four-sided cross, is an ancient symbol that was once used all over the world to symbolise good luck and protection from evil. You can see its shape in Ireland's St Brigid's Cross. But because Hitler used the swastika as the Nazi emblem, most people now associate this shape with Nazism and evil – the opposite of its ancient meaning! In one synagogue in America, a floor that had been paved with a mosaic of a swastika had to be changed after Hitler came to power.

Questions

1. How did the Weimar Republic get its name?
2. Name two problems that the new republic faced.
3. Briefly describe Hitler's life up to the end of World War I.
4. What was Hitler's reaction to Germany's defeat in World War I?
5. What was the full name of the Nazi Party?
6. Name one other important Nazi leader. Give the name of the organisation he led.
7. What was the Munich Putsch?
8. What book did Hitler write? Give three of the aims he set out in it.

Hitler Becomes Dictator

Election poster for the Nazis Party (NSDAP) in 1930. The snake represents the threats to Germany that the Nazis promised to eliminate, such as the Versailles Treaty, communism, inflation, etc. The Jews are portrayed as the main evil, as indicated by the Star of David on the snake's head.

A new approach

By 1925, when Hitler came out of prison, Mussolini had created a dictatorship in Italy. That showed that it was possible to take power peacefully. Hitler decided on a change of tactics. He said:

'Instead of working to achieve power by an armed coup (revolt), we will have to hold our noses and enter the Reichstag...If outvoting them takes longer than outshooting them, at least the result will be guaranteed by their own constitution...Sooner or later we will have a majority and after that – Germany!'

At first this new tactic did not work. The German economy had recovered with the help of loans from American banks. Up to 1929, the Weimar Republic was successful and Germans began to accept it. There was little support for an extreme party like the Nazis. In the 1928 election they only won twelve seats.

Severe economic problems

But in October 1929, an event occurred that would have a very dramatic effect on Germany. The value of stocks and shares fell on the US Stock Exchange. This event was known as **'the Wall Street Crash'**. The American economy collapsed and American banks needed their money back.

The money that Germans borrowed from the American banks had been used to build up the economy and to pay the reparations required under the terms of the Versailles Treaty. Without the US loans, Germany's economy was in serious trouble. Factories closed and millions lost their jobs.

The democratic government was unable to solve the problem. People were desperate and turned to the two undemocratic parties, the Nazis and the Communists. The Nazis went from having twelve seats in the Reichstag (parliament) in 1928 to 230 seats in 1932. These two tables show how the growth of unemployment was linked to votes for the undemocratic parties.

Unemployment grows in Germany	
1928	2.0 million
1929	2.8 million
1930	3.2 million
1931	4.9 million
1932	6.0 million

Election year	Nazis	Communists
1930	107 seats	77 seats
1932 (July)	230 seats	89 seats
1932 (November)	196 seats	100 seats

Hitler becomes chancellor

By 1933 Hitler's party was the largest party in the Reichstag. Despite his dislike of Hitler, the German president, **Paul von Hindenburg,** was persuaded to appoint Hitler as Chancellor (prime minister).

Hitler with President Hindenburg, who was the president of Germany from 1925 until his death in 1934. He was a German war hero from World War I.

The Reichstag (parliament) building on fire in 1933. A Dutch communist, Marinus van der Lubbe, was executed for causing the fire. Some historians believe that the Nazis started the fire themselves to generate public fear of communists.

Establishing a dictatorship

At once, Hitler called another election. The police were brought under Nazi control. SS and SA men attacked other parties and broke up their meetings. A week before the election the Reichstag building was set on fire. Hitler said this act was the communists' signal for a revolution. He used this event as an excuse to pass a law that banned the Communist Party. Over 4,000 of its members were arrested.

Despite the violence and intimidation, the Nazis only won 45 per cent of the votes. But Hitler used the threat of communism to persuade the Reichstag to pass a law called the **'Enabling Act'**. This gave Hitler the power to rule for four years without having to get the approval of parliament. It was to allow Hitler to deal with the threat of communism, but he used it to ban other parties and make himself dictator of Germany.

Hitler acts against the SA

After Hitler took power, the SA grew quickly in size. By 1934, it had over two million members. Its leader, **Ernst Röhm**, was very powerful. He wanted to turn the SA into an army but the German generals opposed his ideas.

Hitler needed the support of the generals. He was also worried by how much power Röhm had. He feared that Röhm and the SA might try to overthrow him. He decided to use the SS to destroy Röhm.

On the night of 30 June 1934, the SS arrested and shot Röhm and other SA leaders, along with some others who had opposed Hitler. In total about 400 people were killed. This episode is known as the **Night of the Long Knives**. Hitler justified his actions by saying:

> *'In this hour I was responsible for the fate of the German people, and thereby I became the supreme judge of the German people. I gave the order to shoot the ringleaders in this treason.'*

This event removed the last traces of political opposition to Hitler.

Questions

1. Why didn't many people vote for the Nazis before 1929?
2. What was the effect of the Wall Street Crash on the German economy?
3. Why did many Germans support the Nazis after 1930?
4. Name the president of Germany and say when he appointed Hitler Chancellor of Germany.
5. How did Hitler take advantage of the Reichstag fire?
6. What was the Enabling Act of 1933 and why was it important?
7. What happened during the Night of the Long Knives?

Life in Nazi Germany 1933–39

Although Hitler destroyed democracy, most Germans supported him. There were a number of reasons for this:

- The Nazis were very good at propaganda. **Joseph Goebbels** was in charge of it. He used radio, newspapers and the cinema to win support for the Nazis. He realised the importance of radio for influencing opinion (there were no TVs) and made cheap radio sets available.
- Goebbels also organised mass rallies with flags, bands and speeches. The most famous rallies were held at Nuremberg every year.
- Hitler ordered the construction of motorways (autobahns) and public buildings. This helped to reduce unemployment. He also began re-arming Germany, and this created jobs in the arms factories. By 1938, Germany had a labour shortage. All Germans could get well-paid work (unless they were Jewish, of course!).
- Hitler ignored the terms of the Versailles Treaty and made the German army powerful again. This restored the Germans' pride in their country.

The Nazis liked to show Hitler as a kind, fatherly man who liked children

The Nazi youth policy

Hitler believed it was important to teach young people to become good Nazis. He said:

> *'When an opponent declares "I will not come over to your side," I calmly say: "Your child belongs to us already...What are you? You will pass on. Your descendants however now stand in the new camp. In a short time they will know nothing else but this new community."'*

Teachers had to belong to the **Nazi Teachers' Association**. All boys had to join the **Hitler Youth** when they were fourteen years old. Girls joined the **League of German Girls**. Great importance was placed on physical fitness in schools, and in the Hitler Youth the boys were shown how to use guns. This was in order to prepare the soldiers of the future.

Hitler driving past his supporters at a Nuremberg rally. These huge demonstrations were carefully staged to show the power of the Nazi party.

Less than 1% of the German population was Jewish. Jews lived in the larger cities. In most German towns and villages there were no Jews at all.

Terror!

When the Nazis took power, they set up a secret police called **the Gestapo** to deal with the communists and anyone else who opposed them. They opened concentration camps to imprison them. The first one was at **Dachau,** outside Munich.

The SS guarded the camps. Conditions in the camps were very brutal. Here are some regulations from Dachau:

> *'Anyone who does the following in the camp, at work, in the sleeping quarters, in the kitchens and workshops, toilets and places of rest will be hanged: discusses politics, carries on controversial talks and meetings, forms cliques* [small groups], *loiters around with others.'*

Brownshirts overseeing a boycott of a Jewish shop. The sign says: 'Germans! Do not buy from Jews!' **If you were the girl on the left, what would you do?**

The persecution of the Jews

Hitler hated the Jewish people. He believed they were to blame for Germany's problems, especially its defeat in World War I.

This was nonsense. There were only 500,000 Jews in Germany out of a population of 80 million. They were just ordinary Germans like everyone else.

When the Nazis first came to power, they organised a boycott of Jewish shops. Then Jews were banned from government jobs. In 1935 the **Nuremberg Laws** were passed. These laws deprived German Jews of citizenship. Jews were forbidden to marry anyone of the German race.

The Night of the Broken Glass

In November 1938, a Polish Jew shot an official at the German embassy in Paris. This led to Nazi-organised attacks on Jews throughout Germany. As a result of the violence, ninety Jewish people were killed and 30,000 arrested. Jewish businesses and synagogues were looted.

There was so much broken glass on the streets that the Germans called it **Kristallnacht** (the night of the broken glass). To add insult to injury, the Jewish community in Germany was then fined one billion marks for the murder of the German official.

From 1941 Nazis made Jews wear a badge with the Star of David to show they were Jews. This left them open to attack.

Because of the Nazis' anti-Jewish policies, over 40,000 German Jews left the country. Among them were twenty Nobel Prize winners, including Albert Einstein. But most Jews were neither famous nor rich. Other countries did not want homeless refugees and they had to remain in Germany.

The Holocaust

Between 1938 and 1941 the Nazis took over large parts of Europe.

By 1942 over eight million Jewish men, women and children were living in territory controlled by the Nazis. That was when the Nazis decided on '**a final solution**' to the Jewish problem. They would kill every one of them.

Responsibility for the task was given to the SS, under the command of Heinrich Himmler. At first Jews were rounded up and placed in ghettos (special areas of cities where only Jews were allowed). The most famous of these was the **Warsaw ghetto**.

An entrance to a concentration camp. The slogan means 'Work Makes You Free'.

From the ghettos, they were taken to extermination camps at **Dachau, Treblinka, Belzec, Maidanek and Auschwitz.** When they arrived at the camps, those too old or too weak to work were sent to gas chambers where they were killed. The rest became slave labourers. Most of them died of overwork and starvation. In all it is estimated that six million Jews were killed at the hands of the Nazis during World War II.

It was not only Jews who suffered as a result of Nazi policies. Poles, Gypsies and handicapped people, whom Hitler also saw as a threat to his German 'master race', were killed as well.

Concentration camp prisoners celebrate their release at the end of the war. **What kind of people do you think they were?**

Questions

1. Give two reasons why Hitler was popular in Germany in the 1930s.
2. What was the Hitler Youth?
3. What was the name of the organisation that young girls had to be members of?
4. Explain the role of the Gestapo.
5. What was the name of the first concentration camp?
6. What were the Nuremberg Laws?
7. Explain what the 'final solution' was and write a paragraph about how Hitler carried it out.

Adolf Hitler – The Main Events

- **1889** Born in Austria.
- **1914–18** Fought on the Western Front.
- **1919** Joined the German Workers Party.
- **1923** An attempted putsch in Munich failed.
- **1924** Wrote *Mein Kampf* while in prison.
- **1929** The Wall Street Crash.
- **1932** Unemployment in Germany reached six million. The Nazis became the largest party in the Reichstag.
- **1933** Hitler was appointed Chancellor of Germany. He banned all other political parties and established a dictatorship. Concentration camps were set up.
- **1934** Night of the Long Knives, power of the SA destroyed.
- **1935** Anti-Jewish Nuremberg Laws.
- **1938** Kristallnacht: attacks on Jews throughout Germany.
- **1939** Germany invaded Poland and started World War II.
- **1942–5** The 'final solution'. Six million Jews killed in concentration camps.
- **1945** Hitler committed suicide.

Review the chapter

1 This is the story of Albert Herzfeld, a victim of Nazi anti-Semitism. Read it and answer the questions that follow.

Albert Herzfeld was the son of a major textile manufacturer from Dusseldorf. He was from a Jewish background but was baptised a Protestant and became an artist. He served in the army in WWI and was awarded the Iron Cross, Second Class.

Once the Nazis came to power, his life began to change: A schoolmaster tenant left his house, because as a civil servant he could not lodge with 'non-Aryans', i.e. Jews. The maid had to go because she was under forty-five years old. Jews were forbidden to employ female servants under the age of forty-five.

The swimming pool in the Kaiser-Wilhelm Park bore a sign saying, 'Jews are not permitted entry.' His artists' club sent him seventieth birthday congratulations and expelled him eight weeks later. In November 1937, a frontier guard confiscated his passport while he was returning from Italy. He was promised that it would be returned when he reached Dusseldorf. This did not happen.

After Kristallnacht, Herzfeld wrote that four-fifths of Nazi Party members that he knew disapproved of what had happened and that the majority of the German population regarded the events with disgust. In December 1938, all Jews were required to surrender weapons. He had to hand over his officer's sabre. In January 1939, he had to sign himself Albert Israel, while his wife became Else Sara.

Herzfeld and his wife were sent to the ghetto at Theresienstadt in January 1942, where he died a year later. His wife died in Auschwitz in 1944. The contents of their home disappeared.

(i) What medal had Albert received in World War I?
(ii) Why did the schoolmaster leave his house?
(iii) What did the sign at the local swimming pool say?
(iv) Why do you think Albert's passport was taken away from him?
(v) What did Albert say was the reaction of most Germans to events during Kristallnacht?
(vi) What law was passed in December 1938?
(vii) From Albert's story, can you say whether the Nazi anti-Semitic policy was racial or religious?

2 Are the following statements true or false? If false, write down the correct statement.
(i) Hitler was born in Germany.
(ii) Hitler served on the Western Front during World War I and won the Iron Cross.
(iii) After the war, Hitler joined the Social Democratic Party.
(iv) Hitler led a revolt in Berlin in 1923.
(v) Hitler's book *Mein Kampf* praised the Treaty of Versailles.
(vi) The Nazis won more than half of the votes in the 1933 election.

3 Write a paragraph on two of the following:
(i) Propaganda in Nazi Germany.
(ii) Kristallnacht and the 'final solution'.
(iii) How the Nazis dealt with their political opponents.

4 Write an account on the following:
'A supporter of the Nazi Party explains how Hitler came to power in Germany.'
Here are some hints to help you with your answer:
- Unhappiness with the Treaty of Versailles
- The formation of the Nazi Party
- The Wall Street Crash and its effects on Germany
- The elections of 1932 and rise in support for the Nazis

(Based on the Junior Certificate, 2001)

Chapter 4

Hitler's Foreign Policy and the Drift to War in Europe

Introduction

People in Europe had hoped that World War I was the 'war to end all wars'. They were wrong. In 1939 another and more terrible war began. Here are the men who were responsible for this catastrophe.

Adolf Hitler: the Führer (leader) of Germany. He wanted Germany to dominate Europe.

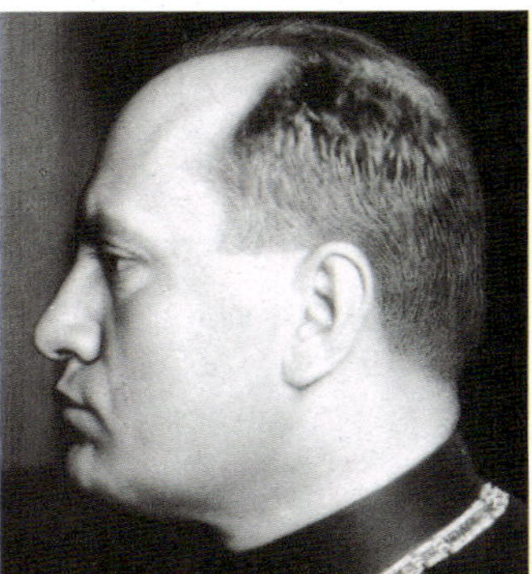

Benito Mussolini: the fascist ruler of Italy. He became Hitler's ally in 1936. He hoped to make Italy the most powerful country in southern Europe.

Neville Chamberlain: prime minister of Britain. He hated war and hoped that by agreeing to Hitler's demands he could avoid one.

Josef Stalin: dictator of the Soviet Union (USSR) and head of the Communist Party. He feared that Hitler planned to destroy communism and conquer the Soviet Union.

What Hitler hoped to achieve

As ruler of Germany, Hitler had three main aims:

- He planned to ignore the Versailles Treaty and build a strong German army.
- He wanted to unite all Germans living in Austria, Czechoslovakia and Poland into a huge German empire, which he called the **Third Reich**. Hitler boasted that it would last a thousand years.
- He then planned to conquer land and resources for the Germans in Eastern Europe and Russia. He called this *lebensraum* (living space).

The Third Reich: 'Reich' is the German word for empire. The first German empire was in the Middle Ages. Luther lived at that time and you read about the Emperor Charles V in Book One. The second empire began in 1871 and collapsed after World War I.

Rebuilding the German army

Under the Treaty of Versailles, Germany could only have 100,000 men in its army. It was not allowed to have submarines, tanks or military aircraft. As soon as he took power, Hitler began to break these rules. At first, he did it secretly in

Hitler with Herman Goering, the commander of the Luftwaffe. He had been a World War I fighter ace.

case France or Britain tried to stop him while his army was still weak. But in 1935, he publicly introduced conscription. He also announced the creation of a new German airforce, the **Luftwaffe**.

What the French and British thought of Hitler's moves

The French were worried by Hitler's actions. They were afraid of a re-armed Germany. But the French would do nothing to stop him without British support.

The British did not want to interfere with Hitler's policies. Many British people came to realise that the Versailles Treaty had been unfair to Germany. As long as Hitler's demands seemed reasonable, they would not stop him. They were also haunted by the memory of World War I, with its huge slaughter. They wanted to avoid another war in Europe at any cost.

These views led to the British policy known as '**appeasement**'. That meant giving in to Hitler in the hope that he would be satisfied and not start another war.

Questions

1. List three of Hitler's foreign policy aims.
2. Which of these policies do you think was most popular in Germany? Explain your choice.
3. Give two examples of how Germany broke the Versailles Treaty in 1935.
4. What was the attitude of the French to German re-armament?
5. Explain what the policy of 'appeasement' was. Give two reasons why British politicians adopted this policy.

The first gamble

In 1935, Mussolini, the Italian dictator, invaded Abyssinia. The League of Nations condemned him. While everyone else was concentrating on Mussolini's actions, Hitler sent his troops into the **Rhineland**. This was forbidden under the Versailles Treaty.

Hitler took a gamble that the French would not stop him. He later said:

'The forty-eight hours after the march into the Rhineland were the most nerve-racking in my life...If the French had then marched into the Rhineland, we would have had to withdraw with our tails between our legs, for the military resources at our disposal would have been wholly inadequate for even moderate resistance.'

The French thought that the German army was far bigger than it actually was. They would not take action without British support, and as a result they did nothing. Hitler had gambled and won. He now believed France and Britain would not stand up to him and was prepared to take further risks.

German troops being welcomed into the Rhineland. **Why do you think they were so warmly greeted?**

Hitler and Mussolini

Between 1936 and 1939 a civil war raged in Spain between those who supported the fascist **General Franco** and those who supported Spain's democratic government. Franco eventually seized power as a fascist dictator. Hitler and Mussolini helped him with troops and equipment. This co-operation led to an alliance between Mussolini and Hitler known as the **Rome-Berlin Axis**. In 1939, they signed a military alliance known as **the Pact of Steel**.

Neville Chamberlain and appeasement

In 1937, Neville Chamberlain became prime minister of Britain. He believed that Britain could not afford another war, so he supported appeasement. This policy was very popular in Britain, where people dreaded war.

The *Anschluss*

Austria, where Hitler was born, was a German-speaking nation, and it was Hitler's goal to join Austria and Germany together (*Anschluss*). The Treaty of Versailles had forbidden this.

After Hitler came to power, he supported the Austrian Nazi Party. In 1934, the Nazi Party had tried to seize control of Austria but the attempt failed. By 1938, Hitler was ready to try again. In February 1938, he forced the Austrian prime minister to include Nazi ministers in his government. When the prime minister called a **referendum** to limit the spread of Nazi control, Hitler ordered the German army into Austria.

Hitler returned in triumph to Vienna. This was the city where before World War I he had lived as a down and out. He said:

> *'If Providence once called me forth from this city to assume the leadership of the Reich, it must have charged me with a mission, and that mission can only have been to restore my dear homeland to the German Reich.'*

This Nazi propaganda poster celebrated the *Anschluss*. The caption says 'One people, one empire, one leader.'

Although the unification of Austria and Germany broke the Treaty of Versailles, the British and French did not take any action to prevent it. They thought most Austrians wanted it and they were probably correct. They were not prepared to risk war by opposing Hitler's actions.

Hitler's victims

Hitler plans to invade Czechoslovakia

Hitler's next target was Czechoslovakia. It was a new country which was set up after World War I. In one region, called the **Sudetenland** near the German border, there were 3 million Germans.

Hitler encouraged the **Sudeten Germans** to demand union with Germany. German propaganda falsely claimed that the Czechs were treating them badly. In the summer of 1938, Hitler announced that he planned to invade Czechoslovakia and seize the Sudetenland.

The Munich Conference brings 'Peace in our time'

The Czechs had an alliance with France and they asked for help. The French would not fight Hitler without British support, but Chamberlain wanted to appease Hitler. He met him twice but they failed to reach an agreement. Around Europe, people expected war.

Then Mussolini proposed a conference of Britain, France, Germany and Italy. They met at **Munich** on 28 September. Although the conference was about the future of Czechoslovakia, Czechs were not asked to attend.

Hitler was given the Sudetenland, provided that he promised that this would be his last demand for territory in Europe. Chamberlain claimed he had won **'peace in our time'**. When he returned home, he received a hero's welcome.

But Hitler had no intention of keeping the agreement. Six months later, in March 1939, he took over the rest of Czechoslovakia. Chamberlain now realised that his policy of appeasing Hitler had failed. Only war would stop him.

Hitler and Chamberlain at the Munich Conference

Map of Poland showing Danzig, East Prussia and the Polish Corridor

Note

Danzig was the port of the Polish Corridor but its people were mainly German. They did not want to be under Polish rule. The solution was to make Danzig a 'free city' under the supervision of the League of Nations. Many Germans did not like this arrangement and Hitler encouraged the people of Danzig to demand the right to unite with Germany.

Poland

Poland was Hitler's next target. Like Czechoslovakia, it was set up after World War I and there were many Germans living in an area of Poland known as the **Polish Corridor** and in the city of **Danzig**.

As with Czechoslovakia, propaganda played an important role. Hitler accused the Poles of mistreating the Germans living there. Hitler demanded the return of Danzig. He expected the Poles to refuse and that would give him the excuse to go to war. He said:

> *'Further successes can no longer be attained without the shedding of blood… Danzig is not the subject of the dispute at all. It is a question of expanding our living space in the east…there is no question of sparing Poland.'*

The conquest of Poland was part of Hitler's policy of *lebensraum*. He believed that Britain and France would give in again but he was wrong. They felt they had to stop Hitler this time, so they supported the Poles. They guaranteed that if Hitler attacked Poland, France and Britain would declare war on Germany. Chamberlain told the House of Commons:

> *'I now have to inform the house that in the event of any action which clearly threatened Polish independence His Majesty's Government would feel bound at once to lend the Polish Government all support in their power.'*

At the Munich conference Hitler promised to leave the rest of Czechoslovakia alone. Six months later he broke that promise. This cartoon shows a worried Chamberlain watching Hitler gobble up the map of Europe. **What did Britain and France decide to do then?**

What Stalin thought

France and Britain were too far away from Poland to help it. Only one country, the Soviet Union, could do that. Its leader, Josef Stalin, had watched with alarm as Hitler took over Czechoslovakia.

- He feared Hitler, who hated communism and talked about conquering Russia.
- But he also distrusted Britain and France, whose leaders were also anti-communist. He suspected that they were encouraging Hitler to attack Russia.

Russian foreign minister Vyacheslav Molotov signs the Nazi-Soviet Non-Aggression Pact in August 1939, while Stalin (in white jacket) looks on

Unlikely allies!

Throughout the summer of 1939, tension built up across Europe. Britain and France held talks with Stalin but there was no agreement. Then on 23 August, the world was astonished to hear that the two bitter enemies, the communist Stalin and the fascist Hitler, had signed a **ten-year non-aggression pact**. They promised not to attack each other for ten years.

What people did not know was that there were secret parts of the pact. The two dictators had agreed to divide Poland and Eastern Europe between them.

The agreement benefited both sides:

- Stalin avoided war with Germany for which Russia was too weak. He also received eastern Poland, Finland and the Baltic States.
- Hitler got western Poland and peace with Russia. That left him free to fight against France and Britain in the West without worrying about having to fight Russia at the same time.

This cartoon appeared soon after the Hitler–Stalin pact. **Look at what the two men are saying. Why did the cartoonist put those words in their mouths?**

The outbreak of World War II

Hitler believed that the news of the Pact would stop France and Britain from going to war if Germany attacked Poland. He was mistaken.

On 1 September 1939, Hitler's troops attacked Poland. Britain and France demanded that he stop. He refused to do so, and on 3 September Britain and France declared war on Germany. World War II had begun.

Although the war had begun in Europe, it would later spread to the rest of the world and would last for almost six years.

Questions

1. What did Hitler do in March 1936 that broke the Treaty of Versailles?
2. What drew Hitler and Mussolini closer between 1936 and 1939?
3. Who became prime minister of Britain in 1937 and what policy did he follow?
4. What was the *Anschluss* and when did it happen?
5. In 1938, why was there a crisis over the Sudetenland?
6. What was agreed at Munich in 1938?
7. What did Britain do after the Germans occupied the rest of Czechoslovakia?
8. What part of Poland did Hitler want?
9. Why was the news of the Nazi-Soviet Pact so surprising to the rest of the world?
10. On what date did World War II begin?

Hitler's Foreign Policy — The Road to War

1933	1935	1936	1938	1939
Hitler left the League of Nations and began to re-arm.	Germany introduced conscription.	German troops entered the Rhineland. France and Britain took no action, policy of appeasement.	Austria was taken over by Germany (the *Anschluss*). After the Munich conference, the Sudetenland became part of Germany.	The Germans occupied the rest of Czechoslovakia. Nazi-Soviet Non-Aggression Pact was signed. Germany invaded Poland and World War II began.

Review the chapter

1 Source Question

Hitler bullied the leaders of countries such as Austria and Czechoslovakia. Read this account of a meeting between the Austrian prime minister and Hitler in 1938 and then answer the questions.

> *'When the Austrian prime minister* [Schuschnigg] *remarked that because of his country's constitution he could not agree to Hitler's demands, Hitler wrenched open the door, gestured for him to leave and shouted in an intimidating tone for General Keitel* [head of the German army]. *After Keitel came in, closed the door and asked for orders, Hitler said: "None at all, have a seat." Shortly afterwards, Schuschnigg signed.'*

(i) Why could the Austrian prime minister not agree to Hitler's demands?
(ii) Explain the method used by Hitler to get the Austrian prime minister to agree to his demands.
(iii) What does this story tell us about Hitler?

2 Source Question

After the Munich agreement, Chamberlain asked Hitler to sign the following document. Read it and answer the questions below.

> *'We, the German Führer and Chancellor and the British Prime-Minister,... regard the agreement signed last night, the Munich agreement... as symbolic of the desire of our two peoples never to go to war with one another again.*
>
> *We are resolved that the method of consultation shall be the method adopted to deal with any other questions that may concern our two countries, and we are determined to continue our efforts to remove possible sources of difference and thus to assure the peace of Europe.'*

(i) How did both leaders promise to deal with problems that arose between their two countries?
(ii) Why do you think Chamberlain was happy with this document?
(iii) Did Hitler keep his promise? Give one reason for your answer.
(iv) Is this a primary or a secondary source? Give reasons for your answer.

3 Picture Source

Study this cartoon and answer the questions below:

(i) Do you think this cartoon supports Hitler or is critical of him? Give one piece of evidence from the picture to support your answer.

(ii) What is the name of the symbol on the flag that Hitler is holding?

(iii) What message do you think this cartoon wants to give?

(iv) Give two reasons why cartoons such as this are useful sources of information for historians.

4 Write a paragraph on two of the following:

(i) The aims of Hitler's foreign policy.

(ii) Appeasement.

(iii) The *Anschluss*.

(iv) The destruction of Czechoslovakia.

(v) The Nazi-Soviet Non-Aggression Pact.

5 Give four reasons why the policies of Adolf Hitler led to World War II.

(Junior Certificate, 2000)

6 Research Topic

Throughout this chapter, many important people have been mentioned. Find out more detail about one of the following:

- Neville Chamberlain
- Herman Goering
- General Franco

Chapter 5 The Early Years of World War II, 1939–43

German troops enter a Polish village. Before they arrived, the German air force had bombed the houses. This combination of bombing from the air followed by a land invasion was called **blitzkrieg**.

Blitzkrieg in Poland

When the Germans invaded Poland on 1 September 1939, they used a newly developed tactic called **'blitzkrieg'**, or lightning war. First, the airforce bombed the Poles, then the Germans sent in large numbers of tanks and soldiers to overwhelm them.

The Poles fought bravely and held out for seventeen days. But on 17 September, Stalin's forces invaded Poland from the east and the Poles were forced to surrender. The two dictators divided the country between them.

The 'phoney war'

Although Britain and France (the **Allies**) had declared war on Germany on 3 September, Poland had surrendered by the time the Allies went into action. British and French troops were sent to France's western border with Germany, but while enemy troops faced each other, there was little fighting. Both sides were using the winter months to build up their strength. As a result this became known as **'the phoney war'**. The Germans called it the **sitzkrieg** (the sitting war).

In April 1940, this situation ended. The German army launched a blitzkrieg attack against the neutral countries of Denmark and Norway and these countries were quickly defeated.

The German advance through the Ardennes region of northern France. This tactic caught the Allies by surprise.

Hitler invades France

Hitler then turned his attention to **the Netherlands, Belgium** and **Luxembourg**. Within days of invasion in May 1940, these small countries surrendered to Germany. France was next.

The French had built a line of forts to protect their border with Germany, which was called the **Maginot Line**. But they had left a gap in the Ardennes region because they thought tanks could not get through the thick forests. The Germans used this weak spot to pour troops and tanks into France.

Also, the French had not built fortifications along their border with Belgium, and German troops were able to enter France across the Belgian border.

The French and British troops were mainly stationed on France's western border with Germany and so were caught unawares. Their armies were forced back by the German advance.

A German postcard celebrating the British defeat at Dunkirk. The British army managed to rescue most of their soldiers and this allowed them to go on fighting. **Do you think the pictures here are realistic or just propaganda? Explain your answer.**

The British escape at Dunkirk

The British retreated towards the English Channel. They were trapped near the port of Dunkirk. It looked as if they would all be captured but a desperate decision was made to rescue them using all available ships.

This rescue attempt was code-named '**Operation Dynamo**'. British ships, trawlers, yachts and even small pleasure boats crossed the English Channel to rescue the troops from the beaches. Under fire from German aircraft, they managed to rescue over 338,000 men in six days. The rescue at Dunkirk made it possible for Britain to go on fighting Hitler.

France surrenders

The French armies retreated south before the advancing Germans. On 14 June, the Germans entered Paris. Eight days later France surrendered.

The Germans then took over northern France and the Channel coastline. This part of France was now ruled directly from Germany. The rest of France was ruled by a French government under German control. It was based in a small town called Vichy and became known as '**Vichy France**' (see map on page 50).

Hitler visits Paris after the defeat of France

Resistance Movements

Many of the peoples conquered by the Germans refused to accept German rule, and resistance groups were formed. Members of these resistance groups operated in great secrecy. They attacked German troops, spied for the Allies and engaged in acts of sabotage such as blowing up railways. In France, they were called the **Maquis**. In Russia and Yugoslavia they were called the **partisans**. Led by Marshall Tito, the partisans in Yugoslavia were very successful and helped to liberate their country in 1945. There were also powerful resistance groups in Norway and Greece.

However, the Germans responded with great brutality to these groups. Many of those captured were tortured and shot. In 1944 a revolt in Warsaw by the Polish Home Army resulted in the Germans completely destroying the city. In 1942 when two Czech resistance fighters assassinated the brutal Nazi ruler of Czechoslovakia, Reinhard Heydrich, the Nazis destroyed the village of Lidice and massacred its 172 male inhabitants. The women and chidren were taken to concentration camps, with less than half returning alive.

Italy joins the war

Mussolini stayed neutral when the war began. But when he saw Hitler's victory over France he joined on the German side on 10 June and invaded southern France. But Mussolini was more interested in conquering North Africa for Italy, and the French managed to stop the Italian advance into France.

Churchill becomes prime minister

In the middle of these disasters, Britain got a new leader. People blamed Chamberlain for appeasing Hitler and on 10 May he resigned.

The new prime minister was **Winston Churchill**. He had always opposed the Nazis and Hitler and criticised appeasement.

Churchill was determined to resist Hitler at all costs. This was clear in the first speech he gave as prime minister:

> *'You ask what is our policy? I will say: it is to wage war, by land, sea and air, with all the might God gave us: to wage war against a monstrous tyranny, never surpassed in the dark, lamentable catalogue of human crime.'*

Winston Churchill (1874–1965) was prime minister of Britain during World War II and he provided the leadership needed to see Britain through the war. Here he is giving his famous 'V' for Victory sign.

His leadership and determination to fight on against the odds inspired the British people to resist Hitler. This was very important, because by July 1940 Britain stood alone against the Nazis.

The RAF and the Battle of Britain

After France fell, Hitler's next target was Britain. He gave the order for **'Operation Sealion'**. This was the codename for the German plan to invade Britain. For the plan to succeed the Germans had to gain control of the skies over Britain. The British were determined to prevent this from happening.

This struggle became known as **the Battle of Britain**. It was fought between the **Royal Air Force (RAF)** and the **Luftwaffe**. The British had one major advantage over the Germans – **radar**. This gave them early warning of German attacks and allowed them to plan their response.

The Battle of Britain began on 13 August 1940 with German attacks on radar stations and RAF airfields. British **Hurricane** and **Spitfire** fighters fought dogfights with German **ME 109s** and **110s**. Each side greatly exaggerated the number of planes that they shot down.

On 7 September 1940 the Germans made a major error. They switched the bombing away from RAF bases and attacked London and other cities. Hitler thought this would make British people demand peace, but in fact it gave the RAF time to recover and rebuild.

The Germans suffered such heavy losses bombing towns and cities that they were forced to switch to night bombing. They had lost the battle for air superiority and Hitler called off Operation Sealion.

During the Battle of Britain, the Luftwaffe lost a total of 1,733 aircraft, the RAF 915.

The Blitz on British cities

The bombing of London and other British cities was called **the Blitz**. It lasted from September 1940 until May 1941. Belfast was heavily bombed in April and May 1941.

During the Blitz, it was the ordinary people who suffered most. In all, about 40,000 civilians were killed. In central London, bombs damaged nine houses in ten.

Coventry Cathedral was destroyed during the German bombing of the city in November 1940. Over 600 civilians were killed in the raid.

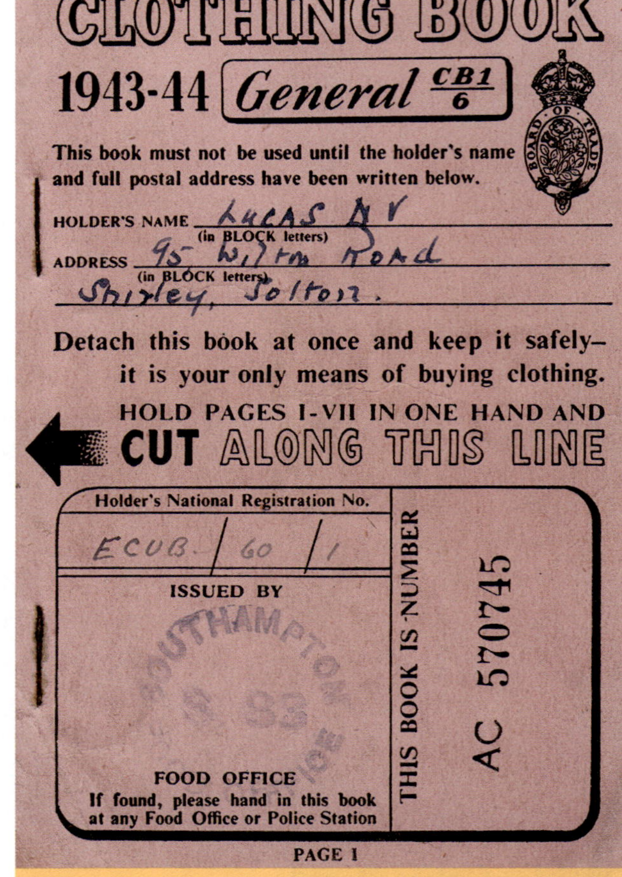

CLOTHING BOOK

1943-44 General CB1/6

This book must not be used until the holder's name and full postal address have been written below.

HOLDER'S NAME LUCAS A V
(in BLOCK letters)

ADDRESS 95 Wilton Road
(in BLOCK letters)
Shirley, Solton.

Detach this book at once and keep it safely– it is your only means of buying clothing.

HOLD PAGES I-VII IN ONE HAND AND CUT ALONG THIS LINE

Holder's National Registration No.
ECUB / 60 / 1

ISSUED BY
SOUTHAMPTON
FOOD OFFICE
If found, please hand in this book at any Food Office or Police Station

THIS BOOK IS NUMBER AC 570745

PAGE 1

A page from a ration book. During the war, most items were rationed in Britain. This was fair and guaranteed that poorer people got food at reasonable prices.

Questions

1. Explain the terms 'blitzkrieg' and 'phoney war'.
2. Name the countries that the Germans attacked in 1940.
3. What happened at Dunkirk?
4. What was Vichy France?
5. Who became prime minister of Britain in May 1940?
6. Give one reason why the British won the Battle of Britain.
7. What was the Blitz?

Map of the German advance in Russia showing Leningrad, Kiev, Moscow and Stalingrad ('Operation Barbarossa')

Operation Barbarossa

By 1941 Hitler realised he was not going to defeat Britain and prepared to invade Russia. He was very confident of victory. He said: *'We have only to kick in the door and the whole rotten structure will come crashing down.'*

Stalin still believed that Hitler would honour the 1939 Non-Aggression Pact. He refused to listen to warnings about Hitler's plans.

On 22 June 1941, Hitler's troops invaded Russia. This was called **'Operation Barbarossa'**. Over three million German soldiers and 10,000 tanks poured over the Russian border. The **Red Army** actually outnumbered the Germans but was very poorly led. Most of its generals had been shot on Stalin's orders in the 1930s. It was no match for the Germans and retreated before them. The Germans captured millions of Soviet soldiers. For example, after the battle for **Kiev** in September 1941, the Germans captured over 650,000 men.

The German advance

The German invasion force was divided into three army groups:

- Army Group **North** advanced on **Leningrad** and soon surrounded it. For 900 days (almost three years), they laid siege to the city. The people of Leningrad suffered horribly from cold and hunger. Over one million of them died during the siege but they held out, and in the end the Germans failed to capture Leningrad.
- Army Group **Centre** reached **Moscow** in December 1941. By then, the winter had set in and the German soldiers were quite unprepared for the intense cold. More soldiers died from frostbite than from Russian bullets. The weather gave the Russians time to regroup and they forced the Germans to retreat from Moscow.
- Army Group **South** was sent to capture the Russian oilfields near the Black Sea. Germany suffered from a shortage of oil and Hitler needed Russian oil. The city of **Stalingrad** stood in the way.

German troops try to keep warm during the cold Russian winter. It was so cold that petrol froze and the tanks couldn't move.

Map of Europe showing the areas under German control in 1942

Marshal Georgii Zhukov, the Russian general who won the Battle of Stalingrad

Stalingrad: the turning point

In August 1942, the German **Sixth Army,** commanded by **General Paulus,** attacked Stalingrad. **Marshal Zhukov** was responsible for the defence of the city. Stalin ordered him to hold Stalingrad at all costs.

For months the battle raged as the Russians and Germans fought for every building. The fighting was so tough that the Germans called it 'the rattenkrieg' or the rat war. While the battle in the city was raging, Zhukov secretly gathered over one million troops to surround the Germans. In November 1942, the Russians attacked and cut off Paulus and his men from the rest of the German army.

Hitler refused to allow Paulus to retreat. An attempt by the Luftwaffe to carry in supplies by air failed. By the end of January, the German position was hopeless. Many of their soldiers were dying of starvation. On 31 January 1943, Paulus surrendered. Over 100,000 Germans were dead and 90,000 were taken prisoner.

The Battle of Stalingrad was Hitler's first major defeat in Europe and proved that the Germans could be beaten. It is seen as the turning point in World War II. After that, the Red Army gained the upper hand. The following summer they defeated the Germans at **Kursk**. This was the largest tank battle of the war. The Russians won many other victories and drove the Germans out of Russia.

The war on the Eastern Front was fought with great brutality. The Russians lost over twenty million in the war. Most of the German soldiers who died in the war lost their lives in Russia.

Note

Conditions for the besieged Germans were very harsh. Temperatures dropped to minus 30 degrees Centigrade. The German bread ration was reduced to just 50 grammes a day. The starving German soldiers were forced to eat their horses.

German prisoners marching into captivity after the battle of Stalingrad. This battle was the turning point of World War II.

A Russian postcard showing Hitler running from 'the nasty Russian climate' and a hail of red missiles

American attitudes to World War II

After World War I, America had adopted a policy called **'isolationism'**. This meant that America kept out of European quarrels. Isolationism was still a popular policy in 1939, so when World War II began, America remained neutral.

But many Americans, including the president, **Franklin D. Roosevelt**, hated everything that Hitler and the Nazis stood for. They sympathised with Britain and tried to help by sending weapons and food.

Franklin D. Roosevelt (1882–1945) was a determined enemy of Hitler. He is the only American president to have been elected for four terms.

Pearl Harbour: the Japanese attack America

In the Pacific, the Americans were worried about Japan, which had become an ally of Germany in 1936. The Japanese had recently conquered parts of China and wanted to expand their empire further.

The Americans opposed this. They banned exports of oil and steel to Japan. This was a problem for the Japanese, who had no oil or steel of their own. They decided to destroy the American Pacific fleet, which was anchored at Pearl Harbour in Hawaii. They hoped that this action would lead to a quick victory and ensure their domination of Asia.

On Sunday 7 December 1941, the Japanese launched a surprise attack on Pearl Harbour. They sank eighteen ships and killed over 3,000 men. As a result of this attack, America declared war on Japan.

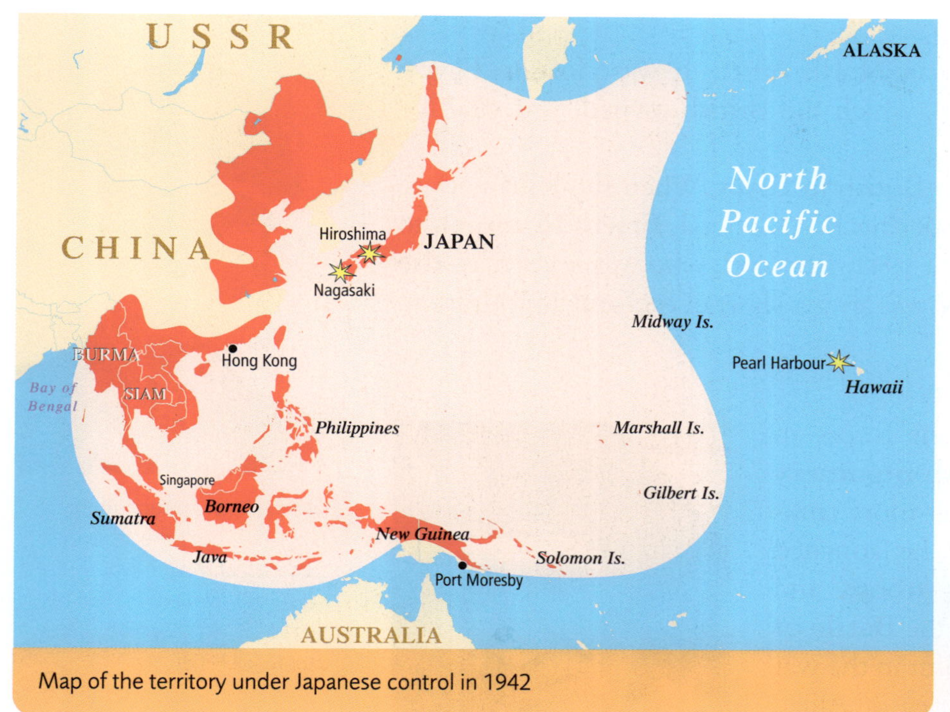

Map of the territory under Japanese control in 1942

The Battle of Midway

At first, the Japanese were very successful. Their armies conquered the Philippines, Singapore, Hong Kong and Burma, as well as many islands in the Pacific.

The turning point came in June 1942. At the **Battle of Midway Island,** the Americans sank four Japanese aircraft carriers for the loss of one of their own. After this, the Americans were on the offensive for the rest of the war in the Pacific.

Germany declares war on America

Hitler was allied to Japan, so when the Japanese attacked Pearl Harbour, he declared war on America. This was a mistake. Hitler, even with his Japanese and Italian allies, could not hope to defeat the combined might of Britain, the USSR and the vast industrial resources of the United States.

America's 'Europe first' policy

The Americans decided to concentrate most of their resources on defeating Germany before dealing with the Japanese. Their first involvement was in North Africa.

One of the ways in which women contributed to the war effort was by stepping into the jobs left vacant by men who had to go off to war. This proved that women were capable of doing work that had traditionally been reserved for men. Some women stayed on in their jobs after the war, and as a result women's career choices became more varied. **Do you see anything strange about the words below this poster encouraging women to do war work?**

The war in North Africa

Before the war, Italy controlled Libya in North Africa. It was close to Egypt, where the Suez Canal was. The Canal, which the British owned, was vital for trade between Europe and Asia.

In 1940, Italian troops attacked the British in Egypt. When the Italians were beaten, Hitler sent the Africa Corps under his best General, **Erwin Rommel**, to help them. They arrived in the spring of 1941. Rommel, who was known as '**the Desert Fox**', defeated the British but he was always short of fuel and ammunition.

The German general Rommel was one of the greatest generals of World War II. He was later forced to commit suicide in 1944 for his part in a plot to kill Hitler.

The Battle of El Alamein

In 1942, the British strengthened their forces in North Africa and appointed **General Montgomery** to lead them. He waited until he had far more tanks than the Germans. In November 1942, he launched a massive attack against Rommel's troops and defeated them. This became known as the **Battle of El Alamein**. It was a major turning point in the war and it marked the beginning of a series of Allied victories over the Germans.

General Bernard Montgomery

American troops now began to arrive in North Africa. They were led by **General Dwight D. Eisenhower**. In May 1943 the British and American armies forced the Germans and Italians to surrender, and they retreated to Italy.

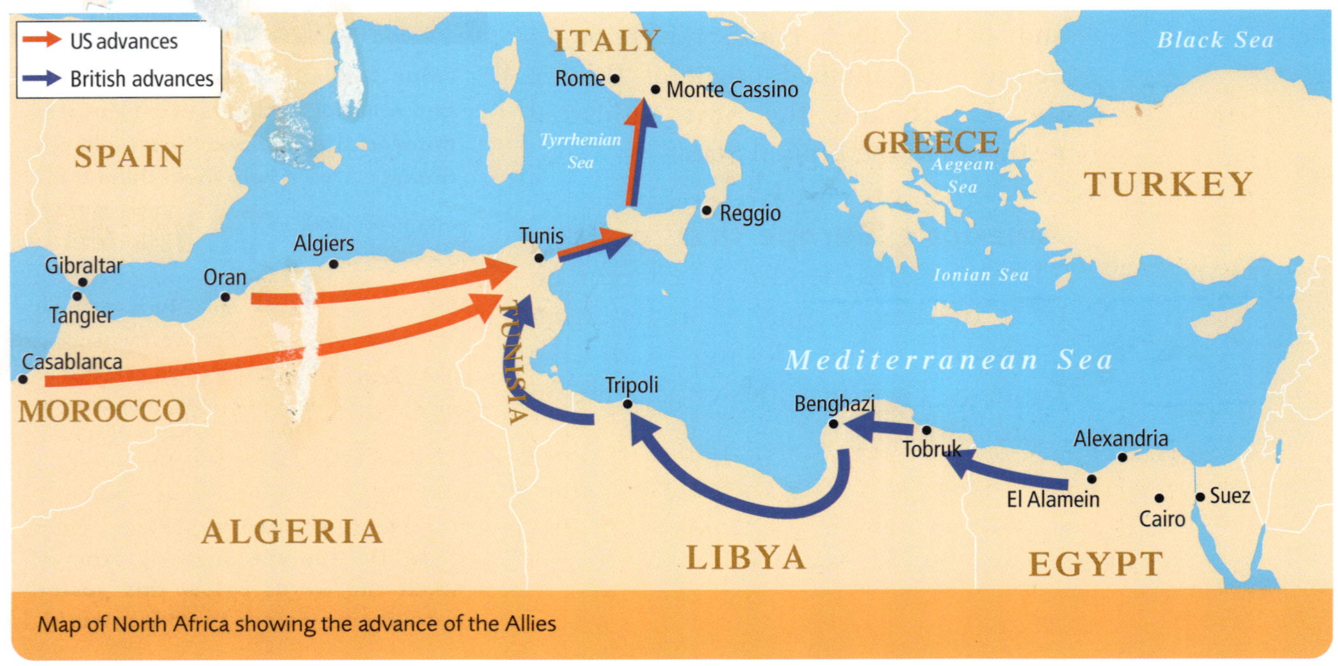

Map of North Africa showing the advance of the Allies

The Allies invade Italy

Two months later, in July 1943, the Allied armies began their invasion of Italy. In September 1943 the Italian king dismissed Mussolini and surrendered. Mussolini was arrested but the Germans rescued him.

From 1943–45 the Allies gradually forced the Germans northward out of Italy. In 1945 Mussolini was captured and shot by Italian resistance fighters.

General Dwight D. Eisenhower was the American general who became the commander of all Allied troops on the Western Front

Questions

1 What was 'Operation Barbarossa'?
2 Name the city that the Germans laid siege to for 900 days.
3 Explain why the Germans failed to capture Moscow.
4 Where were the Germans defeated in 1943?
5 How did Americans first view World War II and why did they change their attitude?
6 Who led the German forces in North Africa? Who led the British forces? Name the major battle between them and say who won.
7 Which country surrendered to the Allies in September 1943? What happened to its leader?

Review the chapter

1 **Source Question**

Ernie Pyle was one of World War II's most popular journalists. Here he describes a night raid on London in 1940 during the Blitz. Read the account and answer the questions that follow.

'It was a night when London was ringed and stabbed with fire. They came just after dark, and somehow you could sense from the quick, bitter firing of the guns that there was to be no monkey business this night.

Shortly after the sirens wailed you could hear the Germans grinding overhead. In my room, with its black curtains drawn across the windows, you could feel the shake from the guns.

Half an hour after the firing started I gathered a couple of friends and went to a high, darkened balcony that gave us a view of a third of the entire circle of London.

The closest fires were near enough for us to hear the crackling flames and the yells of firemen. Little fires grew into big ones even as we watched.

(continued over page)

About every two minutes, a new wave of planes would be over.

Into the dark shadowed spaces below us, while we watched, whole batches of incendiary bombs fell. We saw two dozen go off in two seconds.

The greatest of all the fires was directly in front of us. Flames seemed to whip hundreds of feet into the air. Pinkish-white smoke ballooned upward in a great cloud, and out of this cloud there gradually took shape – so faintly at first that we weren't sure we saw correctly – the gigantic dome of St Paul's Cathedral.

Below us the Thames grew lighter, and all around below were the shadows – the dark shadows of buildings and bridges that formed the base of this dreadful masterpiece.'

(**Note:** Incendiary bombs are dropped to start fires.)

(i) What could be heard shortly after the sirens wailed?
(ii) How much of London could the author see from the balcony?
(iii) What building could the author see?
(iv) Describe the effect the German bombing had on London.

2 Match the items on the left with the items on the right.

Column 1	Column 2
1 Blitzkrieg	**A** Turning point of the war in North Africa
2 Dunkirk	**B** The German bombing of London
3 Operation Sealion	**C** Major Japanese naval defeat
4 The Blitz	**D** German military tactics
5 Battle of Midway	**E** British troops were evacuated from this port
6 El Alamein	**F** German plan to invade Britain

3 Write a paragraph on two of the following:
(i) Germany's early successes in World War II, 1939–41.
(ii) The Battle of Britain, 1940.
(iii) The German invasion of Russia, 1941.
(iv) The war in North Africa.

4 Write an account on the Battle of Stalingrad under the following headings:
- Why the Germans attacked the city
- The main commanders
- The main events during the battle
- The importance of the battle

Chapter 6

The Defeat of Germany and Its Allies

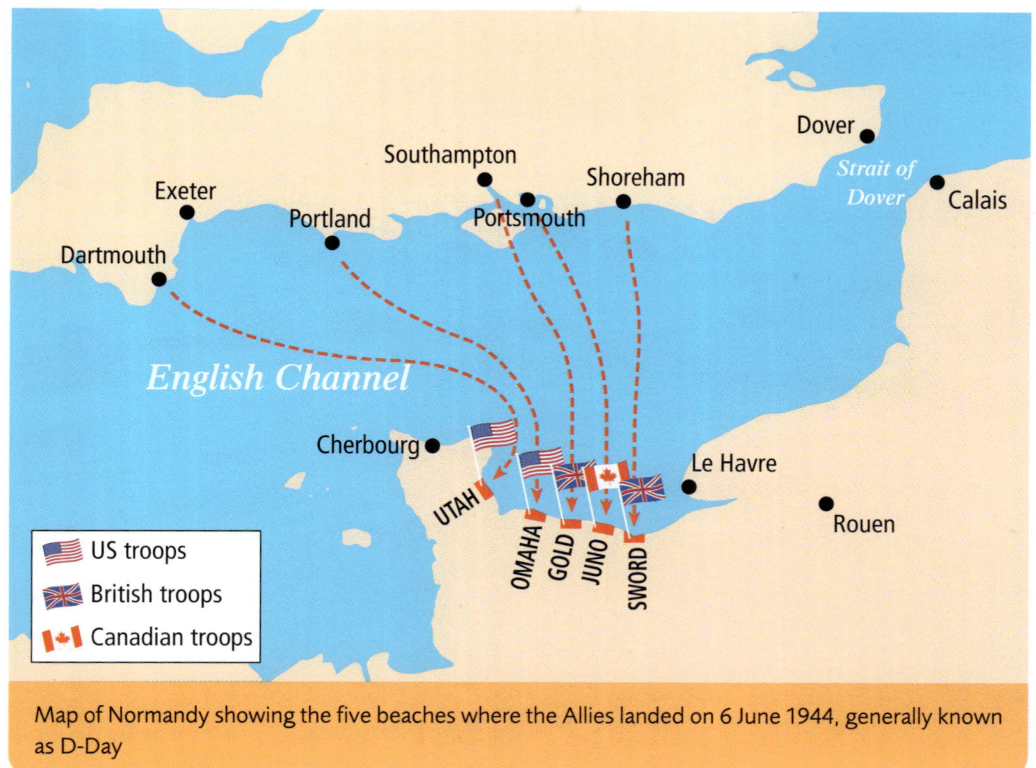

Map of Normandy showing the five beaches where the Allies landed on 6 June 1944, generally known as D-Day

By 1944, the Germans were losing the war.

- On the Eastern Front, the Red Army had driven the Germans out of Russia by January 1944.
- On the Western Front, the British and the Americans gathered their armies to drive the Germans out of France.

Note

To ensure D-Day was a success, the Allies built special tanks called 'funnies' to destroy beach defences such as mines. They built a pipeline under the ocean (called PLUTO) to provide the invading army with fuel. And they constructed artificial harbours called 'Mulberries' on which the troops and their tanks could land.

Planning the invasion of France

Since 1940, the Nazis had controlled France. A 'Free French' government was formed in London by **General Charles de Gaulle**, and he urged the Allies to free his country. Also, Stalin was putting pressure on the British and Americans to invade France. This would open up a 'second front' and help to ease the pressure on Russia. By 1944, they were ready to invade.

In great secrecy, the Allies assembled a huge army for the invasion, which was codenamed **'Operation Overlord'**. They decided to land at Normandy. The Germans knew an invasion was coming but they did not know where the Allies would land. The Allies deceived them into thinking that it would be at Calais, which was the shortest route across the English Channel.

The invasion force consisted of American, British and Canadian troops. Their commander was General Eisenhower. The Allies made careful preparations to ensure that the invasion would be a success.

Allied troops on a Normandy beach. **Do you see the very large number of ships, and also the balloons floating above to protect them from enemy planes?**

D-Day!

June 6 1944 was called **D-Day**. Over 6,500 ships and landing craft sailed towards Normandy. Overhead, 10,000 Allied fighter planes and bombers gave the Allies complete control of the air. Airborne troops were dropped behind German lines and they linked up with the **Maquis** (the French Resistance).

The Germans fought fiercely and the fighting in Normandy lasted until August. When the Germans were finally defeated, the way to Paris was open. The Germans surrendered the city on 25 August. People thought that the war would be over by Christmas.

Churchill and Montgomery studying a map of France after the Normandy landings

Hitler and Mussolini inspecting the damage done by the failed assassination attempt

The 'Bomb Plot'

By 1944 many Germans officers realised they were losing the war and that they would have to get rid of Hitler. In July 1944 an attempt was made to kill him. **Colonel Claus von Stauffenberg** planted a bomb at Hitler's headquarters. Unfortunately, someone moved the bomb and Hitler was only injured. The Gestapo rounded up the plotters and their families. In all, about 5,000 people were executed.

The Allied advance across Germany in 1945

Hitler's last gambles

By the winter of 1944, Germany was under severe pressure from both East and West. But Hitler would not surrender. He had new miracle weapons that he hoped would win the war. These were the **V-1** and **V-2** rockets, which were launched against London. They caused considerable damage but made little difference to the course of the war. In December, the German army launched a surprise attack on the lightly defended Ardennes region on the border with France. The Americans did not expect the attack and the Germans advanced through their lines. This became known as the **Battle of the Bulge**. However, the Germans were short of fuel and the Americans were able to stop them. In January, the Allies counter-attacked and soon the Germans were forced to retreat.

The three main Allied leaders meeting at Yalta in Russia in 1945. **Can you name them?**

Questions

1. Where did Hitler think the Allies would land when they invaded France?
2. When did the Allied invasion force land in Normandy and who was its commander?
3. Give two reasons why the Allied invasion was a success.
4. What was the 'Bomb Plot'? What happened to the plotters?
5. What secret weapons did Hitler launch in 1944?
6. Name Hitler's last offensive in the West. Give one reason why it was a failure.

The end of Hitler's Reich

Hitler had said that the **Third Reich** would last for over a thousand years. It only lasted twelve. By 1945 defeat was inevitable.

- Allied armies were advancing from the East, West and South. They had a vast superiority in both men and equipment.
- Every night Allied air forces pounded German towns and factories. In many raids over a thousand bombers were used. For example, on the night of 13–14 February, the city of Dresden was bombed. About 135,000 people were killed.

The main railway station in Berlin and the buildings around it after an Allied bombing raid in 1945

Russian troops place the Soviet flag on the Reichstag building in Berlin

By the end of March, British, American and French troops had crossed **the River Rhine** into Germany. In April, the Red Army attacked Berlin. American and Russian troops met at the **River Elbe**.

On 28 April, Mussolini was captured and executed in Italy. Two days later Hitler and his new wife **Eva Braun** committed suicide in Berlin. The Russians were only yards from his headquarters.

Hitler had appointed **Admiral Dönitz** as his successor. Dönitz realised that further resistance was useless. On 7 May, German troops surrendered. The war in Europe was over.

Uncovering the Holocaust

As the Allied armies advanced across Germany, they discovered the camps where Jewish people had been gassed. The scenes they witnessed horrified even hardened soldiers. It proved that they had being fighting against an evil regime.

The Nazi leaders at the Nuremberg trials. Goering, on the left of the centre row, was the most senior surviving Nazi at Nuremberg. He committed suicide the night before he was to be executed.

Nazi leaders tried at Nuremberg

After the war, twenty-one leading Nazis were tried at Nuremberg. They were charged with 'crimes against humanity'. Nearly all of them were found guilty. Eleven were sentenced to death and seven others were given long terms in prison.

The war in the Pacific

Meanwhile, in the Pacific, the war with Japan continued. After the Battle of Midway in 1942, the Americans captured many islands. It was clear they were winning but the Japanese refused to surrender. In a last-ditch attempt to stop the Americans, they formed squadrons of suicide or **kamikaze** pilots. These pilots crashed planes full of explosives on to American ships.

Note

The top-secret plan to develop the atomic bomb was called the **Manhattan Project**. It began in 1942 and cost two billion dollars. It was the largest military project during World War II.

Hiroshima and Nagasaki

By the time the war ended in Europe, Japan's position was desperate. Its navy was destroyed and every night American bombers pounded Japanese cities.

In April 1945, President Roosevelt died. The new president, **Harry Truman**, did not want to invade Japan because his advisors told him that it might cost a million American casualties. He decided instead to use a new weapon the Americans had developed. It was the **atomic bomb**.

They had been working on it for years and in July 1945 they had successfully exploded the first one. To save American lives, Truman gave the order to use it.

On 6 August the bomber *Enola Gay* dropped an atomic bomb on the Japanese city of **Hiroshima**. The bomb was called *'Little Boy'*. About 80,000 people died from the explosion and thousands more were to die in later years from the effects of radiation. On 9 August a second bomb called *'Fat Man'* was dropped on the city of **Nagasaki**. It killed a further 60,000 people.

The Japanese were shocked by the bombings and surrendered. World War II was finally over.

Hiroshima after the explosion of the atomic bomb

The American commander, General MacArthur, accepting the surrender of the Japanese in August 1945

The Consequences of World War II

Death and suffering

World War II was the bloodiest war in human history. During it, well over fifty million people died. The vast majority of them were civilians. The racial policies of the Nazis brought untold suffering on the people of Europe, especially the Jews and the Poles. Countless millions were also made refugees. Here is a graph showing the countries with the highest number of deaths during World War II.

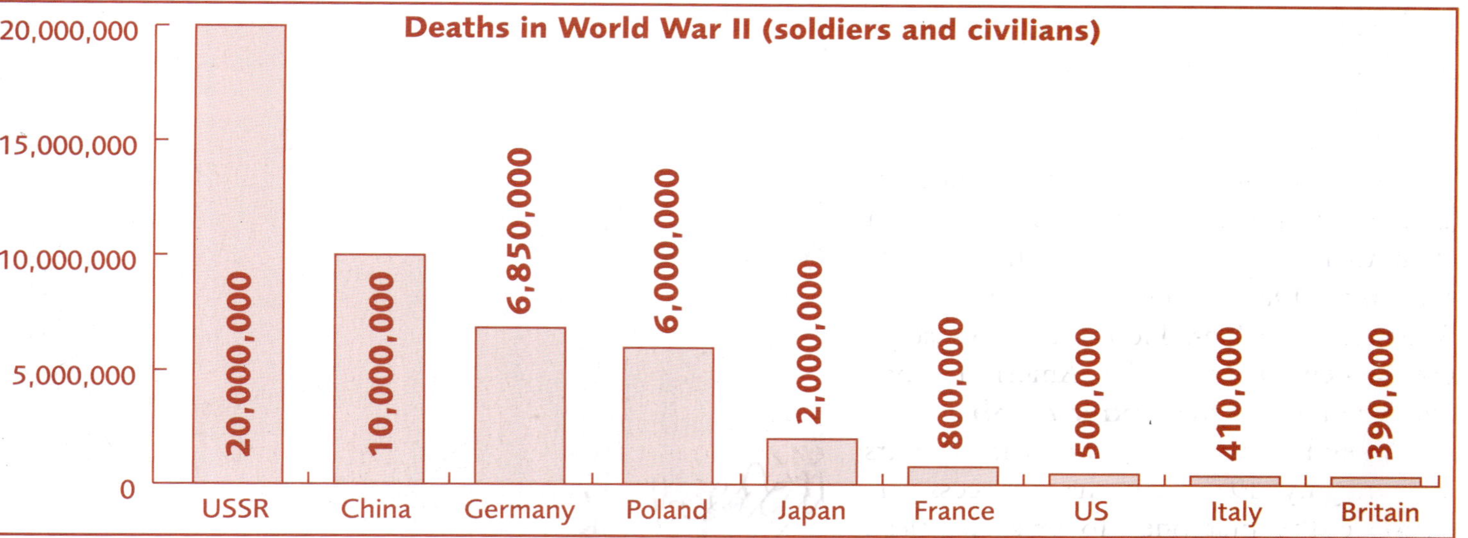

The war also produced great changes in the world. Here are *four* of the main ones:

The Cold War

As a result of the war, the fascist regimes in Italy and Germany were crushed. Japan's plans to dominate Asia were in ruins. Although victorious, France and Britain were weakened by the cost of the war.

The United States and the Soviet Union were left as the two most powerful countries in the world. They became known as the **'superpowers'**. Although allies against Hitler, they disagreed after the war and became opponents. This rivalry led to the **Cold War** (see Topic 1B).

The United Nations

The League of Nations had failed to keep the peace after World War I. But most countries still wanted an international organisation to try to solve disputes between them. The victorious Allies set up a new body called the **United Nations** to keep world peace.

Moves towards European unity

In Europe, many people were determined to prevent another war. They hoped that if old enemies could learn to work together and trust each other, war would be prevented.

This feeling was very strong in France and Germany. They had been enemies for a century and their rivalry was at the heart of the two world wars. The desire to avoid another war between them led to the idea of replacing European rivalries with co-operation. In 1957, six countries set up the **European Economic Community (EEC)** (see Topic 1C) to encourage economic and political co-operation.

African and Asian independence

In 1945, European countries including France and Britain had huge empires in Africa and Asia. But the war had seriously weakened them. They could no longer afford to hold on to their empires. When the native peoples demanded the right to govern themselves, the European countries had to give them their independence. This is called **decolonisation** (see Topic 1D).

Questions

1. Name the city that was destroyed by Allied bombers in February 1945.
2. When and why did Hitler take his own life?
3. Who succeeded Hitler as ruler of Germany? What did he do?
4. Give two examples of the brutality of Nazi rule in Europe.
5. What happened at Nuremberg after the war?
6. What desperate tactics did the Japanese use in the later stages of World War II?
7. How did the war with Japan end?

Main Dates and Battles in World War II

1939	1940	1941	1942	1943	1944	1945
The Nazi-Soviet pact. Germany invaded Poland using blitzkrieg tactics. Britain and France declared war. Stalin invaded eastern Poland.	Germany conquered Denmark, Norway, Holland, Luxembourg, Belgium and France. British troops evacuated at Dunkirk. The Battle of Britain.	Germany attacked Russia ('Operation Barbarossa'). Japanese attacked Pearl Harbour. US entered the war.	Battle of Stalingrad began. Germans defeated at Battle of El Alamein.	German forces surrendered at Stalingrad. Italians and Germans surrendered in North Africa. Italy surrendered to the Allies and declared war on Germany.	D-Day landings in Normandy. France liberated. German offensive in the Ardennes defeated.	Western Allies crossed the River Rhine. Soviet army captured Berlin. Hitler committed suicide and the Germans surrendered. Atomic bombs dropped on Hiroshima and Nagasaki. Japan surrendered.

Review the chapter

1 Source Question

Read the following interview given in 1987 by a Russian general named **Zheltov**. He gave the interview to Albert Axell who was writing a book called *Stalin's War Through the Eyes of His Commanders*.

> **Author:** *Some people blame Stalin for the losses at the start of the war. Do you agree?*
>
> **Zheltov:** *A person who does not do anything is always right. This is the attitude of people who do not know the burden of war. The aim of 'Operation Barbarossa', which Hitler had drawn up, was to strangle us by using masses of tanks and aviation, first of all, and secondly, to divide our country, the people who live in our country, the different republics; to destroy the bond between countryside and the cities. We had to mobilise everything and we had to suffer great losses at the beginning of the war because we were fighting for our land. But we were also fighting for all people, for civilisation…*
>
> **Author:** *Could Russia have defeated Hitler's Germany if the Allies had not invaded France?*
>
> **Zheltov:** *I have written an article for one of our magazines in which I state that we were able to defeat Hitler ourselves. And after three years of severe battles on the Eastern Front, our Allies decided to occupy France because they wanted to get to Berlin as soon as possible.*

(i) Does Zheltov agree that Stalin should be blamed for early Russian losses in the war? Give a reason for your answer.

(ii) From Zheltov's evidence, mention two ways in which Hitler hoped to defeat Soviet Russia.

(iii) According to Zheltov, could Russia have defeated Hitler's Germany on its own?

(iv) What reason did Zheltov give for the Allied occupation of France?

(v) Do you think Zheltov's evidence is reliable? Explain the reasons for your answer.

(Based on Junior Certificate, 1999)

2 Source Question

Read the following description of conditions in the women's compound at **Bergen-Belsen** concentration camp. British soldiers liberated the camp in April 1945.

> *'This was a very large compound containing approximately 23,000. Conditions here were much the same as in the men's compounds except that in a greater proportion there had been attempts to preserve order and some appearance of cleanliness. There did seem, however, to be more cases of extreme starvation amongst the women than the men and in hut 208 conditions were appalling.*
>
> *Practically every inmate was so weak that they could hardly raise themselves and the passage was equally crowded with both living and dead. Not so many dead bodies were left for any length of time in the huts or surroundings, but in the middle of the compound and practically adjoining the children's area was a very large area of naked dead women piled high. It must have contained many hundreds.'*

(i) How many prisoners were housed in the compound?
(ii) Give one difference in conditions between the women's and men's compounds.
(iii) Why were conditions in hut 208 'appalling'?
(iv) What was to be found 'practically adjoining the children's area'?

3 Are the following statements true or false? If false, write down the correct statement.
(i) The commander of Allied troops at the Normandy landings was General Eisenhower.
(ii) The Germans lost more men on the Western Front than on the Eastern Front.
(iii) The V-1 and V-2 weapons attacked New York.
(iv) The Germans won the Battle of the Bulge.
(v) Allied troops crossed the Rhine in 1943.

4 Write a paragraph on two of the following:
(i) The D-Day landings.
(ii) Life in Nazi-occupied Europe.
(iii) The defeat of Japan.
(iv) The consequences of World War II.

5 *'By May 1945, Germany had been completely crushed and had surrendered to the Allies.'* In the light of the above statement, write an account of the reasons for the Allied victory.
(Junior Certificate, 2002)

6 Do you think that the bombing of Hiroshima and Nagasaki were justified? Give two reasons to support your answer.

www War and Peace in Europe on the Internet

Mussolini's Italy

www.library.wisc.edu/libraries/dpf/Fascism/Intro.html This American website contains a variety of visual sources about life in Italy under Mussolini.

http://learningcurve.pro.gov.uk/heroesvillains/mussolini/default.htm This article from the National Archives in Britain examines the invasion of Abyssinia. It asks the question was Mussolini a hero or a villain?

Hitler and Germany

Along with the Second World War, this is possibly the most popular history topic on the Internet. Here is a selection of sites that can help you to find out more about life in Nazi Germany:

www.historyplace.com/worldwar2/riseofhitler/index.html Learn about the rise of Hitler to power from this American website. Contains links to other aspects of Nazi Germany.

www.spartacus.schoolnet.co.uk/GERnazigermany.htm This website is designed for students and deals with nearly every aspect of life and politics in Nazi Germany.

www.bbc.co.uk/history/war/wwtwo/hitler_audio.shtml At this site you can hear Hitler speak. There is a translation to help you understand his poisonous message.

www.calvin.edu/academic/cas/gpa/ At this American website you can find many examples of propaganda posters from Nazi Germany.

World War II

This is only a small selection of the vast number of websites about World War II.

www.bbc.co.uk/history/war/wwtwo/ A collection of articles about World War II from the excellent BBC history website. Contains links to other websites about the war.

www.iwmcollections.org.uk/ The website of the Imperial War Museum in London contains a wealth of information about World War II.

http://search.eb.com/normandy/ You can find the detailed Encyclopaedia Britannica website about D-Day at this address.

www.worldwar2history.net/ This is a very popular site about nearly every aspect of World War II.

ww2archives.net/ This is an American site that contains visual and written sources from World War II.

Getting to Know the Junior Certificate

The syllabus recommends that you should know the following about War and Peace in Europe, 1920–45:

Topic	Description	Approach
International Relations in the Twentieth Century	**1A** War and Peace in Europe, 1920–45.	Since this is a study of International Relations, you do not need to do an in-depth, detailed study of the internal developments in the countries you study. Ordinary Level students need less detail than Higher Level students.

Questions on this topic appear in Questions 1, 2, 3 and 4 on the Higher and Ordinary Level papers. It is also common in Question 6 D in the Higher Level paper. The main subjects to prepare are:

1. The reasons for the rise of fascism in Italy and Germany.
2. The main events in Mussolini's Italy.
3. Life in Nazi Germany.
4. Hitler's foreign policy and the drift to war in Europe.
5. World War II in Europe. This must be studied in detail. The most important aspects of the war are:
   - German successes up to 1941
   - The defeat of France and the Battle of Britain
   - Operation Barbarossa
   - The Battle of Stalingrad
   - D-Day and the liberation of France
   - The reasons why Germany was defeated

Topic 1B

The Rise of the Superpowers

Chapter 1 How Did the Cold War Begin?

What was the Cold War?

After World War II there were only two really powerful countries in the world. They were the United States (US) and the Soviet Union (USSR). They were called the 'superpowers'. From 1945 to 1990 they were rivals in their efforts to become the dominant power in the world. This rivalry created tension between them, which was called the **'Cold War'** because it never became a 'hot' or shooting war.

A war of ideas

The two superpowers had very different ideas about how governments and societies should operate. The table below shows the main economic and political differences between them.

Economic differences	Political differences
The United States believed in the **'capitalist system'**. That meant that ordinary people could own property (houses, farms, shops, etc.). Privately owned businesses supplied most goods and services.	The United States was a **democracy**. That means the people elected the government. In a democracy, citizens also have civil rights like freedom of speech, freedom to travel and the right to a fair trial.
The Soviet Union believed in the **'communist system'**. That meant that ordinary people were not allowed to own property. Everything belonged to the government and it supplied all goods and services like health, housing and education.	The Soviet Union was a **dictatorship**. That meant only one party, the Communist Party, was allowed. In elections people had to vote for it. They had no choice. Citizens also had few civil rights. The government used the secret police to spy on them, and restricted their right to free speech or to travel to other countries.

The start of the Cold War

Before World War II Americans and Russians were suspicious of each other, but during the war they were allies against Hitler. As long as the war lasted they were united in their determination to defeat Nazi Germany.

But in 1945, when it was clear that Germany was beaten, differences between them began to emerge. Two major issues that caused division were:

- What would happen to Germany after the war?
- Which system, capitalist or communist, would the countries of Eastern Europe adopt when the war ended?

Dividing Germany into zones

After Hitler's death, the Allied leaders met at **Potsdam** near Berlin. Roosevelt had died a few months earlier and **Harry Truman** had become the US president. He distrusted Stalin and his policies. A little later Churchill lost the British election and Clement Attlee replaced him.

The Allied leaders agreed to divide Germany into four zones: American, French, British and Soviet. An army from each country would occupy each zone. You can see the zones on the map on page 76.

The British prime minister, Clement Attlee, the US president, Harry Truman, and the Russian leader, Josef Stalin, at the Potsdam conference. This conference was held to draw up a peace treaty after World War II. The differences between the US and the USSR were so great that the conference was a failure.

Berlin divided

Berlin, the German capital, was in the Soviet zone. It too was divided into four zones. To get to their zones, the Americans, British and French (the Western Allies) had to pass through Soviet-controlled territory. Most people did not think this would be a problem in 1945 when the two sides were still on good terms, but it would cause huge problems later.

Eastern Europe becomes communist

During World War II, the Red (Soviet) Army drove the German Army out of Eastern Europe and then occupied Poland, Czechoslovakia, Romania, Bulgaria and Hungary. Can you see them on the map opposite?

The Western Allies wanted these countries to have democratic governments and a capitalist economic system. But Stalin would not agree. He pointed out that in both World War I and World War II, German armies had passed through these countries to invade Russia.

Russia had suffered very badly in these wars. It had lost far more of its people than the United States or Britain. To prevent another invasion, Stalin was determined that Eastern European countries must have 'friendly' (that is communist) governments. He did not intend to give the people in those countries any choice in the matter.

In the Soviet Union after the war, Stalin was treated almost like a god. Russians were told they owed everything to him, including victory over Hitler. Propaganda pictures like this were everywhere. Its caption says: 'To our dear Stalin – the nation.'

Because the Red Army was already in these countries, Stalin got his way. By 1948, he had imposed communist governments on all of them. These were brutal dictatorships that used secret police to spy on the citizens and had concentration camps where thousands died.

The 'Iron Curtain' between East and West

Stalin's treatment of Eastern Europe caused great alarm in the US and Britain. Many believed that he planned to conquer Europe, just the way that Hitler had.

In 1946, Winston Churchill made a famous speech attacking Stalin for forcing communism on Eastern Europe. He said:

> *'From Stettin in the Baltic, to Trieste in the Adriatic, an iron curtain has descended across the Continent. Behind that line lie all the capitals of the ancient states of Central and Eastern Europe – Warsaw, Berlin, Prague, Vienna, Budapest, Bucharest and Sofia. All these famous cities and the populations around them...are subject in one form or another not only to Soviet influence, but to a high and increasing measure of control from Moscow.'*

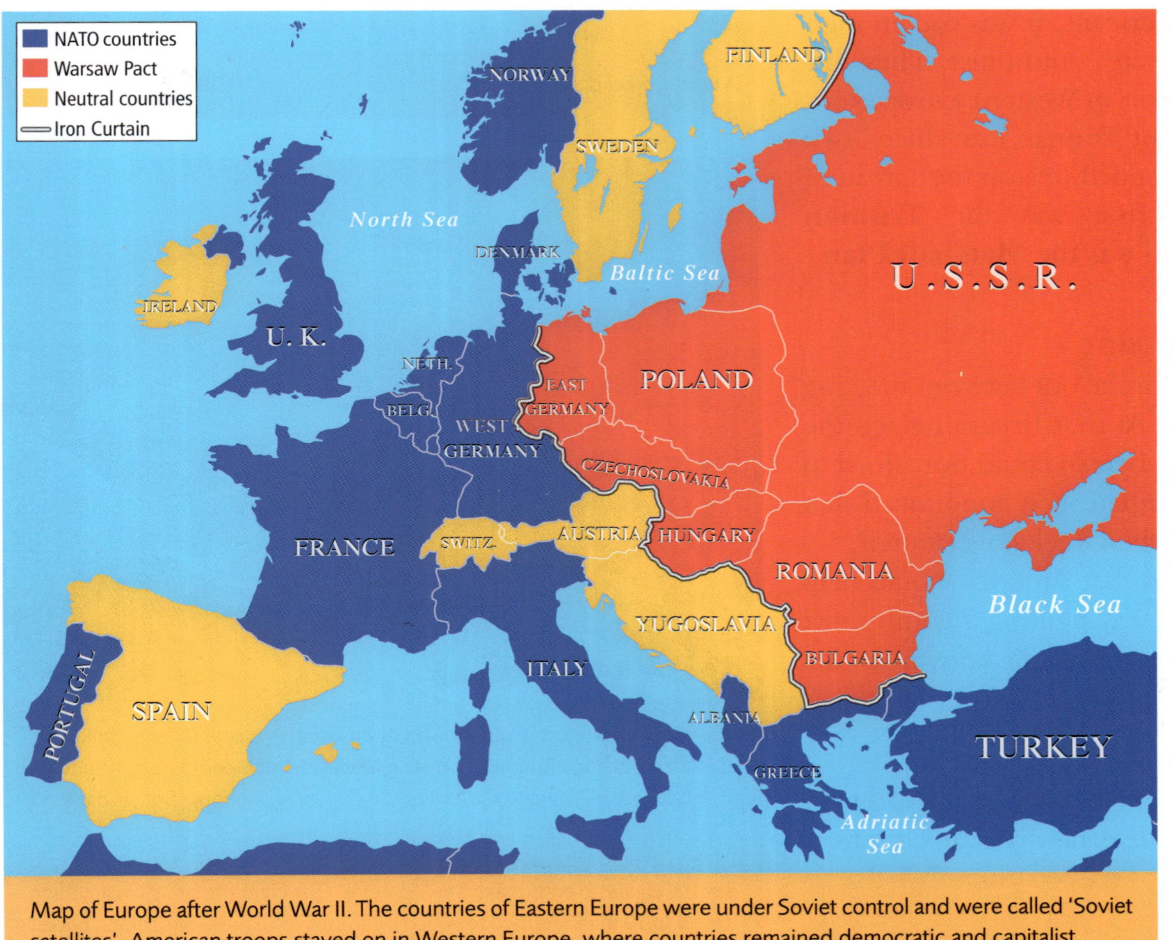

Map of Europe after World War II. The countries of Eastern Europe were under Soviet control and were called 'Soviet satellites'. American troops stayed on in Western Europe, where countries remained democratic and capitalist.

This speech gave a new phrase to the English language. From then on, the term **'Iron Curtain'** was used to describe the line dividing Eastern Europe (which was communist) and Western Europe (which was capitalist). Can you see it on the map?

Support for communism grows in Western Europe

In Western Europe in 1945 and 1946 the effects of war were all around. Whole cities were in ruins, factories were destroyed and millions of refugees were trying to find their way home. Millions of people were homeless, jobless and hungry.

In Italy and France these conditions helped the communist parties to grow. To hungry and desperate people, communism, in which the government provided free housing, health and education, looked more attractive than capitalism. The communists also got credit for leading resistance to the Nazis.

A relief worker doles out soup to the poor of post-war Vienna

America takes action

In elections the communists won many seats. This alarmed the Americans. It was bad enough that Eastern Europe was communist. They did not want that to happen in Western Europe too.

In 1947, President Truman introduced two policies that were intended to stop the spread of communism. The first was the **Truman Doctrine**; the second was the **Marshall Plan**.

The Truman Doctrine

In Greece a civil war broke out between the king and the communists. At first Britain helped the king, but by 1947 the British could not afford to keep sending aid. Truman then announced that America would help the Greek government.

He also promised that America would help any government that was fighting a communist takeover. This promise became known as the 'Truman Doctrine'.

This picture, taken in late 1945, appeared in a newspaper with the following caption: 'Berliners forage among the refuse just dumped by a British truck. The refuse consisted of sweepings from a neighbouring British barracks together with swill from the kitchen. The most prized items are cigarette ends. Then come matchsticks, pieces of wood and any scraps of food. Several cigarette ends make one cigarette. One cigarette brings in anything from 5 to 10 marks, added to which cigarettes have more bargaining power than money.'

President Harry Truman had a sign on his desk which read: 'The buck stops here.' This meant that he took responsibility for the decisions of his government.

General Marshall was one of the most important American generals during World War II. After the war Truman made him Secretary of State.

The Marshall Plan

The Americans also realised that the poor economic conditions in Europe were making the communists popular. To help the Europeans rebuild, the American Secretary of State (foreign minister), George Marshall, announced an aid package of $13.5 billion to European countries. This was known as the 'Marshall Plan'.

Money from the Marshall Plan (known as Marshall Aid) was given to countries provided they had a capitalist economic system. The Americans offered it to the countries of Eastern Europe, but Stalin would not let them accept it. He wanted them to be communist.

Marshall Aid helped Western European countries to recover quickly from the war. By the 1950s their cities were rebuilt and there were jobs for everyone. Ordinary people were better off than they had ever been before. This prosperity undermined support for communism.

These events led to increased suspicion between the US and the USSR. Tension between the two sides grew and this led to the first major crisis of the Cold War, the Berlin Blockade.

Questions

1. Give one economic and one political difference between capitalist and communist countries.
2. Why were the US and the USSR allies during World War II?
3. What issues divided them as the war was ending?
4. Where was the conference held between the Allies after Germany's defeat?
5. What was the 'Iron Curtain'? Who first used the term?
6. In the West, why did many view Stalin's policies in Eastern Europe with alarm?
7. Explain why communism was attractive to many voters in Western Europe after World War II.
8. What was Marshall Aid? How had it changed Europe by 1950?

Case Study 1: The Berlin Blockade

The doctrine of 'containment'

As the tension between the two superpowers grew, the Americans developed a policy called **'containment'**. That meant they would not try to get rid of communism where it existed, but they would try to contain it within those areas and stop it spreading outside them. The Berlin Blockade was the first example of containment in action.

A divided Germany

In 1945, the Allies were determined to punish the Germans for starting the war and for the many atrocities they had carried out during it. The Allies also wanted to make sure that Germany would never threaten Europe again. To punish Germany, the Allies divided it into four zones. The same happened to the capital, Berlin. You can see the zones on this map.

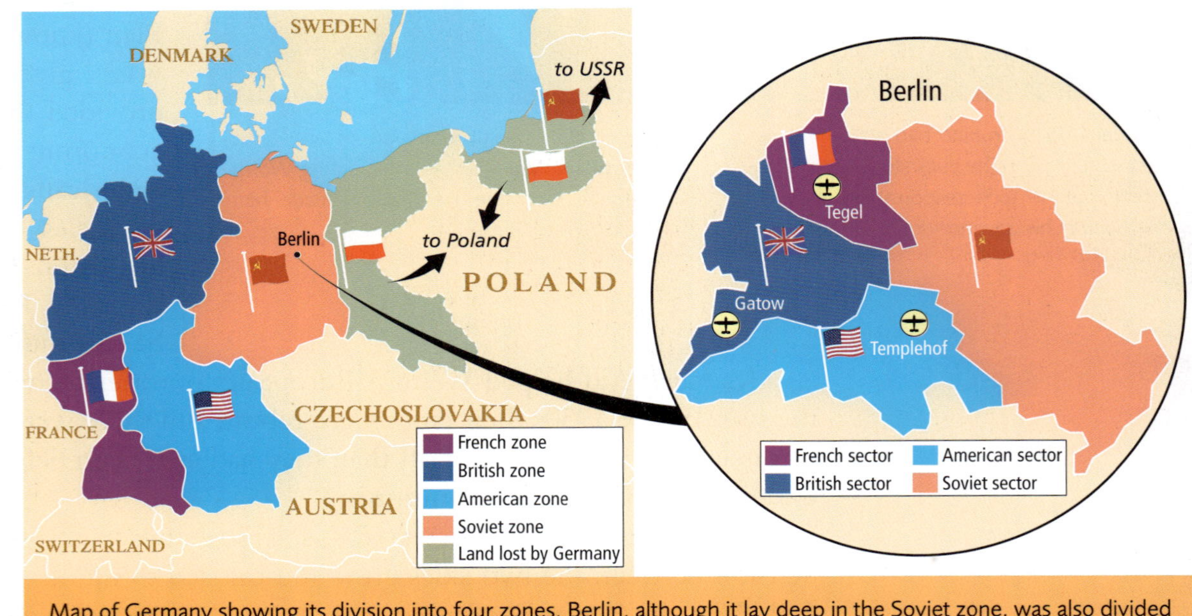

Map of Germany showing its division into four zones. Berlin, although it lay deep in the Soviet zone, was also divided into four by the Allies.

Economic reform and division

But in 1947 when the Americans decided to give Marshall Aid to Europe, they gave it to the Germans too. This was because they believed a prosperous Germany would help economic recovery in the rest of Europe and be a good barrier against the spread of communism.

The British, French and Americans united their zones together to get Marshall Aid. They also gave them a new currency called the **deutsche mark**.

The Americans also offered Marshall Aid to the Soviet zone, but Stalin rejected the offer. He was determined that the part of Germany he controlled must remain communist. He also gave it a separate currency, the **Ostmark**.

Berlin blockaded

Stalin also opposed the introduction of the deutsche mark into the western parts of Berlin. He was worried that an island of capitalism would develop in the middle of the communist zone. When the Western Allies introduced the deutsche mark in West Berlin, he acted immediately.

As you can see from the map, Berlin was deep in the Soviet zone. To get to it, the Western Allies had to cross territory that the Red Army controlled. On 24 June 1948 Stalin closed the roads and railways that led from the western zones to Berlin. He wanted to drive the Western Allies out of Berlin.

The United States, Britain and France decided they had to make a stand against Stalin. If they did not, who knew how far he would go? The American commander in Berlin, General Clay, expressed the attitude of the Western Allies when he said:

Children cheer a plane as it delivers aid to Berlin

'When Berlin falls, Western Germany will be next. If we mean to hold Germany against communism, we must not budge.'

The Berlin airlift

Stalin had not closed the air corridors into Berlin. If he had attempted to do that, it would have meant war. He did not think the Western Allies could bring in enough supplies by air for the 2.5 million people who lived in Berlin.

But the Western Allies were determined not to let Stalin strangle Berlin. They organised an airlift of supplies which was code-named **'Operation Vittles'**. It was an enormous operation, which lasted for 318 days. Huge planes that could carry ten tonnes of supplies arrived every three minutes. On average 5,000 tons of food and fuel were landed every day. If a plane could not land on its first approach, it had to return to the western zone.

During the blockade, Berliners had to live on small amounts of food, which was strictly rationed. There was no fresh fruit or vegetables. They suffered power cuts and had to use candles and oil lamps. However, they never considered giving in. One Berliner wrote: 'The sound of the engines is music to our ears.'

At Easter 1949, an all-out effort to achieve a record airlift was carried out. In a twenty-four hour period, 13,000 tonnes of food were flown into Berlin. This was carried out to show the Soviets that the blockade was not working.

Russian fighters often flew near the Allied planes but they never attacked. Neither side was prepared to go to war over Berlin. Finally, Stalin realised that he could not force the Western Allies out of West Berlin and lifted the blockade on 12 May 1949.

Look

One American pilot, Gail Halvorsen, started dropping small parachutes to the children waving at his plane. They contained bags of sweets. He became known as the 'chocolate pilot' or the 'candy bomber'. This action caught the popular imagination in America and many towns and sweet companies donated sweets. The dropping of sweets became known as 'Operation Little Vittles'.

The Consequences of the Blockade

The Berlin Blockade had a number of effects on relations between the superpowers:

- The Americans had successfully defeated Stalin's attempts to drive the Western Allies from Berlin. Containment had worked. It was to be the main American policy for the rest of the Cold War.
- It deepened hostility and distrust between the two superpowers.
- In 1949 during the blockade, the Soviet Union successfully tested an atomic bomb. Both countries now had the power to destroy the world, and a nuclear arms race began between them.
- To defend Western Europe against the threat of communism, the Western Allies formed a military alliance in April 1949. It was called **North Atlantic Treaty Organisation (NATO)**. It was led by the US, and contained Canada and most countries in Western Europe. In 1955, the Soviet Union set up its own military alliance, **the Warsaw Pact**. Led by the USSR, it included the communist countries of Eastern Europe.

Two Germanies

When the Allies divided Germany into zones in 1945 the arrangement was supposed to be temporary. But the Cold War and the Berlin Blockade made it permanent. From 1948 to 1990 Germany was divided in two:

- The American, British and French zones were united into the **Federal Republic of Germany**, which was usually called **West Germany**. It was a capitalist country with a democratic government elected by the people. Germans were very impressed by the help given to Berlin by the Western Allies. As a result, West Germany was to become a loyal ally of the US during the Cold War.
- The Soviet Zone became the **German Democratic Republic**, which was usually called **East Germany**. But despite its name, it was not democratic. The Communist Party ruled it and there were no elections. A secret police force spied on everyone. It had a communist economy where the state controlled all industry. In the 1950s hundreds of thousands of East Germans left it for the freer and more prosperous West Germany.

Questions

1. What measures did the Allies take to punish Germany after World War II?
2. What were conditions like for ordinary Germans after the war?
3. Give one reason why the Americans gave Marshall Aid to the Germans.
4. What was the name of the new currency that the Western Allies introduced into their zones?
5. What action did Stalin take when the new currency was introduced into Berlin?

6 What was 'Operation Vittles'?
7 How often did planes land in Berlin during the Blockade?
8 Describe conditions for ordinary Berliners during the Blockade.
9 Why did Stalin call off the Blockade?
10 Give two ways in which the Berlin Blockade affected relationships between the US and the USSR.
11 Name the two German states which existed from 1945 to 1990 and mention one feature of each.

Review the chapter

1 **Source Question**
Read this quote from US president Harry Truman, speaking in March 1947, and then answer the questions below.

'At the present moment in world history nearly every nation must choose between alternative ways of life. The choice is too often not a free one. One way of life is based upon the will of the majority, and is distinguished by free institutions, representative government, free elections, guarantees of individual liberty, freedom of speech and religion, and freedom from political oppression.

The second way of life is based upon the will of a minority forcibly imposed upon the majority. It relies upon terror and oppression, a controlled press and radio, fixed election and suppression of personal freedom.

I believe that it must be the policy of the United States to support peoples who are resisting attempted subjugation [forced control] *by armed minorities or by outside pressures. I believe we must assist free peoples to work out their own destiny in their own way.'*

(i) What does Truman mean by 'alternative ways of life'?
(ii) List three differences he mentions between the two ways of life.
(iii) What does he believe the policy of the United States should be?
(iv) Against whom is this policy directed? What was this policy called?

2 Are the following statements true or false? If false, write down the correct statement.
(i) After Franklin D. Roosevelt died, Harry Truman became president of the United States.
(ii) The conference at Potsdam in 1945 left Germany united as one country.
(iii) More Americans and British than Russians died in World War II.
(iv) France and Italy were two countries controlled by the Soviet Union.
(v) The Marshall Plan was aimed at restoring Europe's economy.

3 Write a paragraph on two of the following:
(i) Soviet control of Eastern Europe.
(ii) America's response to the spread of communism.
(iii) The Marshall Plan.

4 Source Question
Read the following account by Eberhard Diepgen, a recent mayor of Berlin. In it, he remembers what life was like during the Berlin Blockade:

> *'I still remember those days very well, even though I was only six years old when the airlift started. We used to live in Spandau, not far from Gatow airport, and day and night we could hear and see the supply planes that landed there. Like all boys in Berlin, I could tell the difference between Dakotas and Skymasters, and I also knew the seaplanes, which landed just beyond Spandau on the Havel and Wannsee lakes. Of course, we schoolboys were fascinated by this spectacle.*
>
> *However, I also remember the supply shortages, the power cuts and food rationing. One day my brother lost our food ration card. For days, we really had trouble at home, because the card could not be replaced. Again and again electricity and gas supplies were cut, also at Christmas in 1948. If you experienced that, you will never forget it. You will always be grateful for those things the following generations take for granted. My generation, in any case, was decisively influenced by the airlift.*
>
> *The Berliners were prepared at that time to defy the siege, the hostage taking. Without the heroic and, above all, prompt action of the Americans, and their readiness to hold out a hand to the defeated Germans, this determination would not have been possible for the Berliners.'*

(i) What airport did Diepgen live near?
(ii) What fascinated the schoolboys in Berlin?
(iii) Give two examples from the text to show that life was hard for ordinary Berliners during the airlift.
(iv) What is the attitude of the author to the Americans? Give two pieces of evidence from the text to support your answer.

5 Write an account of the Berlin Blockade under the following headings:
- Why the Blockade occurred
- The Berlin Airlift
- The results of the crisis

Chapter 2 The Cold War Goes Global

Although the Cold War began in Europe, it soon spread to other parts of the world. The Russians hoped that communism would spread, while the Americans were determined to stop other countries from becoming communist. Events in Korea in 1950 were to lead to the second major crisis of the Cold War.

Case Study 2: The Korean War

Communists gain control of China

In 1949, a long civil war ended in China. The Communist party, led by **Mao Tse-Tung**, won and the mainland of China became communist. Their enemies fled to the island of **Taiwan** and set up a rival government. This government claimed to be the rightful rulers of China.

The communist victory was welcomed by the USSR but it shocked the United States. It seemed as if the communists were winning the Cold War. The US supported the Chinese government in Taiwan and refused to let mainland China join the United Nations. They were also determined to contain communism in Asia. The first test of this determination came in Korea.

Mao Tse-Tung was the communist dictator of China from 1949 until 1976. His victory in the Chinese civil war caused great alarm in Washington. His son was killed in the Korean War.

CHINA
Yalu River
NORTH KOREA
Pyongyang
38th Parallel
Sea of Japan
Seoul
Inch'on
Yellow Sea
SOUTH KOREA
Pusan

Korea: American and Soviet zones of occupation divided by the 38° Parallel

The division of Korea

Japan had conquered Korea in 1910, but after the Japanese were defeated in World War II they had to leave Korea. The Soviets and Americans divided Korea between them. The Russian Red Army occupied the area north of the 38° Parallel and the US army occupied the area south of that (see map).

The division of Korea was supposed to be temporary, but the Cold War made it permanent. In South Korea, a capitalist government emerged, led by **Syngman Rhee**. The Soviets imposed a communist government on North Korea. It was led by **Kim Il Sung**.

North Korea attacks the South

Kim Il Sung wanted to bring the whole of Korea under his control. On 25 June 1950 North Korean troops invaded the South. They advanced rapidly and soon occupied most of the country.

The Americans blamed the Russian and Chinese communists for the invasion of South Korea and were determined to resist it. They asked the United Nations to condemn it and send an army to fight the communists. At that time, the USSR was boycotting the UN, and the American resolution was passed.

Koreans flee the advancing communists. As in most wars, the vast majority of casualties were civilians.

The Korean War

A UN army went to Korea to defend the South. It contained soldiers from sixteen countries, but the majority of them were American. An American General, **Douglas McArthur**, led the UN forces. He was an ambitious man who had made his name commanding US forces in the Pacific during World War II.

General Douglas McArthur in a jeep near the front in Seoul during the Korean War. He was a hero to many Americans because of his record during World War II. He was a good general but interfered in political matters that were none of his business.

On 15 September 1950, McArthur landed troops at **Inchon** behind the North Korean lines. North Korean troops were outnumbered, and by October the UN troops had reached the **Yalu River**, which marked the border between Korea and China.

Stalin sent Russian fighter planes to help the Chinese. They were disguised as Chinese planes and flown by Russian pilots wearing Chinese uniforms. This direct Russian involvement was kept top secret at the time.

China becomes involved

This frightened the Chinese communists. They saw the United Nations advance as a threat. They issued a number of warnings and when they were ignored, China invaded Korea with over 500,000 men. By November, the UN forces were in full retreat.

Peace talks

By April 1951, the two sides were near the 38th parallel. MacArthur wanted to bomb Chinese cities but Truman sacked him and began peace talks.

The talks dragged on for two years. In March 1953 Stalin died and the new Russian leaders wanted to end the war. They put pressure on the Chinese and the North Koreans to stop fighting. On 27 July a ceasefire was agreed. A **demilitarised zone** was established and the borders between North and South Korea returned to where they had been when the invasion began.

The Consequences of the Korean War

The Korean War was to have a number of important results:

- During it over four million civilians and soldiers were killed or wounded.
- It confirmed the permanent division of Korea into a capitalist South and a communist North.
- It was a success for the American policy of containment. South Korea had been saved from a communist takeover.
- It showed that the Cold War was no longer confined to Europe. Disputes were likely to break out between the superpowers anywhere in the world.
- During the Korean War, the Soviet Union helped the North Koreans and the Chinese but did not become directly involved in the fighting. This was to set the pattern for many of the crises during the Cold War. The two superpowers did not confront each other directly. Instead the Russians supported America's enemies and the Americans backed countries opposing the Soviet Union.

Questions

1. What happened in China in 1949? What did (a) the Americans and (b) the Russians think of this development?
2. Explain briefly what happened to Korea after World War II.
3. What started the war in Korea? How did the United Nations react to it?
4. Who led the UN army and what did he do?
5. Why did China intervene in the war?
6. Explain why McArthur was removed as commander.
7. How and in what year did the war end?

Relations Between the Superpowers 1953–61

Nikita Krushchev and 'peaceful co-existence'

Stalin died in 1953 and **Nikita Khrushchev** became leader of the Soviet Union. He condemned Stalin's brutal rule and talked about 'peaceful co-existence' between the superpowers and their allies. This led to hopes that the Cold War might thaw.

But Khrushchev was a committed communist. Just like Stalin, he wanted to protect Russian security by keeping Russian control over Eastern Europe. In 1956 he sent tanks into Hungary to crush an anti-Soviet revolt by the Hungarian people.

Nikita Khrushchev was the most powerful man in the USSR from 1953 until 1964

The arms race

All through the Cold War the two sides competed to build deadly weapons. In the 1950s they developed the hydrogen bomb (known as the H-bomb). It had the strength of over a million tonnes of the high explosive TNT, compared with the 13,000 tonnes of TNT of the bomb dropped on Hiroshima.

They also competed in developing new ways of delivering these weapons of mass destruction. The most important development was in rocket technology. The Nazis had begun this with their V-1 and V-2 rockets towards the end of World War II. After the war, both the US and the USSR got German scientists to work for them. They produced long-range ballistic missiles that could carry nuclear weapons for thousands of miles.

The space race

Competition in rocket technology led to the space race. The Soviet Union won the first rounds. In October 1957 they launched the earth's first man-made satellite. Called Sputnik, it captured the world's imagination.

After Sputnik, the Soviet Union launched more satellites. One contained a dog, Laika. In 1961 they sent Yuri Gagarin into space. He was the first human being to orbit the earth and look at it from space.

The Soviet achievement shocked the Americans. Khrushchev boasted that the Russians were far ahead of the Americans in developing missiles. Although this was not true, the Americans believed him and this frightened them. They began to invest heavily in space exploration.

Yuri Gagarin was the first man in space in 1961. This was a great propaganda victory for the Soviets.

Cold War rivalry led to the development of space technology

John F. Kennedy was President of the United States from 1961 until 1963, when he was assassinated in Dallas, Texas.

Kennedy and Khrushchev

In 1961, John F. Kennedy became president of the United States. He met Khrushchev at Vienna in June. The two did not get on and Khrushchev thought he could bully his younger American rival. Soon after, another crisis developed over Berlin.

Berlin again

Although the Western allies had successfully defeated Stalin's blockade in 1948–9, Berlin remained a problem. It became worse in the late 1950s as the two German states developed very differently.

- Capitalist West Germany grew rich. There were plenty of jobs and its people enjoyed one of the highest standards of living in Europe. They had plenty of food and good housing as well as cars, televisions and foreign holidays.
- Life in communist East Germany was much less comfortable. People worked long hours, pay was not good and there were few consumer goods like cars or televisions. In addition, travel outside the countries in the Warsaw Pact was banned and the secret police spied on everyone.

Note

After he was elected, Kennedy promised that by the end of the 1960s America would have a man on the moon. On 20 July 1969, Neil Armstrong and Edward Aldrin stepped down from the lunar module *Eagle* to become the first people on the moon. Back on earth millions of people were glued to their television sets watching this momentous event in human history. The space race continued through the 1970s and 1980s.

In the mid-1950s East Germans began to leave in their thousands for the prosperous West. The East German government could not stop them. All East Germans had to do was go to East Berlin, walk across the frontier and they were in the West. West Berlin was like a hole in Eastern Europe through which people could escape.

The Berlin Wall

The communist leaders of East Germany decided they had to plug the hole. Most of the people who were leaving were skilled engineers and scientists – the kind of people they needed if they were to build up the East German economy.

On the night of 13 August 1961, the border between the two parts of Berlin was sealed and the building of the Berlin Wall began. It was huge and lined with barbed wire. There were landmines on either side of the wall and watchtowers where armed guards stood day and night.

From 1961 until 1989, the Berlin Wall was the symbol of the division between East and West. It also symbolised the failure of communism. The Germans called it the 'Wall of Shame'. Over 200 East Germans who attempted to escape across it died. Border guards shot most of them.

Soldiers building the Berlin Wall in 1961, to separate the two parts of Berlin

Questions

1 Who became the ruler of the Soviet Union after Stalin? Why was there hope that he would improve superpower relations?
2 Why did the Soviets intervene in Hungary?
3 What was the arms race?
4 Who was the first man in space?
5 Who became US president in 1961?
6 Why was the Berlin Wall built in 1961?
7 Explain why many regarded the wall as a symbol of the failure of communism.

Case Study 3: The Cuban Missiles Crisis

Events in Berlin heightened tension between the superpowers. This tension was to lead to the most dangerous episode in the Cold War, the Cuban Missiles Crisis in 1962.

This map shows Cuba and the United States. As you can see, Cuba is very close to the coast of the US. The circles on the map show the range of the different missiles that the Russians planned to install on the island of Cuba. Nearly all of the major cities in the US could be hit by these missiles.

Fidel Castro and the Americans

Cuba is an island ninety miles off the south coast of the United States, just below Florida. Up until 1959 rich Americans often went there on holiday to enjoy the beaches and spend money in the bars and casinos of the capital, Havana. US businesses owned the major Cuban industries – sugar and tobacco. The Americans supported the ruler of Cuba, a corrupt dictator called **General Batista**.

Castro shakes hands with Khrushchev on a state visit to Moscow in 1963

In 1959 **Fidel Castro** led a popular revolt that overthrew Batista. His government then took over the American-owned companies. This angered the Americans and they stopped all trade with Cuba.

In 1961 President Kennedy approved a plan to help anti-Castro Cubans invade Cuba and overthrow Castro. A CIA-trained force of 1,500 men landed in **the Bay of Pigs** but Castro easily defeated them. This defeat embarrassed the Americans.

US intelligence photograph of soviet missile sites in Cuba, 1962

The Crisis begins

Castro then turned to the Soviet Union for help. Khrushchev saw a chance to gain an advantage over the US in the arms race. In return for Soviet help in buying Cuban sugar and cigars, as well as supplying weapons, Khrushchev persuaded Castro to let him place missiles in Cuba. From there Soviet missiles could easily hit American cities like Washington or New York (see map).

But the Americans quickly found out what was going on. They noticed that more Soviet ships were heading for Cuba. American spy planes called **U-2s** flew high above Cuba, photographing everything that was happening on the ground. They could clearly see that the Soviets were building launching sites for missiles.

Kennedy acts!

When Kennedy saw what was happening he had two options:

1 Attack the missile sites in Cuba and risk immediate war with the Soviet Union.
or
2 Blockade the island and prevent Soviet ships from arriving at Cuba with weapons.

An American warship and a Soviet cargo ship during the crisis

After an intense discussion with his advisors, Kennedy chose to blockade Cuba. On 22 October 1962, he called a press conference and informed the world that the USSR was placing missiles in Cuba. He said that the US navy would stop and search all ships heading for Cuba and that:

'All ships of any kind bound for Cuba from whatever nation or port will, if found to contain cargoes of offensive weapons, be turned back.'

Kennedy knew that at that very moment Soviet ships carrying missiles were crossing the Atlantic. If they did not stop, it could mean World War III – a nuclear war!

For three days, the world held its breath. There was panic buying in the US as people stocked up on food. Then the Soviet ships turned back. They were only half an hour from the American warships.

An agreement is reached

After secret negotiations between the Americans and the Russians, an agreement was reached. The Russians agreed to withdraw their missiles from Cuba. In return, the Americans promised not to invade Cuba and to withdraw missiles they had in Turkey, a country that bordered the Soviet Union. War had been avoided, but only just!

The Consequences of the Cuban Missiles Crisis

- Both superpowers were aware of how close they had come to nuclear destruction. That frightened them and marked a turning point in their relationship.
- One major problem during the crisis was that there was no direct way for the two leaders to contact each other. They now agreed that a hotline would be set up connecting the **White House** and the **Kremlin**. That meant that if another crisis occurred, Soviet and American leaders could talk directly to each other.
- In 1963, the two superpowers signed the **Partial Test Ban Treaty**. It banned the testing of nuclear weapons above ground. Concern about pollution caused by the tests lay behind this agreement. This was the first of a number of agreements between the superpowers that helped to ease the tension during the Cold War.

Questions

1. Who took over the government of Cuba in 1959? What did he do to anger the Americans?
2. Why did the Cubans turn to the Soviet Union for help?
3. What did the Soviets want in return for their help? Explain why they wanted it.
4. How did the Americans find out what the Russians were up to in Cuba?
5. Why were the Americans so worried about Russian missiles in Cuba?
6. What option did Kennedy choose to prevent Russian ships from reaching Cuba?
7. What agreement between the Americans and the Russians ended the Cuban Missiles Crisis?
8. Give one consequence of the crisis.

Review the chapter

1 Write a paragraph on two of the following topics:
   (i) The background to the Korean War.
   (ii) The main events during the Korean War.
   (iii) The main consequences of the Korean War.

2 The following extract is from taped discussions between John F. Kennedy and his advisors during the Cuban Missiles Crisis. Most of Kennedy's military advisors favoured an attack on Cuba, except the Minister for Defence, Robert McNamara.

> **19 October 1962**
>
> **Robert McNamara:**
> *'Any air strike would have to be directed not solely against missile sites, but against the airfields, aircraft and all potential nuclear storage sites. There would be potential casualties of Cubans in at least the hundreds, more likely 2–3,000. You're going to kill an awful lot of people, and we're going to take an awful of heat on it.'*
>
> **John F. Kennedy:**
> *'If we go in and take the missiles out we reduce the danger to the United States. But we greatly increase the chance of the Russians taking Berlin by force. Which leaves me with only one alternative, which is to fire nuclear warheads and begin a nuclear exchange.'*
>
> **Air Force Chief General Curtis Le May:**
> *'We don't have any choice except direct military action right now. I don't share your view that if we knock off Cuba, they're going to knock off Berlin. This blockade and political action I see leading into war. This is almost as bad as the appeasement at Munich. I think that a blockade, and political talk, would be considered by our friends and neutrals – and I'm sure a lot of our citizens – as a pretty weak response. You're in a pretty bad fix, Mr President.'*

   (i) Give one reason why Robert McNamara argued against an attack on Cuba.
   (ii) According to Kennedy, what was the benefit of taking the missiles out?
   (iii) If the Russians took Berlin, what was the alternative open to Kennedy?
   (iv) What did General Curtis Le May feel was the only choice?
   (v) Did General Curtis Le May agree with the blockade of Cuba? Give one piece of evidence from the text to support your answer.

2 Are these statements true or false? If false, write down the correct statement.
   (i) In 1956, Khrushchev supported the people of Hungary against their communist rulers.
   (ii) The Berlin Wall was built to stop people leaving East Germany.
   (iii) Kennedy and Khrushchev met in London in 1961.
   (iv) Sugar and tobacco were Cuba's main exports.
   (v) In response to Castro's economic policies, the US increased trade with Cuba.
   (vi) The Bay of Pigs led to the overthrow of Castro.

3 Write an account on the Cuban Missiles Crisis under the following headings:
   - Background to the crisis
   - The main events during the crisis
   - The results of the crisis

Chapter 3 The End of the Cold War

The Cuban crisis and the changes that followed it helped to ease the tension between the two sides. Although there were many more crises between 1963 and 1985, never again was the threat of war so close.

Soviet stagnation under Brezhnev

Khrushchev was forced to retire in 1964. His successor, Leonid Brezhnev, who ruled from 1964 to 1982, failed to develop the economy and by the 1980s the Soviet Union was far behind the West in technological development.

Mikhail Gorbachev and Ronald Reagan, the US president, at a meeting in Moscow in 1988

Mikhail Gorbachev and Glasnost

In 1985 an energetic young leader named Mikhail Gorbachev emerged. He wanted to open up Russian society. This policy was called **glasnost** (Russian for 'openness'). He allowed people to criticise the government and he met the citizens on the streets.

Gorbachev also wanted to reshape the Russian economy by allowing ordinary people to own private property and develop private enterprises. This was called **perestroika** (restructuring).

1989: the year of miracles

Gorbachev's reforms were welcomed by the people of Eastern Europe. Some careful reforms began there, especially in the economic area.

But the key question was – how far would Gorbachev allow these reforms to go? In 1989 he visited East Germany and made it clear that the Soviet Union would not send in tanks to protect the communist governments of Eastern Europe.

This was the signal people needed. Within weeks those governments collapsed, one by one. They were replaced by democratically elected governments which adopted a capitalist economic system.

The fall of the Berlin Wall

The most spectacular event was in Berlin. Ever since it was built in 1961, the Berlin Wall symbolised the failure of communism and the division of Europe.

On the night of 9 November 1989, the communist rulers of East Germany suddenly announced that the Wall was open. While an amazed world watched on TV, thousands of East Berliners poured through the gates and into West Berlin. Some of them greeted relatives in the West whom they had not seen since the Wall had been built almost thirty years before.

Germans sit on the Berlin Wall celebrating the opening of the border between East and West Germany. Soon bits of the Wall were being sold as souvenirs.

The end of the Soviet Union

In 1991 communist hard-liners, angered by Gorbachev's reforms, tried to take over the Soviet Union. They were defeated. This was the signal for the break-up of the Soviet Union. Although dominated by Russia, it was officially a union of eighteen separate republics. Now many of these republics became independent.

In Russia, Gorbachev had to resign and Boris Yeltsin became president. He approved a new democratic constitution and adopted the capitalist economic system. The Cold War had ended in victory for the Western system of democracy and capitalism.

Note

Among the countries that became independent after the collapse of the Soviet Union were the Ukraine, Latvia, Lithuania, Estonia and Belarus. Another was Georgia, where Stalin was born.

Questions

1 Who became the ruler of the USSR in 1985?
2 What was his policy of 'Glasnost'?
3 How did Gorbachev help to end communism in Eastern Europe?
4 Name three countries that removed their communist government in1989.
5 What happened in Berlin in November 1989?
6 What happened to the USSR in 1991?

Review the chapter

1 Why do you think 1989 is called the 'year of miracles'? Give three reasons to support your answer.

2 Write a paragraph giving the main reasons for the fall of the Soviet Union.

www The Cold War on the Internet

www.coldwar.org/index.html An American website dedicated to the Cold War. If you click on resources on the menu, you will find links to a vast number of websites relating to the Cold War.

http://learningcurve.pro.gov.uk/coldwar/default.htm This site from the British National Archives is designed to help students understand the Cold War.

www.cnn.com/specials/cold.war/ Excellent site from the American TV network, CNN. All aspects of the Cold War are covered with timelines, primary documents and much more.

Getting to Know the Junior Certificate

The syllabus recommends that you should know the following about The Rise of the Superpowers.

Topic	Description	Approach
International Relations in the Twentieth Century	**1B** The Rise of the Superpowers	You need to know the different ideologies of the two superpowers, why tension arose between them after World War II, and three important crises that brought them close to war.

This topic usually come up in Questions 3 and 4 on the Higher and Ordinary Level papers and in Question 6D on the Higher Level paper. Students should prepare the following for the exam:

1 Why the Cold War began after World War II
2 The Berlin Blockade 1948–49
3 The Korean War 1950–53
4 The Cuban Missiles Crisis

Topic 1C

Moves to European Unity

Chapter 1 The Origins of the European Economic Community

Europe devastated by war

In the first half of the twentieth century, Europe experienced two terrible wars.

- In World War I millions of young men died between 1914 and 1918. After it, people hoped desperately for peace but instead a worse war began in 1939.
- By the time World War II ended in 1945, most of Europe was devastated. Millions of people were dead. Savage bombing had left whole cities in ruins. The survivors huddled in the ruins, often starving, without work or hope. Around Europe millions of people were homeless refugees with no country to call their own.

What caused the wars?

Despairing people asked: how could this have happened and what could they do to prevent it from happening again? Here are some of the answers they came up with.

- **Hatred and rivalry caused the wars:** Both wars grew out of hatred and rivalry between countries, and especially between France and Germany. If hatred and rivalry could be turned into friendship and co-operation, then another war might be avoided.
- **Dictators ignored human rights:** Dictators like Hitler, Mussolini, Stalin and Franco caused great suffering by ignoring human rights. Only democratic governments could uphold human rights.
- **Hitler started the war:** A fascist dictator, Hitler, started World War II. Democratic governments do not usually begin wars. Therefore it is important to encourage and support democratic governments.
- **Poverty helped fascists or communists win power:** In the 1920s and 1930s many people in Europe were very poor. They voted for fascist or communist parties because these parties gave them hope for a better future. Therefore, democratic governments must ensure their people had jobs, houses, education and health care so that they would not be tempted to support fascists or communists in the future.

The leaders of a new Europe

Among those who reached these conclusions were the three men below. After the war they worked to create a peaceful, democratic and prosperous Europe.

Jean Monnet was a French businessman and civil servant who had opposed the Nazis. After the war he was asked to plan the French economy.

Robert Schuman was a French politician who joined the French Resistance to fight against the Nazi occupation of his country. After the war he became French prime minister.

Konrad Adenauer was a German politician who had opposed Hitler and was imprisoned. In 1949 he became the Chancellor of the new German republic.

Defending human rights: The Council of Europe

When World War II ended, the horrors of the Nazi concentration camps showed what misery dictators could inflict. In 1949 ten democratic governments, including Ireland, set up the Council of Europe to foster democracy and respect for human rights.

The Council drew up the **European Convention on Human Rights**. The rights that the Convention lists include:

- The right to a fair trial
- The right not to be tortured
- The right to privacy
- The right to travel

All governments that join the Council guarantee these rights to their citizens. The Council also set up the **European Court of Justice** to see that governments keep their promise. Citizens from any member state who feel their government is treating them unjustly can go to the Court to get justice.

The inaugural meeting of the Council of Europe at Strasbourg University in 1949

Only democratic governments can join the Council of Europe. As democracy expanded in Europe, more countries joined and today it has 34 members. As well as defending democracy, the Council has encouraged co-operation and friendship among European people.

Economic co-operation among European countries

Monnet and Schuman believed that peace and democracy depended on prosperity. The best way to achieve this, they believed, was to encourage economic co-operation between countries. This belief produced a number of organisations.

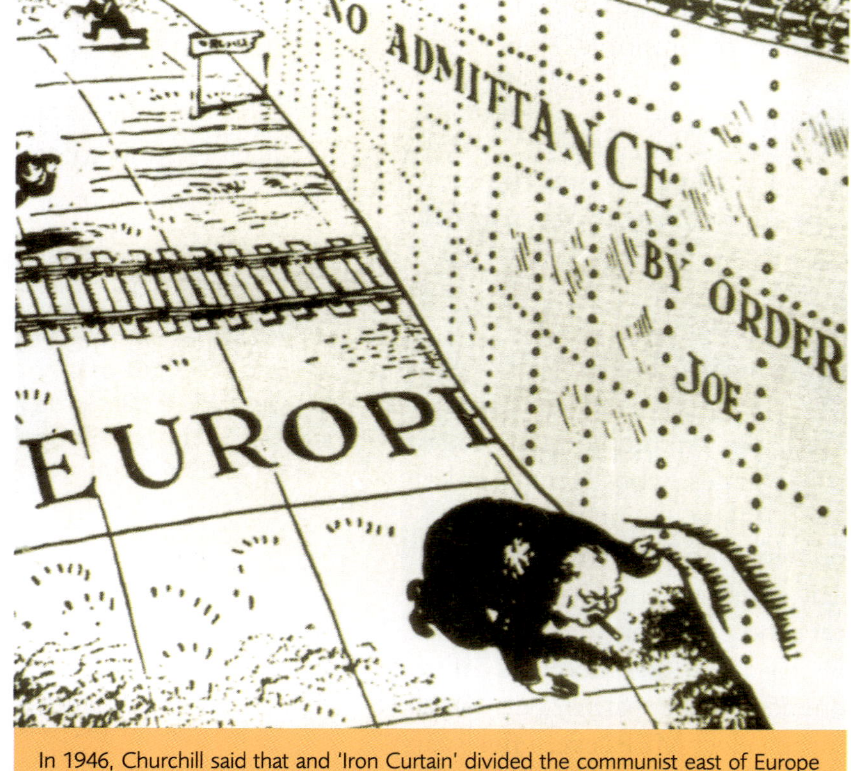

In 1946, Churchill said that and 'Iron Curtain' divided the communist east of Europe from the capitalist west. Fear of the spread of communism encouraged European unity.

- **The Organisation for European Economic Co-operation (OEEC):** After the war, the United States feared that Stalin planned to conquer Western Europe. To prevent that, the Americans gave money (Marshall Aid) to European governments to help them develop their economies. The OEEC was set up to distribute the money. As a result of this investment, the economies of Western Europe recovered quickly from the war.

- **The Benelux Union:** Belgium, the Netherlands and Luxembourg suffered badly during the war. When it was over, their leaders decided to work together to rebuild their economies. They formed the **Benelux Union**. Goods, people and money could pass freely between them. The Union was a success and by 1950 they had become prosperous. This suggested that co-operation rather than competition could create prosperity.

- **The European Coal and Steel Community:** After the success of the Benelux Union, Jean Monnet and Robert Schuman suggested that France and Germany share their coal and steel industries. These two countries were old enemies, so this was an extraordinary idea. The German Chancellor, **Konrad Adenauer**, agreed but at first French people were reluctant to join. They only agreed when Italy and the Benelux countries joined as well. In 1951, these six countries formed the European Coal and Steel Community. To the surprise of the French people, it was a great success.

The Treaty of Rome and the start of the European Economic Community (EEC)

The six countries then decided to co-operate in other economic areas. After talks, they agreed that:

- People, goods and services could pass freely between them.
- They would set up a **Common Agricultural Policy** (CAP), which would give farmers guaranteed prices to grow more food. The CAP was set up just ten years after Europe nearly starved in the war. It was so successful that within ten years, the EEC had a problem with huge food surpluses (called 'wine lakes' and 'butter mountains').
- They would have a **Social Policy**, under which richer areas like Germany would help poorer areas like southern Italy to improve their roads, telephones, etc.
- They would work for political as well as economic unity.

These commitments were included in the **Treaty of Rome**. Six countries signed it in 1957, and on 1 January 1958 the **European Economic Community (EEC)** came into existence.

The institutions of the EEC

The Treaty of Rome set up four main institutions to run the EEC. They still operate today.

- **The Council of Ministers** is the main decision-making body. It consists of government ministers from the member states who meet regularly. They decide on the policies that the EEC will follow.
- **The European Commission** consists of two members from each large country and one member from each small country. The Commissioners propose changes to the Council of Ministers and carry out their decisions.
- **The European Parliament**. From 1958 to 1979 the members of the European parliament (MEPs) were appointed by the parliaments of the member states. Since 1979 the people of Europe elect MEPs every five years. Ireland elects 15 MEPs, but that number will decline as the EU expands. The parliament has less power than the other institutions but its power is growing.
- **The European Court:** This consists of judges appointed by the member states. Its job is to see that the members obey the rules of the Union.

Questions

1. Name three of the men who helped to start the search for European unity. Why did they start and what did they hope to achieve?
2. Write a short account of the Council of Europe.
3. Name two of the institutions that laid the foundations of the EEC and write a short account of each of them.
4. Give the main terms of the Treaty of Rome.

The EEC succeeds

When the EEC was set up, many people were sceptical. Nothing like this had ever been tried before. How could once bitter enemies co-operate? But they were soon proved wrong. Within ten years the EEC was peaceful and prosperous. Its people had one of the highest living standards in the world. This success encouraged other countries to apply to join. The most important of these was Britain.

Britain, Ireland and the EEC

Although the British were involved with the Council of Europe, they refused to join the EEC when it was set up. They had close ties with America and their empire and they thought these were enough.

But as the EEC prospered, the British economy lagged behind. The British government realised their mistake and applied to join. This presented the Irish government with a problem. In 1961 Ireland sold over 90 per cent of its exports to Britain. If Britain went into the EEC, Ireland had to go in too, although the Irish economy was still backward.

HAPPY NEW YEAR, NEW EUROPEANS!

Irish Independent

MONDAY, JANUARY 1, 1973

GOOD MORNING, EUROPE!

Historic moment as we go into E.E.C.

FROM DAVID HAWORTH, OUR MAN IN BRUSSELS

THIS MORNING we join a potential new superpower, which possibly will one day rival the U.S. and Russia. The formal enlargement of the European Common Market, to include Ireland, Denmark and Britain came at midnight last night.

The headquarters of the European Commission in Brussels — (Picture: courtesy E.E.C.)

A headline from the day Ireland joined the EU. **What date was that? What was the EU called then? What building does the photo show?**

In 1961 the Taoiseach, Seán Lemass, applied to join on the same day as Britain. But the French President, General de Gaulle, blocked Britain's entry. He thought they were too close to the Americans, whom he did not trust. The delay gave the Irish economy more time to develop.

When de Gaulle retired, the British applied again. In 1972 the talks succeeded. The Irish government sought the people's approval in a referendum. Over 70 per cent voted for membership and Ireland joined the EEC on 1 January 1973, along with Denmark and Britain.

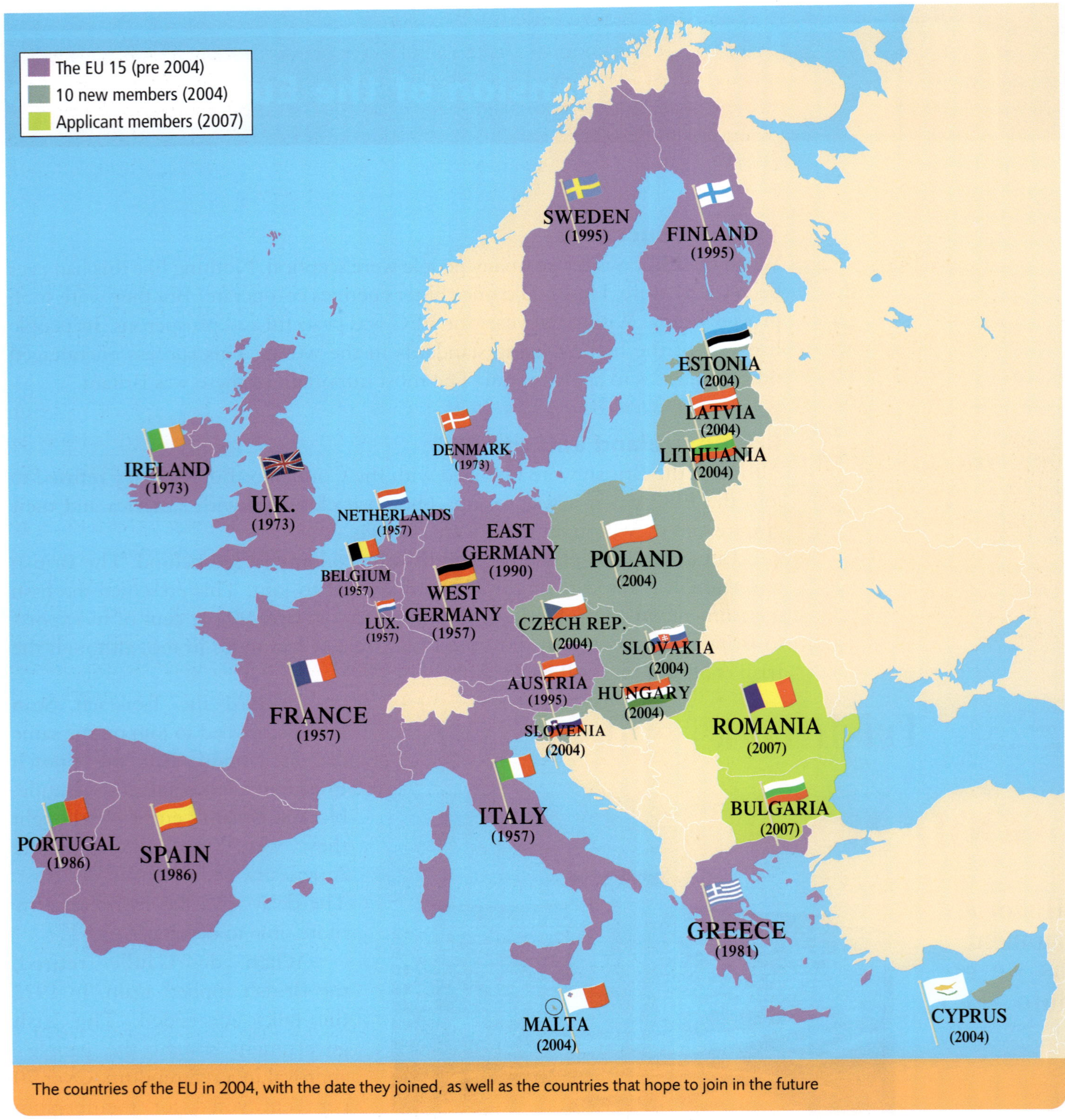

The countries of the EU in 2004, with the date they joined, as well as the countries that hope to join in the future

Expanding the European Union

Since then, more countries have joined the European Union. The biggest group of new members came from Eastern Europe. After World War II, the Soviet Union controlled this area and forced communist dictatorships on the people. When the Soviet Union fell in 1990, the countries of Eastern Europe ended communism and became democracies. All applied to join the EU, though it took a while for them to develop their economies sufficiently.

Jacques Delors, the French politician who was head of the EU Commission from 1985 to 1995

Changing the EEC into the EU

Until the 1980s the members of the EEC concentrated on developing economic co-operation. Then in 1985 a Frenchman, **Jacques Delors**, became head of the Commission. Between 1985 and 1995 he encouraged many changes in the Community.

- **1985: the Single European Act:** Under it members agreed to bring their taxation systems into line and to remove any remaining barriers to trade and free movement of people. It also increased the power of the European Parliament.
- **1989: The European Monetary System:** the members agreed to try to reduce inflation and keep their currencies in line with each other.
- **1992: The Maastricht Treaty:** The Maastricht Treaty turned the EEC into the **European Union**. Members agreed to much closer political co-operation. This included the establishing of a common currency called the **euro**. It began to operate on 1 January 2002, when most members gave up their local currencies, and euro notes and coins went into circulation.

How the EU has affected Europe

The EU has had a profound impact on the countries of Europe.

- Apart from a short war in the Balkans after Yugoslavia collapsed, there has been no war in Europe for sixty years.
- The governments of the EU are all democracies that respect the human rights of their citizens.
- The EU created a huge market of over 300 million people who move freely and trade freely across the Continent.
- The EU has brought prosperity to its citizens, most of whom enjoy a high standard of living.

How membership of the EU has affected Ireland

Being a member of the EU has changed Ireland profoundly.

- Membership of this large international union has allowed a small, poor country to have more influence on events than it could have had on its own.
- It has created greater equality with Britain because the two countries must negotiate as equal partners in the Union. This has encouraged co-operation in bringing peace in Northern Ireland.
- The Common Agricultural Policy has brought prosperity to rural areas in Ireland. The Structural Fund has paid for better roads, telecommunications and education.
- Ireland's access to the European market is an important reason why large multinational companies have set up factories here.

Questions

1. Explain how Ireland joined the EEC.
2. List and describe three major changes in the EEC since Ireland joined in 1973.
3. Name all the countries that have joined the EU since 1973. Where did the biggest group of new members come from?

Review the chapter

(i) Name two politicians associated with the moves to European Unity after World War II.
(ii) Describe the major moves towards European Unity between 1945 and the Treaty of Rome in 1957.
(iii) Write an account of the growth of the European Union between 1957 and the Maastricht Treaty in 1992. *(Junior Certificate, 2003)*

www The European Union on the Internet

http://europa.eu.int/abc/history/index_en.htm You can read about the progress towards European Unity and examine key events at the official site of the European Union.

www.let.leidenuniv.nl/history/rtg/res1/ The History of the European Union from a website run by a Dutch University.

Getting to Know the Junior Certificate

The syllabus recommends that you should know the following about Moves towards European Unity:

Topic	Description	Approach
International Relations in the Twentieth Century	**1C** Moves towards European Unity	You need to know the reasons, both economic and political, why people wanted European unity after 1945, what they hoped to achieve by it and the extent to which these aims have been achieved.

This topic usually comes up in Questions 3 and 4 on the Higher and Ordinary Level papers and in Question 6D on the Higher Level paper. Students should prepare the following for the exam:

1. Events leading to the Treaty of Rome, 1957.
2. The Growth of the European Union.
3. The Maastricht Treaty, 1992.

Topic 1D

India – A Study in Asian Nationalism

Chapter 1 What Was India Like Under British Rule?

Note

Colonialism is when a strong country takes over a weaker country and makes use of its resources. India was a colony of Britain.

Colonialism

In the eighteenth and nineteenth centuries European countries had the strongest armies and the strongest economies in the world. This allowed some of them to conquer parts of Asia and Africa. This is called **colonialism**.

After World War II many of the colonies in Asia and Africa became independent. This chapter tells the story of how one colony, India, won its independence from British rule.

In 1900 the British Empire was the biggest in the world. This map shows the areas that Britain ruled. India was one of them. The British thought so highly of it they called it the 'Jewel in the Crown'.

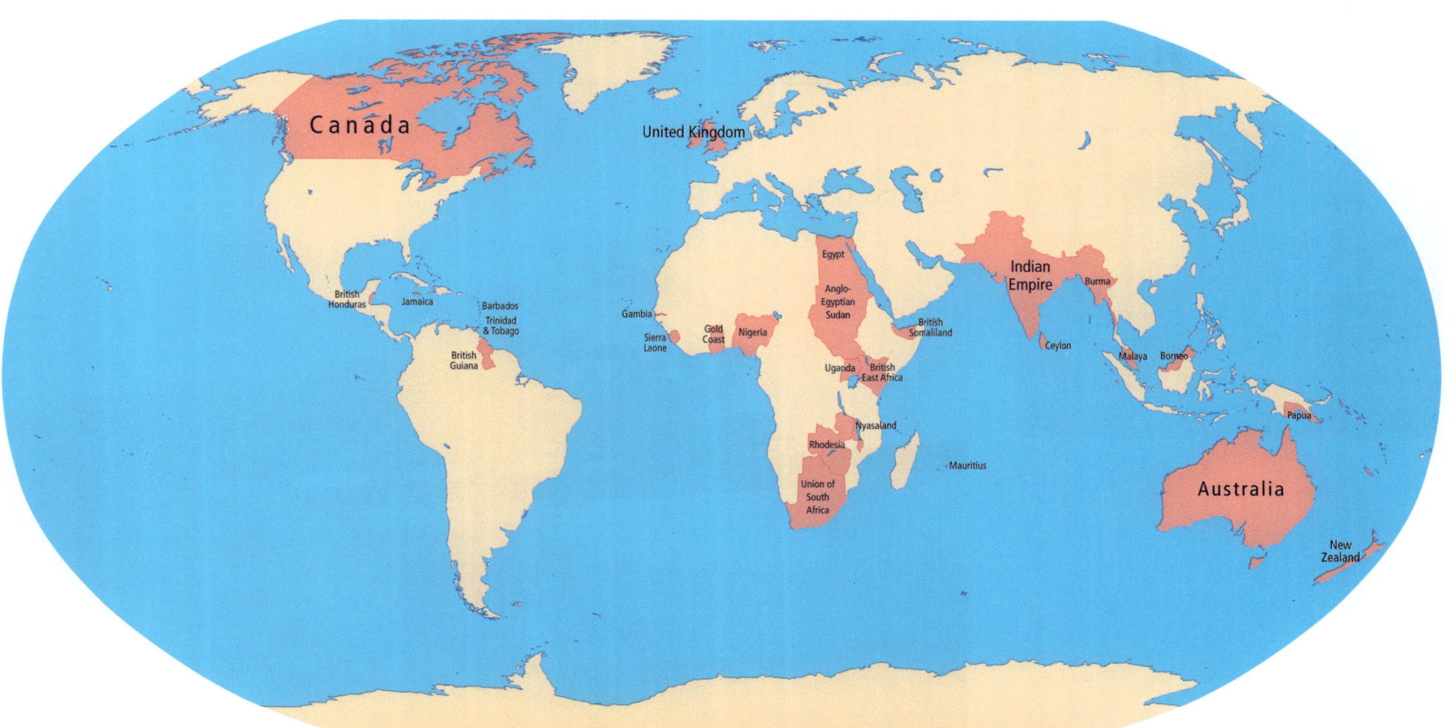

The British Empire in 1900. The British boasted that the sun never set on their empire. **Can you name three other countries, apart from India, that Britain ruled?**

India in the British Empire

India had a population of about 300 million in 1900. This made it an important market for British goods. Indians bought cloth, steel, machines and other things from Britain. In return, the British bought tea, dyes, raw cotton and other raw materials from India.

Was British rule good for India?

The following sources tell us about relations between the British and the Indians. Study them and then answer the questions that follow.

Source A

This picture shows an Indian child attending school

Source B

From a letter written to *The Times* by a British army officer serving in India:

> *'I must say that I have been struck with the arrogant and repellent manner in which we often treat natives of rank, and with the unnecessary harshness of our treatment of inferiors. The most scrubby mean little representative of the white race…regards…himself as infinitely superior to Indians with a genealogy* [family history] *of a thousand years.'*

Source C

A train passing through a rural Indian village

Source D

Indians officers in the British army

Source E

British troops fighting Indians

Source F

Mahatma Gandhi, leader of India's campaign for independence, wrote in 1909:

> *'I admit you are my rulers…but although you are the rulers; you will have to remain as servants of the people. It is not we who have to do as you wish, but it is you who have to do as we wish…The common language of India is not English but Hindi. You should learn it.'*

Questions

1 Do you think the British treated the Indians well? Select two pieces of evidence from the sources to support your answer.

2 Do you think the British and the Indians mixed much? Pick out three pieces of evidence to support your answer.

Advantages of British rule

In some ways British rule was good for India:

- The British built railways that linked the different parts of India together.
- They set up schools where Indians got a good education.
- They encouraged irrigation (bringing water to desert areas), which increased the amount of food Indian farmers could grow.
- They set up courts where Indians got a fair trial.
- They tried to end some customs such as 'sati'. This was a Hindu Indian custom in which a widow was burned to death on her husband's funeral pyre. The woman could either commit suicide or be forcibly burnt alive by her in-laws.

A painting showing the Hindu custom of Sati

Disadvantages of British rule

But some Indians pointed out that there were disadvantages to British rule.

- The British imposed heavy taxes on India.
- Cheap British cloth ruined the Indian cloth industry and put many poor Indians out of work.
- Most of the important jobs in India (civil servants, judges, and teachers) went to British people and not Indians. Only Europeans could hold posts worth over £500 per year.

The Congress Party

Some wealthy Indians went to school in Britain. There they found that even poor men could vote for the government of their choice. But in India, Indians could not vote for their government.

These Indians realised that British rule was unfair. They wanted Indians to rule themselves. They set up a political party called **the Congress Party** to work for Indian independence.

Crowds of supporters of the Muslim League

The Muslim League

There were many religious groups in India, but the two main ones were the **Hindus** and the **Muslims**. Over 70 per cent of Indians were Hindu, while 25 per cent were Muslims.

It was mainly the Hindus who supported the Congress Party. This worried the Muslims. They were afraid that if India won its independence, Muslims would be out-voted by the Hindus. To protect themselves, the Muslims set up their own party, **the Muslim League**. It too worked for independence for India.

During World War I, Britain and America said they were fighting for democracy and 'self-determination' (letting people rule themselves). This encouraged more Indians to demand independence. The Congress Party and the Muslim League grew in strength.

Questions

1. What does colonisation mean?
2. What European country ruled India before World War II?
3. Name three advantages and three disadvantages of that country's rule for India.
4. Give two reasons why some Indians wanted independence.
5. What were the names of the two main religious groups in India? What percentage of the population was in each group?
6. What two parties were set up to fight for independence for India? What was the difference between them?
7. Read the quote in Source F on page 111.
   (i) How does Gandhi feel about British rule in India?
   (ii) Does he want complete independence for india? Give a reason for your answer.

Chapter 2 Who Was Mahatma Gandhi?

Gandhi

After World War I, the Indian Congress Party got a new leader. His name was Mohandas Gandhi. He came from a wealthy Hindu family. At nineteen he went to England to study law. After that he went to South Africa. Many Indian people lived there and they were very badly treated. Gandhi used his skill as a lawyer to protect them. He returned to India in 1914, joined the Congress Party and campaigned for Home Rule for India. He tried to unify all classes and religious groups behind the campaign.

Mahatma Gandhi in Downing Street, London. Even there he dressed like an Indian peasant.

The 'Mahatma'

The poorest people in India were the peasants (farmers). Gandhi went to live among them in their villages. He ate the same simple food they ate and dressed like them in a simple robe. Like them he learned to spin and make cloth. He used the spinning wheel as the emblem of the Congress Party. His actions impressed the peasants. Here at last was a leader who sided with them.

They called him 'Mahatma', which means 'great soul'. Gandhi won over the peasants to the Congress Party. By 1930 Gandhi had a huge following.

Non-violent opposition to the British

Gandhi hated violence. He believed a corrupt political system could be overcome by peaceful means. He wrote: *'I object to violence because when it appears to do good, the good is only temporary: the evil it does is permanent.'* He asked Indians to boycott British courts, to stop buying British goods and not to work for the British.

His most famous campaign was about the price of salt. Most Indians needed salt to keep their food fresh. But the British government controlled the price of salt and kept the price high. Gandhi led thousands of Indians on a 200 mile (320km) protest march to the Indian Ocean. Here the protesters made their own salt by evaporating seawater. The British put Gandhi in prison but that only made him more popular. In the end the campaign was successful and the price controls were removed.

Indian women and children gather salt water, which they will evaporate to make salt. Gandhi favoured this kind of peaceful protest.

Muslims from India protesting in London in 1946. **What are they demanding?**

Hindus and Muslims

Gandhi became convinced that India would never be really free as long as it remained part of the British Empire. The British also realised they would have to give the Indians more say in government. They set up elected local councils to deal with local matters.

The Congress Party won most of the seats in these councils and this worried the Muslim League. Its leader, Muhammed Jinnah, said that if the British left India, the Muslims must have their own state.

The Hindus objected to this idea because it would partition India (divide it in two). There were riots between Hindus and Muslims.

Note

After World War II Europeans were no longer able to control their large empires. They began to grant their colonies independence. This is called **'decolonisation'**.

Independence

In 1939 Britain went to war with Germany. Gandhi demanded independence as India's price for helping Britain during the war.

When the war ended in 1945 Britain had neither the men nor the money to keep the empire going. The British announced that they would leave in 1947.

The Partition of India

The British tried to get the Congress Party and the Muslim League to rule India together but they failed. Finally in 1947 they agreed to partition the country. The Muslims got their own state, which is called **Pakistan** (see map on next page). The rest became the Republic of India.

Gandhi had not wanted partition. He said in 1946: *'Before partitioning India my body will have to cut into two pieces.'* However, the alternative to partition seemed to be civil war between the Hindus and the Muslims. So at the last minute Gandhi urged the Congress Party to accept partition.

The division didn't happen peacefully. Nearly one million people died in riots between Hindus and Muslims. Terrified Hindus fled from Pakistan to India and terrified Muslims fled from India to Pakistan.

Riots in Calcutta in 1948

Gandhi killed by Hindu protestor

Gandhi went from village to village trying to stop the slaughter. Wherever he went he made peace. He turned again to non-violent protest. He went on hunger strike, saying he would not eat until the violence stopped. He also said that India would have to give back the 550 million rupees (€50 million) it was holding from Pakistan.

Gandhi failed to bring peace between the Hindus and the Muslims. Then a fellow Hindu, Nathuram Godse, who felt that Gandhi had betrayed the Hindu cause, shot him on his way to a prayer meeting in 1948. Gandhi, who was seventy-eight, died from three wounds to the chest.

India at the time of partition. The eastern province of Pakistan became an independent state called Bangladesh in 1971.

India after independence

Pandit Nehru became the leader of India after Gandhi's death, and his family have played a prominent role in Indian politics ever since. A big problem India faced was deciding on the border between it and Pakistan. There were bitter riots over Punjab and Bengal in particular, because both Hindus and Muslims lived there. Can you see these places on the map? Later there were wars with Pakistan over Kashmir and Bangladesh. The last war between India and Pakistan was in 1999.

When the Indians designed a flag for themselves, they included Gandhi's spinning wheel emblem

India's increasing population

India's population has grown very fast since 1947. Over one billion people now live in India. There is a lot of poverty and many social problems such as dowry abuse. A dowry in India was a traditional custom where the bride's family made a payment in cash or property to the bridegroom's family. In 1990 nearly 5,000 women were killed, often burnt, because their husbands did not feel they had brought a large enough dowry to the family.

But India has also been very successful. It has become one of the top ten industrial powers in the world. Since 1947 it has become the world's largest producer of rice. It is the world's largest exporter of tea and computer programmes and it has one of the biggest film industries in the world.

Pandit Nehru

Questions

1. What does 'Mahatma' mean? How did Gandhi get this name?
2. Why did Gandhi and the Congress Party have a huge following by 1930?
3. What is non-violent protest? Give an example of two such protests that happened in India.
4. What were the two main religious groups in India? What was the relationship between them?
5. Explain what is meant by 'decolonisation' and say why European countries began to decolonise after World War II.
6. Describe how independence came to India.
7. Why was India partitioned?
8. Write down two problems and two successes that have affected India since 1947.

Review the chapter

1 Here is a quote from Gandhi:
'I have nothing new to teach the world. Truth and non-violence are as old as the hills. All I have done is to try experiments in both on as vast a scale as I could.'

(i) Explain what Gandhi meant by non-violence.
(ii) Give an example of the non-violent tactics he used.
(iii) Would you agree that his experiment in non-violence was on a vast scale? Explain your answer.

2* (i) In a named African or Asian country, mention one leader who led the movement towards independence.
(ii) Mention the colonial power that controlled the country that you have named.
(iii) Write an account of the independence struggle in that country after World War II.

(Junior Certificate, 2001)

3 Write about a named leader in the movement for the independence of a named country in Africa or Asia. *(Junior Certificate, 1999)*

4* (i) Write about the movement for independence of a named country in Africa or Asia.
(ii) Write about the experiences of that country after securing its independence.

(Junior Certificate, 1998)

* Questions 2 and 4 above show what Junior Certificate exam questions on this topic are like. Since you have studied India, you should use what you know about India to answer them.

www India on the Internet

www.itihaas.com/modern/index.html A timeline with links about India's struggle for independence.

www.historyofindia.com As the name suggests, you can find out about the history of India at this website.

www.mkgandhi.org An Indian website dedicated to Mahatma Gandhi.

www.famous-quotesandquotations.com/mahatmagandhi-quotes.html Famous quotes from Gandhi.

Getting to Know the Junior Certificate

The syllabus recommends that you should know the following about India – A Study in Asian Nationalism:

Topic	Description	Approach
International Relations in the Twentieth Century	**1D** India – A Study in Asian Nationalism	You need to know what British rule in India was like, why the Indians wanted independence, how they achieved it and how India has developed since independence.

This topic usually comes up in Questions 3 and 4 on the Higher and Ordinary Level papers and in Question 6D on the Higher Level paper. Students should prepare the following for the exam.

1 The colonial background of India.
2 India's independence movement.
3 India's post-colonial experience.

Section 2

Political Developments in Ireland, 1900–2000

Topic 2A

Political Developments in Ireland, 1900–1921

Chapter 1 Ireland at the Start of the Twentieth Century

Ireland then and now

Ireland changed greatly in the twentieth century. In this section we will look at these changes and the reasons why they happened. But first look at these two maps. They show the most important changes.

This map shows Ireland today. Look at these three points.

(i) The island of Ireland is divided in two: the Republic of Ireland and Northern Ireland.

(ii) Northern Ireland is part of the United Kingdom along with Britain.

(iii) Ireland and the United Kingdom are both part of the European Union.

This map shows Ireland around 1910. Compare it with the map above.

(i) The island of Ireland was united.

(ii) All of it was part of the United Kingdom along with Britain.

(iii) There was no European Union; instead the Continent was divided into several powerful empires, which would soon be changed forever by World War I.

1800–1922: Ireland in the United Kingdom

In Book One, Section 9, you read about the Act of Union. It made Ireland part of the United Kingdom. This is what that meant:

- Ireland, England, Scotland and Wales were all in one state called the **United Kingdom (UK)**. The official head of that state in 1910 was King George V.
- Laws for all these countries were made by the United Kingdom parliament in Westminster. Irish voters elected 105 MPs to go to Westminster and help to make these laws.
- The head of the government of the United Kingdom was the **Prime Minister**, who lived in London. He appointed two ministers to run Ireland. They were called the **Viceroy** and the **Chief Secretary**. The Viceroy lived in this house in Phoenix Park in Dublin.

Aras an Uachtaráin where the President lives today. Until 1922 it was the home of the Viceroy, the King's representative in Ireland.

Questions

1. List three important differences between Ireland in 1910 and Ireland today. Which do you think mattered more to Irish people? Explain your choice.
2. Where were the laws for Ireland made in 1910?
3. What were the two people who were responsible for running Ireland called? Who appointed them?

Was It Good For Ireland to Be Part of the United Kingdom?

Unionists and nationalists

In 1910 the people in Ireland were divided in their attitude to the United Kingdom.

- Those who thought the United Kingdom was bad for Ireland were called **nationalists**.
- Those who thought the United Kingdom was good for Ireland were called **unionists**.

The Harland & Wolff shipyard was the world's biggest. Here we see The *Olympic* liner almost complete in 1911 and, beside it, its sistership the *Titanic*. Some 20,000 men worked in the shipyards and this largely accounted for Belfast's prosperity.

	Nationalists	Unionists
Who they were	Most Irish Catholics were nationalists. There were about 3 million of them. They were a majority in all parts of Ireland except the north-east.	Most Irish Protestants were unionists. There were about 1 million of them. They were scattered around Ireland but the majority were in the north-east around Belfast.
What they wanted	Nationalists wanted Ireland to have its own parliament and elect a government to run Irish affairs.	Unionists wanted Ireland to stay in the United Kingdom.
Why they wanted it	(i) Catholics felt that the British, who were mostly Protestant, discriminated against them in jobs. (ii) Most of Ireland was poor. Between 1800 and 1910 it experienced famine and emigration. Nationalists felt they could manage the Irish economy better than the British had.	(i) Unionists feared that the Catholics, who outnumbered them, might persecute them if Ireland had its own parliament. (ii) Belfast was prosperous in 1900, even when the rest of Ireland was poor. Unionists thought that might end if Ireland left the United Kingdom.

Political parties

Both nationalists and unionists had their own political parties who worked to achieve their aims.

- Unionists voted for the **Unionist Party**. In 1910 their leaders were **Edward Carson** and **James Craig**. They elected about twenty of the Irish MPs at Westminster. They tried to persuade the British to keep Ireland in the United Kingdom.
- Nationalists voted for the **Home Rule Party.** In 1910 its leader was **John Redmond**. Nationalists elected over eighty of the Irish MPs at the Westminster parliament. There they tried to persuade the British to give Ireland its own parliament.

John Redmond

Edward Carson

Extreme nationalists / republicans

Not all nationalists agreed with the Home Rule Party. A small number were extremists. They believed that the only way that Ireland would get its freedom was to fight for it.

Many extreme nationalists belonged to a small secret society called the **Irish Republican Brotherhood (IRB)**. That is why extreme nationalists are also called **republicans**. IRB men swore an oath to fight for an Irish republic and not to tell anyone what they were planning. In 1910 two men, **Sean McDermott** and **Tom Clarke**, were leaders of the IRB.

This diagram shows the main differences between the Home Rulers and the republicans.

Sean McDermott

Tom Clarke

	Home Rule	Republic
What did it mean?	Ireland would have a parliament making laws about Irish home affairs like education or health. The British would still decide on foreign affairs like trade or war.	Ireland would be completely independent of the British. It would control both home and foreign affairs. The British would have no say in what Ireland did.
Who would be the head of state?	The King / Queen of Britain.	A president elected by Irish people.
How to achieve it?	By peaceful persuasion.	By a violent rebellion against the British.

In 1910 most Irish nationalists disapproved of violence. Therefore they supported John Redmond and the Home Rule Party. Then a number of developments changed that. By 1918 the Home Rulers were defeated and the republicans had won the backing of the majority of nationalists.

Questions

1 In Ireland in 1910, what was a nationalist? What kind of people were nationalists and how many of them were there?
2 In Ireland in 1910, what was a unionist? What kind of people were unionists and how many of them were there?
3 What political party did unionists support and who led it in 1910?
4 What political party did most nationalists support and who led it in 1910?
5 Give (i) two reasons why nationalists wanted Ireland to leave the United Kingdom and (ii) two reasons why unionists wanted Ireland to stay in it.
6 What was a republican and what did republicans want?
7 Name the main republican organisation and its leaders. How did it plan to win a republic for Ireland?
8 Which did most nationalists support in 1910: Home Rulers or republicans? Explain why that was.

New Cultural and Political Movements

New cultural movements

The start of the twentieth century was an exciting time in Ireland. New ideas and new movements emerged which helped to form the very different Ireland we have today.

Note

Anglicisation = becoming like the English. This started in Ireland with the plantations.

Were the Irish becoming too like the English?

Nationalists wanted Ireland to have its own government. They said that the main reason for this was that Irish people were different from the English. But throughout the nineteenth century the things that made the Irish different slowly vanished.

- The Irish language was the most obvious difference between the English and the Irish, but by 1900 only 14 per cent of Irish people knew any Irish. The rest spoke only English.
- Irish people were reading books and newspapers that came from England and which carried English ideas.
- Irish people were playing games like rugby, cricket and soccer, which had been invented in England.

Nationalists were worried by these developments. If the Irish got more like the English, how could they claim the right to rule themselves? To avoid this, some nationalists set up movements to strengthen Irish culture.

Michael Cusack

The Gaelic Athletic Association

In 1884 **Michael Cusack**, a teacher from Clare, set up the **Gaelic Athletic Association (GAA)**. It drew up rules and organised competitions for Irish games like Gaelic football and hurling. The most important competitions led to the All-Ireland finals each year.

Membership of the GAA grew quickly after 1900. Soon each parish had its own club, electing its own leaders and organising its own matches. This gave many Irish men their first experience in running a democratic movement.

The Gaelic League

Douglas Hyde, founder of the Gaelic League and later the first president of Ireland

In 1893 **Douglas Hyde** and **Eoin MacNeill** set up **the Gaelic League**. It wanted to end the decline of the Irish language. The League

- set up classes where people could learn Irish
- encouraged Irish dancing and music
- printed books and a newspaper in Irish.

Young men and women joined the League to learn Irish and have fun at the céilís it organised. They included Eamon de Valera (who met his wife through the League) and Michael Collins. The League produced a newspaper, *An Claidheamh Soluis*, which was edited by Patrick Pearse. The Gaelic League encouraged many people to study Irish and halted the decline of the language.

Douglas Hyde was a Protestant. He hoped a shared love of Irish would unite Protestants and Catholics, unionists and nationalists. But the opposite happened. People who wanted to save Irish thought that only an Irish government could do that. They became more extremely nationalist. In 1915 the IRB gained control of the League and Hyde resigned in disgust.

An Claideam Soluis

[An Claidheamh Soluis.]

Agus Fáinne an Lae.

[Registered as a Newspaper.]

Dublin, June 13, 1903

One Penny.

The Gaelic League paper, *An Claidheamh Soluis*, encouraged Irish music, dancing and story-telling as well as learning Irish

The Abbey Theatre at the time it was opened

The Literary Revival and the Abbey Theatre

Around the 1890s a number of poets and playwrights began to write about Irish subjects in English. The most important poet was **W. B. Yeats**.

In 1904 Yeats helped Lady Gregory to set up the **Abbey Theatre**. It put on plays about Irish subjects. The most famous play was *The Playboy of the Western World* by J. M. Synge, which was put on in 1908.

Many nationalists were not sure what to make of the Literary Revival. Poets and playwrights wanted to write the truth as they saw it and not just propaganda for nationalism. When Synge's play was first put on there was a riot in the Abbey, because nationalists thought it showed Irish people in a bad light.

Questions

1. What reason did nationalists give for wanting to be independent of Britain? Why was that reason becoming weaker by 1910?
2. Name the organisation that was set up to support Gaelic games. Who set it up?
3. Name the organisation that was set up to revive the Irish language. Who set it up? What did he hope it would do? What happened to that hope?
4. Name one writer who wrote in English about Irish subjects.
5. What was set up in 1904? Name two of the people involved.

New political movements

Several new political movements also began around the start of the twentieth century. Some were nationalist, others were not.

Arthur Griffith, the founder of Sinn Féin

Sinn Féin

A Dublin journalist called **Arthur Griffith** wanted Ireland to be independent of Britain. He did not think Home Rule gave Irish people enough freedom, but he also disliked the violence that the IRB planned. In 1905 he put forward a plan for winning more independence without violence. This was what he suggested:

- Irish MPs would refuse to go to the Westminster parliament. They would stay in Dublin, form their own government and ignore the British government.
- Griffith said that the British would have to accept this and leave. This would achieve freedom peacefully.
- To reassure the unionists, Griffith said Ireland should keep the king as head of state, rather than having a republic.

In 1905 Griffith set up a new party to put his ideas into practice. He called it Sinn Féin (Irish for 'ourselves'). At first some nationalists supported Sinn Féin. But that changed in 1910 when the Home Rulers at last persuaded the British government to agree to give Home Rule to Ireland (see next chapter). Now nationalists did not see a need for any further change.

The Labour Movement

Many of the people who lived in Irish towns and cities were very poor.

- They worked for low wages and lived in dreadful slums.
- They could not afford good food, so their health was bad.
- They could not afford to send their children to school, so they had very little education.

James Connolly introduced socialist ideas into Ireland

Around Europe, there were people who thought this kind of thing was unfair. They were called socialists. Socialists wanted decent living conditions for everyone.

- Some socialists wanted a revolution to get rid of the old system. They hoped to replace it with a new kind of society where everyone would have equal treatment. In Ireland **James Connolly** put this idea forward.
- Other socialists thought the workers should join together to form trade unions and demand better wages and conditions. In Ireland **James Larkin** supported this idea.

The 1913 lockout

Larkin set up the **Irish Transport and General Workers' Union (ITGWU)** to work for better wages. (Today it is known as SIPTU.) At first it was successful and this worried the employers. In 1913 they demanded that workers resign from Larkin's union. When they would not, their employers locked them out.

The lockout lasted for months. During it, Connolly formed the **Irish Citizen Army** to protect the workers from the police. In the end the workers lost and Larkin went to the USA. Connolly was left in charge of the ITGWU and the Citizen Army.

Some women turned to violent protest when their demand for the vote was ignored. This got attention but little sympathy.

Women demand right to vote

Around 1900 women also began to demand their rights. Since 1850 they had gradually been allowed to go to university and to become lawyers and doctors. But while even the most ignorant man could vote, no woman could.

This angered Hanna Sheehy Skeffington. She campaigned for the 'suffrage', as the right to vote was called. She and others went to prison for their cause.

Note

Women who campaigned for the vote called themselves **suffragists**. To belittle them, hostile newspapers christened them **'the suffragettes'**.

Hanna Sheehy-Skeffington

In 1918 the British government finally gave the vote to women over thirty. (Men could vote at 21!). Women in Britain and Northern Ireland did not get equal citizenship until 1928, but the new Irish Free State gave equal citizenship to women in 1922.

Questions

1 Who founded Sinn Féin? What did he want and how did he plan to achieve it?
2 Give one important difference between Sinn Féin and the Home Rule Party.
3 What were 'socialists'? What did they hope to achieve? Name two important Irish socialists.
4 Write a paragraph on the 1913 Lockout in Dublin.
5 Who could vote for MPs in 1910? Who campaigned to have that changed? Explain why.

Review the chapter

1 Select two cultural or political movements that appeared at the start of the twentieth century and write an account of them. You should include the people who founded them, their aims and their achievements.

2 In 1912 a leading Home Ruler said: 'Women's suffrage will, I believe, destroy the home and destroy the headship of man laid down by God'.
   (i) What point is the cartoon making about the future of men?
   (ii) Do the quote and cartoon agree or disagree? Explain your answer.
   (iii) Why did some men oppose votes for women?

3 Are the following statements true or false? If false, write down the correct statement.
   (i) Arthur Griffith founded the Gaelic League.
   (ii) The IRB wanted Home Rule for Ireland.
   (iii) The Gaelic League wanted to save the Irish language.
   (iv) W.B. Yeats played hurling for the GAA.
   (v) James Connolly locked out Dublin workers in 1913.

John Redmond and Home Rule at last

From 1900 **John Redmond** was the leader of the Home Rule Party. He was good at negotiating with British leaders. In 1910 he at last persuaded the British prime minister, **Herbert Asquith**, to agree to give Ireland Home Rule. It was due to begin in 1914.

Carson's campaign to stop Home Rule

Unionists were horrified at the idea of Home Rule. Their leaders, **Sir Edward Carson** and **Sir James Craig**, were determined to prevent it. They began to resist it in various ways.

Edward Carson signing The Ulster Covenant in 1912

- They organised mass demonstrations and protests. The biggest was in September 1912 when about 500,000 people signed the Ulster Covenant promising to oppose Home Rule by 'all means'.
- They encouraged unionists to form armed groups to resist Home Rule. These groups were called the **Ulster Volunteers**. At first they drilled with wooden guns, but in 1914 they bought guns and ammunition in Germany. They imported guns into Ireland at Larne in County Antrim. After that nationalists had to take the unionist objections seriously.

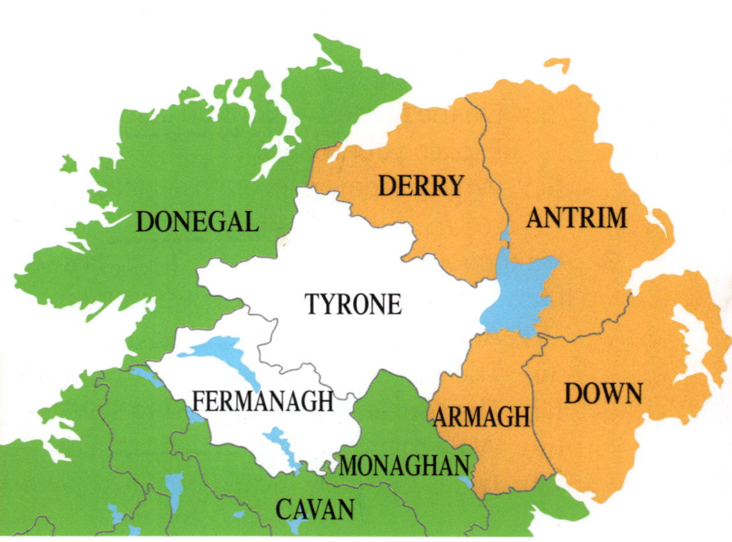

In four counties of Ulster, unionists were in a clear majority. Nationalists were in the majority in the west and south. But two counties, Tyrone and Fermanagh, were evenly divided. Both sides wanted to claim them.

There was a little man
And he had some little guns,
But his guns were made of wood, wood, wood.
He armed some Ulster Bhoys
With these pretty little toys,
And told them to kill all they could, could, could.

Who is the man in the hat? Explain the word written on it. Read the verse beneath the picture. What does it mean? These words were written by a nationalist. Does he take the 'Ulster Bhoys' seriously? What event changed the opinion of the nationalists?

The Irish National Volunteers and the IRB

Nationalists were angry at what the unionists were doing. In 1913 **Eoin MacNeill**, one of the founders of the Gaelic League, suggested they copy the unionists. He set up the **Irish National Volunteers** to support Home Rule.

But unknown to MacNeill, some leaders of the Irish Volunteers were also in the secret IRB. They planned to use the Volunteers to fight for an Irish republic. They too bought guns in Germany and smuggled them into Ireland at Howth in July 1914.

Talking about partition

There were now two armed groups in Ireland. Prime Minister Asquith feared there might be a war between them. He persuaded Redmond to talk to Carson about dividing Ireland into two parts:

- one part for the unionists in the north-east and
- the rest of Ireland for nationalists.

This was called **partition**.
Reluctantly Redmond agreed to partition. But he and Carson could not agree where the border between the two parts should be.

- Carson wanted the unionists to have six of the Ulster counties.
- Redmond said that the unionists were only entitled to the four in which they were in a majority. The map opposite shows the areas they argued about.

World War I postpones the Home Rule crisis

Redmond and Carson were discussing partition when the German army invaded Belgium in July 1914. Both unionists and nationalists were shocked by Germany's action. When Britain declared war on Germany, Carson and Redmond agreed to postpone their talks. Each leader called on his Volunteers to join the British army and fight for the freedom of small nations like 'little Belgium'.

Questions

1. Name the British prime minister who promised to give Ireland Home Rule and the Irish leader to whom he made that promise. When was Home Rule due to begin?
2. Name two unionist leaders at this time. Say two things they did to try to stop Home Rule. Which do you think would influence the British more? Explain your answer.
3. Explain what 'partition' means. Why did the British prime minister suggest the partition of Ireland?
4. How much territory did Carson want and how much did Redmond think Carson should have?
5. Why did talks between Carson and Redmond suddenly stop in 1914?

Ireland in the First World War

How Irish people responded to the start of World War I

Irish people, both nationalists and unionists, were angry that Germany had invaded Belgium. Volunteers answered their leaders' call and joined the British army to fight against Germany.

This is the reason one Home Ruler, Tom Kettle, gave for going:

> *'We started the National Volunteers to defend the liberties of Ireland. Well, if you are engaged in a work of defence, you must carry it out in the proper place and the proper place now is not in Ireland but on the plains of France and Flanders* [Belgium].*'*

This government recruiting poster used the same idea.

The British government produced many recruiting posters. Some, like this one, tried to encourage men to stop German aggression in Belgium.

Irishmen in World War I

In all, about 206,000 Irishmen fought in World War I.

- Unionists formed the Ulster Division. Their worst time came at the **Battle of the Somme in 1916** when 5,000 of them were killed on the first two days of fighting alone.
- Nationalists formed the 16th (Irish) Division. They also fought at the Somme, where Tom Kettle (above) was killed. Their worst battle was at Gallipoli when Britain tried to invade Turkey, which was allied to Germany.

In all, about 30,000 men from Ireland died in fighting between 1914 and 1918.

Questions

1. What did the two Irish leaders tell their Volunteers to do after Germany invaded Belgium?
2. Read what Tom Kettle said. What reason does he give for the Irish Volunteers being started? Why did he think that had changed in 1914?
3. How many Irishmen fought in the First World War? Name the two units in the British Army where most of them fought. How many Irishmen died in the war?

Review the chapter

1 Write a paragraph on the Home Rule crisis of 1912–14.

(Junior Certificate, 1997)

2 This was one of many cartoons that unionists produced in their campaign against Home Rule.

(i) Who does the man represent? What does 'Ulster' want him to do?

(ii) According to the cartoon, what will happen to Ireland if the link with Britain breaks?

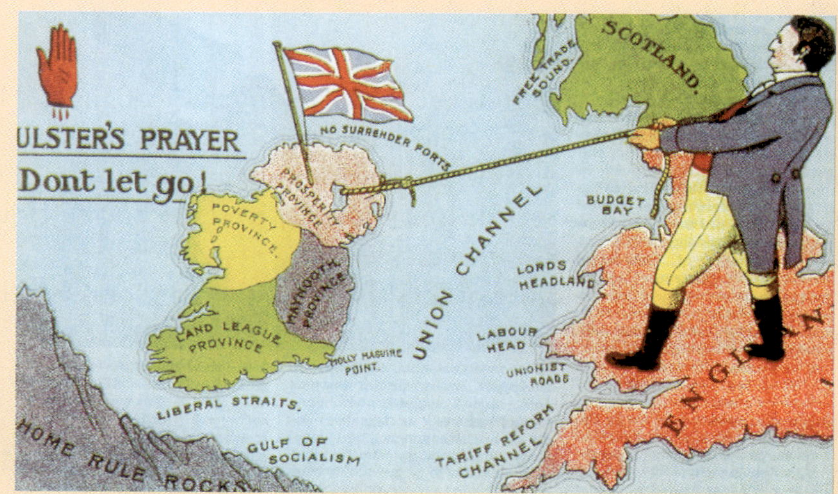

3 These are two more recruiting posters.

(i) In Source A what 'chums' is the Irishman urged to join?

(ii) Why did the people who made the poster think this would appeal to Irishmen?

(iii) In Source B what Irish characteristic did this poster appeal to?

(iv) Which poster was most likely to appeal to nationalists and which to unionists? Explain your choice.

Source A

Source B

Chapter 3 The 1916 Easter Rising

The 'Sinn Féin Volunteers'

In 1914 John Redmond called on the Irish Volunteers to fight for Belgium's freedom. But some Volunteers, led by Eoin MacNeill, did not agree with this. They felt they should not fight for the freedom of any country until their own was free. They preferred to stay in Ireland, ready to resist in case Britain broke its promise to give Home Rule after the war.

Arthur Griffith, the founder of Sinn Féin, supported them. For that reason they were usually called the 'Sinn Féin Volunteers'.

The IRB sees its opportunity

MacNeill did not plan to fight the British. But unknown to him Sean McDermott and Tom Clarke, who were leaders of in the IRB, had different ideas. The IRB had a saying: 'England's difficulty is Ireland's opportunity.' McDermott and Clarke thought that Britain's difficult war with Germany was a golden opportunity to start a rebellion against British rule. With the 11,000-strong Sinn Féin Volunteers and help from Germany, they believed they had a good chance of success.

Patrick Pearse (1879–1916)

As soon as the war started, the IRB leaders began to make plans. They asked **Patrick Pearse** to join them. He was the son of an English stonemason. As a young man he joined the Gaelic League, edited their newspaper and wrote poems in Irish. In 1908 he set up an all-Irish school, St Enda's.

Patrick Pearse

Pearse loved the Irish language. He believed it was the soul of Ireland. If it died out, Ireland would have lost its soul. He thought that only an Irish republic could protect it. This idea led him to join the IRB in 1913. Clarke and McDermott, who wanted to stay out of the limelight, let Pearse become their spokesman.

James Connolly (1868–1916)

In 1916 the plotters also invited the socialist leader, James Connolly, to join them. Connolly believed that the British Empire was behind the evils of poverty. He wanted to overthrow it. He thought about using the Irish Citizen Army, which had been set up to defend the workers during the 1913 lockout, to start a revolution but it was too small. So when the IRB offered him a chance to join them, he accepted.

Joseph Plunkett drew up the plans for the Easter Rising. By 1916 he was dying from TB. On the night before he was executed he married his fiancée Grace Gifford in his prison cell.

Getting help from Germany

Clark and McDermott sent **Roger Casement** to Germany to ask for help. The Germans would not send soldiers but they agreed to send a shipload of arms. The ship, the *Aud*, was to arrive in Kerry at Easter 1916. This was to be the signal for fighting to begin.

Fooling MacNeill

Most Volunteers, including their leader MacNeill, knew nothing of these plans. They did not want a violent rebellion, so the plotters had to trick MacNeill into ordering the Volunteers to fight.

On the Wednesday before Easter they showed him a letter. It said the British were going to arrest him and all the other nationalist leaders. The letter was a forgery but MacNeill did not know that. He told the Volunteers to get ready to resist.

Then on Saturday he heard that the British navy had captured the *Aud* and its load of arms. MacNeill realised he had been deceived and cancelled the fighting. He published this order in the Sunday papers.

Deciding to fight on Easter Monday

The plotters met on Easter Sunday. Their plans were in ruins, but they decided they must try anyway. They sent word out to the Volunteers to start to fight on Monday.

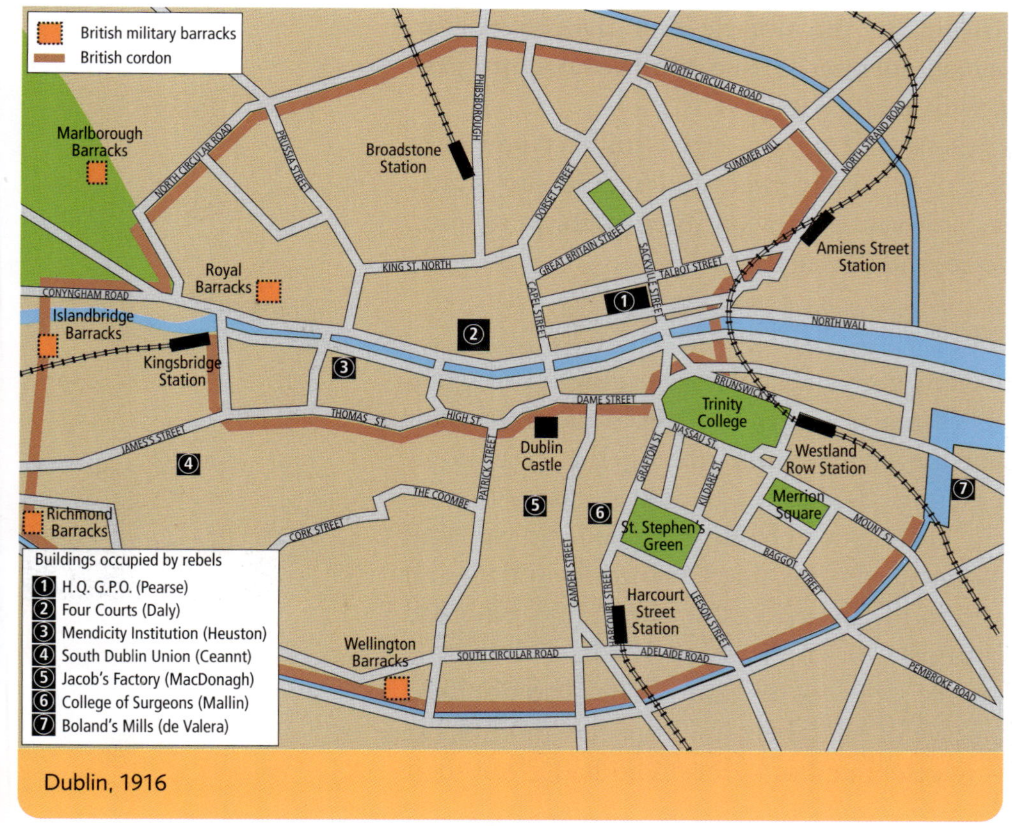

Dublin, 1916

On a sunny Bank Holiday morning the Volunteers marched out to seize buildings around Dublin. Because of the cancellation, only 1,500 turned up, almost all of them in Dublin. As they set out, Connolly told one of his followers: 'We are going out to be slaughtered'.

Connolly and Pearse made their headquarters in the GPO on O'Connell Street. From the steps, Pearse read the Proclamation of the Republic while the Irish tricolour was raised above the building. Other Volunteers took over buildings in other parts of the city. You can see them on this map.

Easter Week

The area behind O'Connell Street, reduced to ruins by shells from the British gunboat *Helga*

The rising caught the British by surprise. They sent in troops and put the country under military rule. They knew the rebel headquarters was in the GPO. They concentrated their attack on it and left other areas alone. They brought a gunboat up the Liffey and shelled O'Connell Street, reducing it to ruins.

Trapped by the gunfire, ordinary Dubliners suffered badly. They could not go to work and there was no food in the shops. Over 300 of them were killed in the crossfire.

On Thursday, the GPO caught fire and Connolly was badly wounded. Pearse ordered the Volunteers to move to the nearby streets. Here they saw the suffering the fighting was causing. On Friday Pearse ordered them to surrender and by Saturday the city was quiet.

Punishing the rebels

The British felt betrayed by the rising. In the middle of a dangerous war, the rebels had joined with their German enemies. Prime Minister Asquith gave the British army a free hand to deal with them.

The army rounded up 3,000 people and set up secret military courts to try the ringleaders. They sentenced over ninety men and women to death. The executions began at once. Each morning two or three men were shot. Pearse, Clarke and McDonagh were among the first to die.

Reactions to the rising

Immediately after the rising, people were angry at the damage caused. But when word came of the executions, people's mood changed. They transferred their anger to the British. John Redmond begged Asquith to stop the executions. Reluctantly, he agreed. After fifteen men had been shot, he told the army to stop.

Connolly was the last man to die. He had been badly wounded and was shot tied to a chair. The rest of the prisoners, who included Eamon de Valera and Countess Markievicz, were sentenced to life in prison. Another 1,500, who had not been tried, were sent to prison camps. One of them was Michael Collins.

The executions changed Irish people's view of the rising. They had not liked the fighting but they admired the courage of the rebels. Within a few months the dead leaders of the Easter Rising were celebrated as heroes who had given their lives for Ireland.

Questions

1 Why did some Volunteers not accept Redmond's advice to join the British in fighting for Belgium? Who was their leader and what were they called?
2 Who saw the war as 'Ireland's opportunity'? Explain what that meant.
3 Name three of the men involved in the plot and say where they looked for help.
4 What did MacNeill and the rest of the Volunteers know of the plot? How was MacNeill persuaded to give the order to fight?
5 Why did MacNeill cancel the order? What did the plotters do?
6 What did the British do with the leaders of the rising? How did this affect people's view of what happened?

Review the chapter

1 Write a paragraph on the Easter Rising of 1916. *(Junior Certificate, 1997)*

2 Joseph Marshall was the Chief Steward in Trinity College on Easter Monday 1916. This is part of his report:

> *'There were six porters on duty within the College on the above date between 9 am and 2 pm. In the course of my rounds I heard that the Sinn Féiners had seized the General Post Office and other public buildings in the city. I immediately directed the porters, Halpin and Wilson, to shut and lock the Front Gate of the College and to make the Gate perfectly secure. I took from my office a large padlock with a strong chain attached and put it on the gate myself, together with arming the porters with Fenian pikes which I had seized while in the D.M.P.* [Dublin Metropolitan Police] *in 1867. I also directed the porters to invite into the College all passing soldiers for safety, many of whom entered College and became very useful later in defence of the College…*
>
> *I directed Acting Porter Crawford to inform the Provost of the Sinn Féin rising…. I armed myself with my old historic revolver and my Tipperary blackthorn which I brought into use in the wild riots in Dublin in September 1913.'* (From Georgina Fitzpatrick, *Trinity College and Irish Society 1914–22, a selection of documents*, Trinity College, 1992)

(i) What news did the Chief Steward hear in the course of his rounds? Was that news correct?
(ii) Look at the map on page 137. Was Trinity College near the scene of the action?
(iii) List four things the Chief Steward did as a result of what he heard. Which do you think would be the most useful? Explain your choice.
(iv) Did the Chief Steward approve or disapprove of the Sinn Féiners? Pick out two things in the text that support your opinion.
(v) How long did the rebellion last?

(Based on the Junior Certificate, 1995)

Chapter 4 The Victory of Sinn Féin, 1916–18

A new British prime minister

Late in 1916 **David Lloyd George** became prime minister of Britain. His sole aim was to win the war with Germany. He hoped to persuade the Americans to join on the British side. But many Americans disapproved of the way Britain ruled Ireland, so to please them he freed the people imprisoned after the Easter Rising.

David Lloyd George became prime minister late in 1916 and remained in power until the end of 1922

New leaders

The men who were freed became the new leaders of the nationalists. Here are three of them:

- **Michael Collins** was from Cork. As a young man, he worked in London where he joined the Gaelic League and the IRB. In the rising he fought in the GPO. When he was freed he began to rebuild the IRB and the Volunteers.
- **Arthur Griffith**, the founder of Sinn Féin, was not involved in the fighting. But people called it the 'Sinn Féin rebellion' so he was imprisoned anyway. When he was freed he began to rebuild his Sinn Féin party, which was now much more popular than it had been before.
- **Eamon de Valera** was the last of the new leaders to be freed. He was born in New York but brought up in Ireland. He joined the Gaelic League and later the Volunteers. During Easter Week he commanded the Volunteers in Boland's Mills. He was sentenced to death but the executions stopped before it was his turn to die.

Michael Collins

Arthur Griffith

Eamon de Valera

1917: De Valera becomes the leader of Sinn Féin

In 1917 nationalists who approved of the rising joined the Sinn Féin Party, which grew rapidly. It defeated the Home Rule Party in a number of by-elections. But Sinn Féin supporters were divided about several issues.

- *What kind of independence would they look for?* The IRB wanted a republic but Griffith and others would settle for less.
- *Who would be the leader?* Griffith had the best claim but the IRB did not approve of him because he was not a republican.

When de Valera was freed he worked to unite the various groups. At a party meeting in October, Griffith stepped aside and de Valera was elected as leader. A few days later, the Volunteers also elected de Valera as their leader. Griffith and Collins also had important positions in these two organisations.

The Home Rule Party used a green flag with a golden harp as the Irish flag. You can see it in the poster (Source A) on page 135. But Sinn Féin used green, white and orange in its banners, and after independence these colours became the colours of Ireland's national flag.

What Sinn Féin wanted

The Sinn Féin leaders decided they wanted Ireland to be a republic, completely independent of Britain. They planned to get MPs elected who would not go to London. Instead they planned to set up an Irish parliament called **Dáil Éireann**. It would elect an Irish government and ignore British officials.

They also hoped the Americans would support their demand. When the United States entered World War I in 1917, President Woodrow Wilson said they were fighting for the right of small countries to choose their own governments.

1918: conscription makes Sinn Féin popular

At first, moderate nationalists were nervous of Sinn Féin. It was linked to the fighting of Easter Week and most nationalists disliked violence. But in 1918 an event occurred that won them over to Sinn Féin.

Early in 1918 the Germans made one last desperate attempt to win the war. Britain needed extra troops to stop them. Lloyd George decided to conscript young Irishmen (i.e. force them to serve in the British army). Nationalists were appalled. The Volunteers threatened to fight any attempt to impose conscription. The British response was to arrest de Valera, Griffith and other leaders.

In the end, the British did not try to enforce conscription because the war ended before the extra men were needed. But Sinn Féin and the Volunteers got the credit for stopping it.

The general election of 1918 was the first time women had the opportunity to vote and also to stand for election. Sinn Féin was the only party that put forward women candidates. Winifred Carney stood in Belfast and Constance Markievicz in Dublin. Markievicz was elected.

The 1918 election

As soon as the war ended, Lloyd George called a general election. This was the first election in which women could vote, though not yet on equal terms with men. In this election, Irish voters could choose between three parties:

- The Unionist Party led by Carson and Craig. It wanted to keep part of Ireland in the United Kingdom.
- The Home Rule Party. It wanted Ireland to have a parliament with power over Irish home affairs while the British still looked after foreign issues like trade or war. Redmond died shortly before the election and the new leader was John Dillon.
- The Sinn Féin Party led by Eamon de Valera. It promised that its MPs would stay away from Westminster, set up Dáil Éireann and declare an Irish republic.

Here are the results:

	Before	After
Unionists	18 MPs	26 MPs
Home Rulers	78 MPs	6 MPs
Sinn Féin	7 MPs	73 MPs

Sinn Féin had won. Now it had to keep its promises.

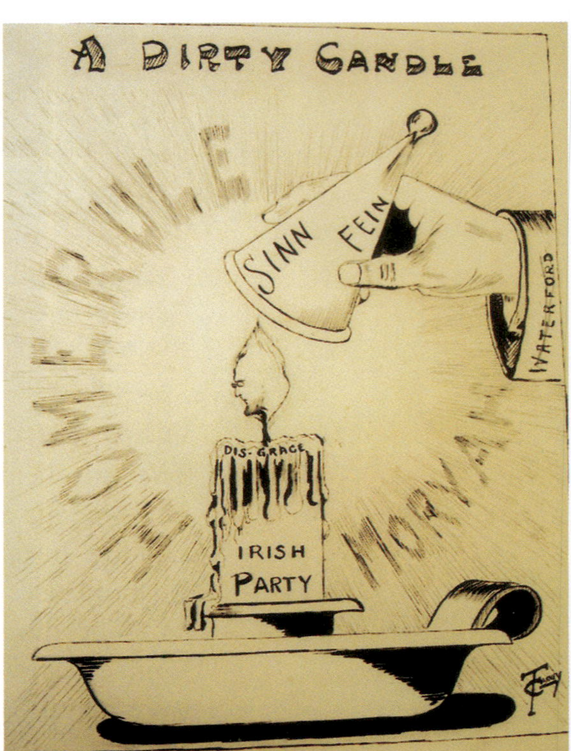

A Sinn Féin comment on the results of the 1918 election. Which party is represented by the 'dirty candle'?

Questions

1 Three new leaders emerged after the Easter Rising. Name them and in each case write two sentences about his life up to then.
2 Explain how Eamon de Valera became leader of Sinn Féin in 1917. What did Sinn Féiners want and how did they propose to get it?
3 What does 'conscription' mean? Explain how conscription affected developments in Ireland in 1918.
4 List the three parties in the 1918 election and say who led each party and what they wanted to achieve.
5 What were the results of the 1918 election?

Review the chapter

1 Give two reasons why the Sinn Féin Party was so successful in the 1918 general election.

2 Match the items on the left with the corresponding items on the right.

Column 1	Column 2
1 Sir Edward Carson	**A** Home Rule leader
2 Arthur Griffith	**B** British prime minister
3 John Redmond	**C** Howth gun-running
4 Herbert Asquith	**D** Leader during 1913 strike and lockout
5 The Irish Volunteers	**E** Founder of Sinn Féin
6 James Larkin	**F** Unionist leader in Ireland

(Based on the Junior Certificate, 2002)

Chapter 5 Dáil Éireann and the War of Independence

The First Dáil

In the 1918 election Sinn Féin MPs had promised not to go to the British parliament at Westminster but to set up an Irish parliament, Dáil Éireann, in Dublin. On 21 January 1919 they kept that promise.

The first meeting of Dáil Éireann only lasted three hours.

- It declared Ireland was a republic.
- It promised a ***democratic programme*** of social reforms.
- It picked people to go to the peace conference in Paris (see Topic 1A) to ask other countries to accept Irish independence.

Note

MPs are members of the British parliament. When Sinn Féin set up Dáil Éireann, the members called themselves **TDs**. That means *Teachtaí Dála* or delegates to the Dáil.

The Dáil government

The Dáil met again on 1 April. It elected Eamon de Valera as President (i.e. Prime Minister /Taoiseach) and he appointed ministers.

- Griffith was Vice-President and Minister for Home Affairs. He was in charge of police and the courts.
- Collins was Minister for Finance, in charge of taxes and government spending.
- Cathal Brugha was Minister for Defence, in charge of the Volunteers. They soon changed their name to the Irish Republican Army (IRA).
- Countess Markievicz, the only woman TD, was Minister for Labour.

Countess Markievicz was the only woman elected to the British parliament in the 1918 election. But she belonged to Sinn Féin and took her seat in Dáil Éireann rather than Westminster.

De Valera in America

Sinn Féin sent representatives to the Paris peace conference to ask other countries to recognise the Irish republic. But Lloyd George easily persuaded them not to listen to the Irish.

De Valera thought the Irish Americans could persuade the American government to change its mind. In June 1919 he went to the United States. He failed to win American backing for Irish independence but he raised $4 million for the struggle. He stayed there until December 1920.

Griffith and the Dáil government

While de Valera was away, Griffith led the Dáil. He wanted it to ignore British officials and run the country itself. This idea worked in some areas.

YOU CAN

Buy Dail Eireann Bonds To-day

RECOVER IRELAND FOR THE IRISH.
RE-PEOPLE THE LAND.
HARNESS THE RIVERS.
PUT HER FLAG ON EVERY SEA.
PLANT THE HILLSIDES AND THE WASTES.
SET THE LOOMS SPINNING.
ABOLISH THE SLUMS.
SEND HER SHIPS TO EVERY PORT.
SET THE HAMMER RINGING ON THE ANVIL.
GARNER THE HARVEST OF THE SEAS.
DRAIN THE BOGS.
SAVE THE BOYS AND GIRLS FOR IRELAND.

Hand your Subscription to your Local Member of the Dáil, or his Representative in your Parish.

YOU CAN RESTORE IRELAND'S HEALTH, HER STRENGTH, HER BEAUTY, AND HER WEALTH.

This advertisement for Dáil Bonds lists the things that Collins said the money was needed for. **What is missing from the list?**

- Collins organised a loan to cover expenses. People lent the Dáil £350,000 (over €20 million in today's values). This, and the money de Valera raised in the US, paid for wages, propaganda and guns.
- Griffith helped set up Sinn Féin courts to replace British courts. The Volunteers acted as a police force to replace the British-run Royal Irish Constabulary (RIC).
- Local councils switched their support to the Dáil government.

Violence begins

Griffith had a dream that independence could be won by these peaceful means alone. But some Volunteers were convinced that the only way to win independence was to fight for it. On 21 January 1919 at a place called **Soloheadbeg** in County Tipperary, a small group of Volunteers killed two policemen in an ambush and seized the dynamite they were protecting. This was the start of a war for Irish independence.

Collins's spies

Michael Collins shared these views. He was also the Volunteer's Director of Intelligence and he had a network of spies around the country. They included post office clerks, railway men, policemen and even officials in the British headquarters in Dublin Castle. These spies kept him informed of what the British were up to, and Collins used this information to outwit them.

Collins was also determined the British must not find out what the Volunteers were planning. He set up a group called the 'Squad', whose job was to murder anyone suspected of being a British spy. They killed with ruthless efficiency. This worried Sinn Féiners like Griffith, who felt murder dishonoured the cause of Ireland.

Note

After the Dáil declared a Republic, the Volunteers began to call themselves the Irish Republican Army (IRA).

The IRA's guerrilla war

Collins passed on the information his spies gathered to local IRA leaders. This helped them to organise a guerrilla war against the British forces. Among the most famous local commanders were Liam Lynch and Tom Barry in Cork, Seán Tracy in Tipperary and Seán Mac Eoin in Longford.

In 1919 the IRA attacked RIC barracks and killed policemen. Gradually they drove the police out of small towns and villages. At Easter 1920, they burned many RIC police stations.

What is a guerrilla war?
In a guerrilla war, a few soldiers attack their enemy with ambushes, bombs and assassinations. Since the guerrillas do not wear uniforms, they can hide among ordinary people after each attack. Their enemies have no way of telling who were the killers and who is an innocent civilian. These tactics are the only way a small, poorly armed force can fight a bigger one.

Lloyd George and the Black and Tans

While this was going on, the prime minister Lloyd George was at the peace conference in Paris. Only at the end of 1919 did he turn his attention back to Ireland.

Lloyd George thought IRA men were gangsters and murderers. He was determined to destroy them. He wanted that job to be done by policemen, but by then few Irishmen wanted to join the RIC. So Lloyd George began to recruit policemen in Britain.

Jobs were scarce in Britain after the war. Unemployed soldiers were glad to find any well-paid job, and many of them joined the RIC. Because there were not enough police uniforms to go around, some of them were dressed in a mix of dark green police and khaki army uniforms. From this came their nickname, the 'Black and Tans'.

The Black and Tans in Ireland

When the Black and Tans arrived in 1920, the IRA guerrilla war was in full swing. That year the IRA killed 182 policemen, many of whom were Black and Tans.

The Black and Tans struck back ruthlessly. They searched houses for arms. Anyone on the streets after 10 pm was arrested and some were beaten up. As their lorries thundered down country roads, they fired at people and animals along the way.

Black and Tans searching for arms on a street in Dublin

Sometimes, when the IRA killed a policeman, the Black and Tans went on the rampage. They burned houses, smashed up towns and killed prisoners. In December 1920 they burned the centre of Cork. The British encouraged these actions, hoping to frighten people out of supporting the IRA. In fact it had the opposite result. Even people who disliked what the IRA had done backed them against the Black and Tans.

In December 1920 Black and Tans burned part of Cork city in retaliation for an ambush by the IRA

Main events in the war

The war between the IRA and the British forces lasted from 1919 to July 1921. Here are some of the main events.

Note

RIC=
Royal Irish Constabulary

- When the Lord Mayor of Cork, **Terence Mac Swiney**, was imprisoned, he demanded that the British treat him like a prisoner of war. When they refused, he went on hunger strike. He died after 73 days without food. This made headlines around the world.
- In an IRA ambush in a Dublin street, a seventeen-year-old British soldier was killed. **Kevin Barry**, an eighteen-year-old student who had taken part in the ambush, was captured and hanged for murder. People protested at the execution because Barry was so young.

- Late in 1920, Michael Collins found out that the British were sending spies to Ireland. On Sunday 21 November, he sent his 'Squad' to these men's homes and shot thirteen of them. Later that day, Black and Tans surrounded Croke Park where a GAA match was in progress. They suspected the killers were in the crowd. They opened fire, killing twelve people. That night, three Volunteers who had been arrested earlier were killed in Dublin Castle. The police said they were trying to escape but no one in Ireland believed them. This day is known as the Republic's 'Bloody Sunday'.
- In 1921 the war got worse. The IRA formed 'flying columns' of full-time Volunteers who moved from place to place helping local commanders to set up ambushes. The British rounded up large numbers of young men and interned them in prison camps. This made it harder for the IRA to get guns or fight.

By the early summer of 1921 the IRA needed to stop fighting and start talking.

Questions

1. When was the first Dáil formed? Name three ministers in the first Dáil government.
2. Where was de Valera between 1919 and 1920? Why was he there?
3. Describe the part played by Michael Collins in the war of independence.
4. Who were the Black and Tans? What did they do during the war of independence?
5. What happened on 'Bloody Sunday'?
6. How did the IRA fight in 1921 and how did the British respond?

Review the chapter

1. **Research Topic**
   Select one of the following episodes in the war of independence and find out more about it:
   (i) The hunger strike of Terence McSwiney
   (ii) Bloody Sunday (November 1920)
   (iii) The Burning of Cork (December 1920)
   (iv) An important episode in the war in your area.

2. **People in History**
   Write about a republican during the war of independence in Ireland, 1919–21.
   (Junior Certificate, 2001)

Chapter 6 Partition, Treaty and Civil War, 1920–23

Lloyd George and the unionists

Although Lloyd George wanted to defeat the IRA, he knew that he would have to talk to the Sinn Féin leaders in the end. But first he had to deal with the unionists.

Their leader, Sir Edward Carson, told Lloyd George that they wanted to have the six north-eastern counties of Ireland for themselves. There were now no nationalist leaders in London to oppose this, so Lloyd George gave the unionists what they asked for.

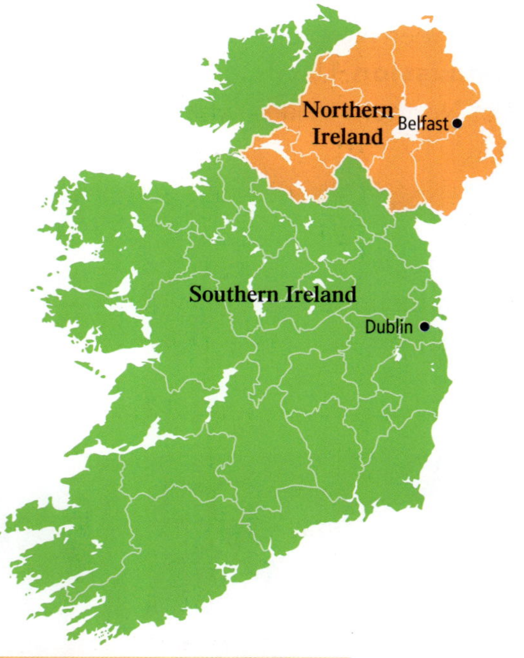

In 1920 Lloyd George used the Government of Ireland Act to partition Ireland into two parts, which he called 'Southern Ireland' and 'Northern Ireland'. Nationalists never accepted 'Southern Ireland', but unionists set up Northern Ireland in 1921.

The Government of Ireland Act partitions Ireland in 1920

In 1920 Lloyd George got the British parliament to pass the **Government of Ireland Act**. It partitioned (divided) Ireland into two parts:

- One part had six counties and was called **Northern Ireland**. It was to have a parliament in Belfast. This gave the unionists their own state within the United Kingdom. Carson, who was old and tired, retired. When Northern Ireland was set up in 1921, James Craig became its first prime minister (there is more about this in Topic 2C).
- The other part had twenty-six counties and was to be called **Southern Ireland**. It was to have a Home Rule parliament in Dublin.

By now de Valera was back from America. He and the other Sinn Féin leaders would not accept Home Rule or partition. The IRA continued to fight until July 1921. Then Lloyd George offered de Valera a truce so that talks could begin on a peace treaty.

December 1921: a Treaty is signed

In October 1921, de Valera sent Griffith and Collins to London to talk to the British.

- They wanted to have a republic, completely independent of Britain.
- They wanted to end partition by bringing Northern Irleand back under Irish rule.

The negotiations for a Treaty with Britain lasted until December. Then Lloyd George offered these terms:

1. Ireland would be called the Irish Free State.
2. It would have a lot of independence, including its own army, flag, stamps, coins and passports. It would also be able to protect its industry from British competition.
3. But it would not be a republic. Instead it would be a **Dominion of the British Commonwealth** (Empire). That meant the king would be head of the Free State and TDs would have to take an oath to be loyal to him. This is called 'Dominion Status'.
4. To protect the coast of Ireland, the British navy would continue to use three Irish ports.
5. Three men would be appointed to decide where the boundary between Northern Ireland and the Free State should be. They were to be called the **Boundary Commission**. Lloyd George assured Griffith and Collins that the Commission would give the parts of Northern Ireland where nationalists lived to the Irish Free State.

Collins and Griffith said they must go back to Dublin to show these terms to de Valera. But Lloyd George threatened to start the war again if they did not sign then and there. Reluctantly, at 2 am on 6 December 1921, the Irish representatives signed the Anglo-Irish Treaty.

Debating the Treaty

Nationalists were divided about the Treaty with Britain. Many were glad that peace had come at last. But de Valera was angry that Griffith and Collins had signed without consulting him. Some IRA leaders also disapproved. They did not want to settle for anything less than a full republic.

The Dáil debates the Treaty

A few days after the Treaty was signed, the Dáil met to discuss it. The TDs had a long and bitter debate.

These were the Irishmen who went to London to negotiate with Lloyd George. **Can you find Griffith and Collins?**

Here are some of the points that the two sides made.

Arguments in favour of the Treaty by Griffith, Collins and the pro-Treaty side	Arguments against the Treaty by de Valera and the anti-Treaty side
1 The Treaty gave Ireland control of trade, its own army and flag. This was far more than Home Rule, even if it was not full freedom.	**1** The Free State would not really be free because it was still in the British Empire and the British king would be its head of state.
2 Once the British left, it would be easy to take further steps towards a republic.	**2** Because Britain was near Ireland it would be easy for them to go on interfering in Ireland if their king was our head of state.
3 The IRA had not really beaten the British. If war started again, they would certainly lose.	**3** The republic had existed since 1916. Republicans had taken an oath to be loyal to it. They would break that oath if they swore an oath to the king. It would be better to go back to war.

On 7 January 1922 the Dáil voted on the Treaty.

- 64 TDs voted for it.
- 57 TDs voted against it.

De Valera resigned as president and he and his followers walked out of the Dáil. Griffith took his place, with Collins as his second-in-command.

Divisions over the Treaty

Outside the Dáil, people also argued about the Treaty. It divided families and friends. In April, IRA leaders who opposed it took over the Four Courts and other buildings in Dublin. But Collins did not want to fight his friends, so he left them alone. He tried to keep the peace by making a pact with de Valera but it soon collapsed.

In June 1922 there was a general election. Voters had a choice between candidates who supported the Treaty and candidates who opposed it. This is the result.

The pro-Treaty side of Sinn Féin:	**58 TDs**
The anti-Treaty side of Sinn Féin:	**35 TDs**
Other parties (almost all pro-Treaty)	**35 TDs**

The Civil War, 1922–23

This election result showed Collins that the majority of voters supported the Treaty. A few days after it he ordered the Irish army to attack the IRA in the Four Courts. De Valera then joined the IRA. This was the start of a bitter civil war, which lasted for almost a year.

Within a week, the Irish army defeated the IRA 'Irregulars' in Dublin. The IRA had more support in Munster and was able to hold out a little longer there. But by August, Collins had defeated them there as well. The Irregulars then fought a guerrilla war, with ambushes and atrocities on both sides.

When the Dáil accepted the Treaty, the British began to leave. This picture shows British troops marching out of an army barracks and Irish troops marching in.

Early in August 1922, Griffith died of a stroke. Ten days later Collins was killed in an ambush at **Beal na mBlath** in Cork. After this double loss, **William T. Cosgrave** became head of the Irish Free State government. He took a strong line against the IRA. When it continued its campaign of burning, murder and ambush, he had over 70 IRA men executed.

The IRA had not consulted de Valera about the civil war. When he saw they were losing, he tried to get them to stop fighting. At last, in May 1923, they agreed to put away their guns. The civil war was over, but it caused a lot of damage, cost a great deal of money and left a legacy of bitterness behind it.

The body of Michael Collins lying in the Pro-Cathedral in Dublin

Questions

1. Name the two Irish leaders who went to London to negotiate a Treaty. Who was the British prime minister they dealt with?
2. Give four of the main terms of the Anglo-Irish Treaty of 1921. Why was de Valera angry when it was signed?
3. Where was the Treaty debated? Name two people who supported it and two of the arguments they used. Name two of the people who opposed it and two of their arguments. What was the result of the vote on the Treaty?
4. Describe how the civil war began.
5. How did William T. Cosgrave become leader of the pro-Treaty side?

Review the chapter

1. Explain the following terms in relation to the war of independence and the civil war (1919–23):
   (i) Black and Tans;
   (ii) Flying Columns;
   (iii) Bloody Sunday;
   (iv) The Government of Ireland Act;
   (v) Dominion Status;
   (vi) Irregular forces.
   (Junior Certificate, 2000)

MAY FLOWERS

2. This cartoon appeared in May 1922.
   (i) Name the two men.
   (ii) Who does the 'girl' represent?
   (iii) Using evidence in the picture and your knowledge of what was happening at the time, say what each of the men is trying to persuade her to do?
   (iv) In 1922, which side did she support?

Topic 2B

Independent Ireland, 1921–2000

Chapter 1 The Cumann na nGaedheal Government, 1922–32

Irish political parties grow from the Treaty split

The Treaty with Britain split the Sinn Féin party that had won the 1918 election. This split, and the civil war that followed, are the origin of our two main political parties today. This diagram shows how they formed.

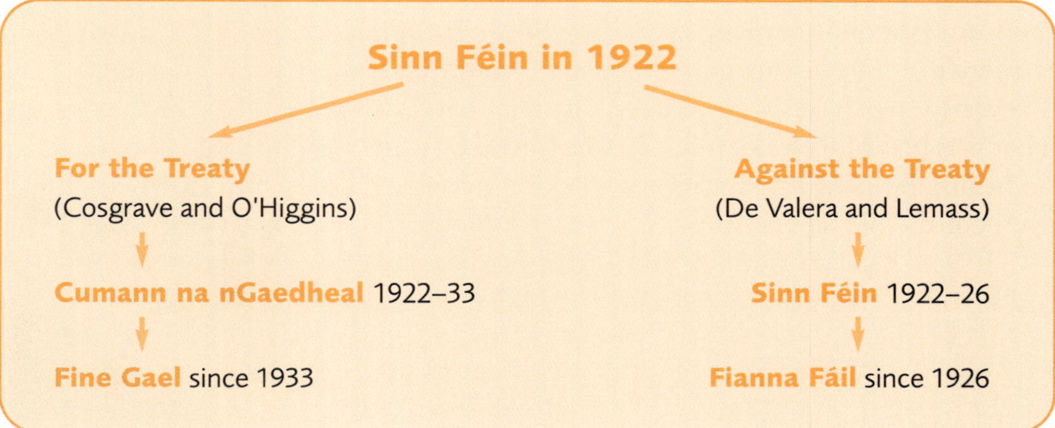

William T. Cosgrave

The government of the Irish Free State

During the civil war the pro-Treaty TDs formed a party called **Cumann na nGaedheal**. These two men were its leaders.

- **William T. Cosgrave** was the head of the Irish government from 1922 to 1932. He was a good leader who restored peace and order after the civil war.
- **Kevin O'Higgins** was Minister for Justice. He took a tough line against the IRA during the civil war. IRA men murdered him in 1927.

Setting up a new Irish state

When they won the civil war, the Cumann na nGaedheal leaders had to set up the Irish Free State.

- They drew up a democratic constitution. Under it, all laws were to be made by an elected Dáil and Senate. All men and women over twenty-one could vote in elections. But because of the Treaty, all TDs and Senators had to take an oath to be loyal to the king.

Kevin O'Higgins

- They set up a civil service, army, police and courts.
- They brought in Irish coins and notes.
- They made the Irish language compulsory in schools.

The army mutiny

During the civil war the Irish army got very big. Cumann na nGaedheal wanted to cut the number of soldiers to reduce costs. Some of soldiers protested but O'Higgins sacked them. In the Irish Free State, he insisted, the army must obey the elected government.

How Cumann na nGaedheal managed the economy

The Irish Free State earned most of its income by selling food to Britain. Cumann na nGaedheal encouraged farmers to improve quality so that sales would increase. They also kept taxes low to keep farmers' costs down. That was good for the rich but left little money to spend on health, housing or education for poorer people. They even cut the old age pension.

It was hard to develop industries because Ireland had no oil or coal to drive factories. In 1923 they decided to build a big hydro-electric station on the Shannon. They started the Electricity Supply Board (ESB) to send electricity around the country.

A view of the ESB hydro-electric scheme on the Shannon

Cumann na nGaedheal's foreign policy

Cosgrave and O'Higgins wanted the world to see the Irish Free State was an independent country like France or Belgium. To show this, they joined the newly formed **League of Nations** in 1923.

But the Treaty also forced them to belong to the **British Commonwealth**. That was a limit on Irish freedom, so Cosgrave and O'Higgins set out to make the members of the Commonwealth as free as possible. They were helped by Canada and South Africa, who wanted the same thing.

In 1931 the British agreed to their demands. They passed **the Statute of Westminster**, which said that all Commonwealth members were free to change any laws the British made for them. Because of this, when de Valera destroyed the Treaty, the British could do nothing about it.

British Commonwealth
After World War I empires went out of fashion, so the British renamed theirs as the 'British Commonwealth'.

The Boundary Commission

The Treaty said that a three-man **Boundary Commission** would look again at the border between the Free State and Northern Ireland. This commission began work in 1924. The members visited areas along the border and spoke to local people. But to everyone's surprise they decided to make only minor

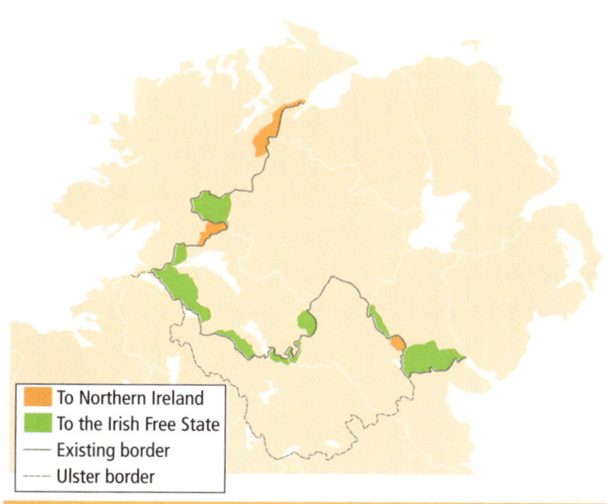

Irish Boundary Commission proposed changes, 1925

changes. They even suggested that bits of Donegal be given to Northern Ireland.

Cosgrave refused to accept this. As a result, the border between Northern Ireland and the Free State was left unchanged from what it had been in 1920.

De Valera sets up Fianna Fáil

After 1922 Eamon de Valera led the anti-Treaty part of Sinn Féin. His followers would not take the oath to the king and so could not enter the Dáil. But de Valera found this frustrating. When the Boundary Commission failed, he was not able to criticise the government in the Dáil.

He suggested that Sinn Féin go into the Dáil but the IRA rejected his proposal. So he left Sinn Féin. Helped by **Sean Lemass**, he formed a new party called **Fianna Fáil**. He said Fianna Fáil TDs would enter the Dáil if the oath were removed.

Even after Fianna Fáil entered the Dáil, it had close links with the IRA. Cosgrave hoped this would stop people voting for Fianna Fáil, as this poster shows. But many people overcame their dislike of violence and supported Fianna Fáil because of its economic policies.

Fianna Fáil enters the Dáil

In 1927 the IRA murdered Kevin O'Higgins. Cosgrave brought in the **Electoral Amendment Act**. It said that all TDs must take the oath or give up their seats. De Valera swallowed his pride and took the oath.

Fianna Fáil's promises

De Valera wanted to win the next election. He promised people that if they voted for him, he would

- dismantle the Treaty
- create more jobs by putting tariffs (taxes) on foreign goods coming into Ireland. That would make them too expensive for people to buy. De Valera hoped this would encourage Irish businessmen to set up factories in Ireland.
- give better pensions to poor people and build better houses for people living in slums.

Fianna Fáil wins the 1932 election

In 1930 a great **economic depression** swept the world. Everywhere factories closed and people were put out of work. Like most leaders at the time, Cosgrave had no idea how to deal with the depression. Many Irish people thought de Valera and Fianna Fáil might do a better job. When the election was held in 1932, Fianna Fáil won.

Cosgrave hands over peacefully

At that time in Europe, dictators like Hitler and Mussolini were overthrowing democracies (see Topic 1A). When Fianna Fáil won, many people wondered uneasily if Cosgrave might not do the same thing. Was he likely to hand over to a man he had beaten in a bitter civil war only ten years before?

On the day the Dáil met to elect a new government, some of the Fianna Fáil TDs had guns in their pockets. But Cosgrave was a democrat. When he was defeated in the Dáil, he quietly stepped aside and let de Valera be elected head of government in his place.

Questions

1. Name two important members of the Cumann na nGaedheal government.
2. List four things they had to do to set up the Irish Free State.
3. Describe three features of Cumann na nGaedheal economic policy.
4. How did Cosgrave strengthen Irish independence between 1922 and 1932?
5. What was the Boundary Commission? Describe the work it did in 1924–25.
6. Explain why de Valera set up a new party in 1926. What was it called? Why did it not enter the Dáil until 1927?
7. Give three reasons why Fianna Fáil won the 1932 election. Why did some Fianna Fáil TDs not expect Cosgrave to hand over power after Cumann na nGaedheal lost?

Review the chapter

1. Explain the importance of three of the following during the period 1922–32: The army mutiny, the Boundary Commission, the Shannon Scheme, the Electoral Amendment Act of 1927; the Statute of Westminster. *(Junior Certificate, 2003)*

2. Write an account of the achievements of the Cumann na nGaedheal government 1922–32. *(Junior Certificate, 2000)*

3. Are these statements true or false? If false, write down the correct statement.
   (i) Cosgrave opposed the Anglo-Irish Treaty of 1921.
   (ii) The Boundary Commission gave large parts of Northern Ireland to the South.
   (iii) IRA men assassinated Kevin O'Higgins.
   (iv) The Statute of Westminster limited Irish freedom.
   (v) De Valera set up a new party called Cumann na nGaedheal.

The Fianna Fáil Government, 1932–39

The Blueshirts

Cosgrave handed over power to de Valera, but he did not trust him to act in a democratic manner. Fianna Fáil's close links to the IRA strengthened this fear. In 1932 and 1933, IRA men attacked Cumann na nGaedheal meetings. A group of former Free State soldiers called the **Army Comrades Association (ACA)** helped Cumann na nGaedheal people to defend themselves.

In 1933 the ACA got a new leader. He was **Eoin O'Duffy**, an admirer of Mussolini. He dressed the ACA in blue shirts and began using the fascist salute. When O'Duffy announced a big march in Dublin, de Valera claimed this was like Mussolini's 'march on Rome' (see Topic 1A). He banned the march and outlawed the Blueshirts.

Setting up Fine Gael

To Cosgrave this looked like a threat to democracy. Was de Valera about to become a dictator? To stop him, he joined O'Duffy. Together they formed a new party called **Fine Gael**.

Eoin O'Duffy at a Blueshirt rally. **Can you see anything to suggest that the Blueshirts were fascists?**

Fine Gael chose O'Duffy as its first leader. It was a disastrous choice, because O'Duffy was a fascist. He let the Blueshirts get involved in riots with the Gardaí and threatened to invade Northern Ireland. Within a year, Cosgrave got rid of him and became the leader of Fine Gael himself.

De Valera outlaws the IRA

Soon after this, de Valera split with the IRA. They committed several murders which shocked people. De Valera begged them to give in their guns. When they refused, he outlawed them.

In 1939, some IRA men set off bombs in Britain. De Valera got the Dáil to pass the **Offences Against the State Act**. It allowed him to imprison IRA members without trial.

Eamon de Valera speaking at a public meeting. Before radio and TV, this was how political leaders got their message across to the voters.

Keeping promises

Fianna Fáil won the 1932 election because they promised:

- to undo the Treaty and
- to create jobs

Once they took power they set about keeping these promises.

Undoing the Treaty

De Valera hated the Treaty, and the Statue of Westminster gave him the opportunity to change it:

- As soon as he took over in 1932, he got the Dáil to remove the oath to the king.
- He insulted the Governor General who was the king's representative in Dublin and forced him to resign.
- Finally in 1936 he got the Dáil to remove the king as head of the Irish Free State.

A new Constitution: *Bunreacht na hÉireann*

These changes meant the Constitution that Cosgrave produced in 1922 no longer worked. So in 1937 de Valera wrote a new one. He called it ***Bunreacht na hÉireann***. Here are some of its main points:

- The country was called Ireland (or Éire in Irish which was to be the 'first official language').
- Articles 2 and 3 claimed control over the whole island of Ireland, not just the twenty-six counties. (After a referendum in 1998, these Articles were replaced as part of the Northern Ireland peace process).
- The head of state was a **president**, elected by all the people. The first president was Douglas Hyde, who had founded the Gaelic League.
- The Dáil was to elect the head of the government, who was to be called the **Taoiseach**.
- All religions were guaranteed freedom but the Catholic Church was given a special position because the majority of people belonged to it. This was changed in 1972.

In the 1930s Lemass encouraged industrialists to set up factories. The cartoonist claimed Lemass had opened so many factories he had to start a factory making keys for opening factories.

How Fianna Fáil managed the economy

In 1932, when Fianna Fáil won, the country was in the middle of a depression. They promised to create jobs and to protect Irish industries with taxes (tariffs) on imports.

An economic war with Britain

First Fianna Fáil put tariffs on hundreds of imports from Britain. They also stopped paying **land annuities** to the British government. They said they would invest the money in Irish industry instead.

Naturally this annoyed the British, who were already angry about the oath being removed. They hit back by putting taxes on the cattle the Irish sold to Britain. Fianna Fáil then put more taxes on goods coming from Britain.

This exchange of tariffs is called the **economic war**. It damaged farming. Prices for cattle fell and farmers were badly off.

Manufacturing industry did better. De Valera appointed Seán Lemass to develop it. He encouraged Irish businessmen to start factories making shoes, cutlery, clothing and furniture. These industries provided jobs but they were small and inefficient.

Note

What were land annuities?
Until c. 1900, land in Ireland belonged to landlords. Most of them were descended from the undertakers who got estates in the plantations. After a big agitation, the British agreed to lend money to Irish farmers so that they could buy their farms. The farmers were to repay the loans in annual instalments called 'land annuities'. Cosgrave had handed this money to the British.

Lemass set up Aer Lingus to develop air travel. Fianna Fáil also developed Foynes in Co. Limerick as a terminus for transatlantic flights. The planes were flying boats which landed in the water. All through World War II Foynes remained in use, but after that it was replaced by Shannon Airport

Making peace with Britain

By 1938 de Valera had achieved everything he wanted. In Europe, Hitler was threatening war. It was time to make peace with Britain, where a new prime minister had just been elected. His name was **Neville Chamberlain**. He too was worried by Hitler. He decided to make a generous peace with de Valera in the hope that when the war came, Ireland would support Britain against Germany.

The 1938 Anglo-Irish Agreements

After talks in London, de Valera and Chamberlain signed the Anglo-Irish Agreements in 1938. The Agreements said:

- Ireland would make a once-off payment of £10 million for the annuities.
- Both countries would reduce the tariffs on each other's goods.
- To win Irish backing in the war, Chamberlain handed over the three ports that the Treaty allowed the British navy to use.

The Agreements ended the quarrel between Britain and Ireland, but a bigger quarrel was about to break out in Europe – World War II.

Questions

1. Who were the Blueshirts? Explain how de Valera dealt with them.
2. Write a paragraph about the IRA in the 1930s.
3. Describe how de Valera dismantled the Treaty.
4. When did de Valera introduce his Constitution and what was it called? List four important points about it.
5. Which Fianna Fáil minister was in charge of industrial development in the 1930s? Describe his main policies.
6. Why did de Valera make peace with Britain in 1938? List the three main parts of the Anglo-Irish Agreements of that year.

Review the chapter

1. Write an account of the following: the Blueshirts; relations between the British and Irish governments in the 1930s. *(Junior Certificate, 2001)*
2. Write an account of the economic war. *(Junior Certificate, 2000)*
3. Write an account of the achievements of the Fianna Fáil government from 1932 to 1939. *(Junior Certificate, 1999)*

Chapter 3

Neutral Ireland in the Second World War

Declaring neutrality

In September 1939, Hitler invaded Poland. France and Britain declared war on Germany and World War II began. De Valera at once declared that Ireland would remain **neutral**. He did this to show that Ireland was independent of Britain. Most people supported this policy because it avoided the suffering that war brings.

Note

The LDF later became known as the FCA (Fórsa Cosanta Áitiúil).

The Defence Forces

Before the war the Irish army only had 7,700 men and few guns or aircraft. After the war started, thousands joined the army to defend their country in case of invasion by Germany. By 1940 the army had 37,000 men. Another 250,000 joined the Local Defence Force (LDF) as part-time soldiers.

But they had very little equipment to fight with. De Valera tried to buy weapons from the Americans but they refused to sell him many. The defence forces would have had little chance of success if Ireland had been invaded.

The threat from the IRA

The IRA was the main threat to neutrality. Early in 1939 they set off bombs in Britain. They also had contacts with the Nazis, who sent spies to Ireland to link up with them.

De Valera feared this would give the British an excuse to invade Ireland. He imprisoned over 500 IRA members and when three went on hunger strike, he let them die. German spies were also quickly rounded up.

Seán Lemass

The problem of food and fuel supplies

Before the war, Ireland imported many of the things people needed, like tea, flour, fruit and oil. They were carried here in British ships. When war began, German submarines attacked British ships. This seriously reduced imports. To deal with the problem, de Valera appointed **Seán Lemass** as **Minister for Supplies**. Lemass then

- ordered farmers to grow more wheat for flour
- rationed tea and sugar to ensure that everyone got a fair share
- set up a shipping company to carry goods to Ireland.

But in spite of his efforts there were severe shortages.

Shortages of food

Fruit like oranges and bananas disappeared from the shops. Tea and sugar were scarce. The weekly ration was 1/2 ounce of tea (about one tea bag) and half a pound of sugar for each person.

The only flour was what the farmers could grow. To make sure none of it was wasted, Lemass ordered bakers to use the whole wheat. This produced brown bread and people grumbled a lot about it. But unlike people elsewhere in Europe, they never starved.

A wartime cartoon from *Dublin Opinion*. In the caption the man is saying: 'I have an ancient name, a reputation for honour and integrity, a large and well-ordered estate in the country and eight pounds of tea'.

Shortages of fuel

Petrol was scarce. Private cars were banned and bus and train services were cut in half. Everyone used bicycles, and some people in country areas went back to using horses.

Coal came from Britain, which now needed all that it produced. What little they sold to Ireland was used to make electricity or gas. Lemass ordered that electricity was only to be used for cooking and light. It was cut off at other times. Gas was only to be used for cooking. An official called a **'glimmer man'** went around to see that these rules were obeyed.

Irish turf replaced imported coal as the main fuel. It ran trains, but very slowly. The journey from Cork to Dublin took eight hours in a turf-fired train. In summer, people went out to the bogs to cut enough turf to see the country through the winter.

Fuel shortages damaged industry too. Factories had to close or go on short time. That put many people out of work and thousands emigrated to Britain looking for work or to join the British forces.

Another cartoon from *Dublin Opinion*. In the caption the woman is saying: 'Glory be! The glimmer man!'

Bombing

Because Ireland was neutral, it was spared the suffering war brought to many people around Europe. But bombs did fall in various places. The worst incident was in May 1941 when a German plane dropped a bomb on the North Strand in Dublin. It damaged three hundred houses and killed thirty-four people.

Bomb damage in Dublin in 1941

Note

Although Ireland remained neutral during World War II, 43,000 people from the Republic joined the British army to fight against the Germans.

Why was Ireland able to stay neutral?

Many countries wanted to stay neutral in the war but they were attacked. Ireland remained neutral because no one attacked it.

- The Germans would have found it difficult to invade because Britain lay in between. Anyway Hitler was more interested in attacking Russia.
- Britain and its ally, the United States, had a large army in Northern Ireland. They could easily have crossed the border if they wanted to. Fortunately they did not. One reason was that de Valera secretly followed a pro-British policy. This gave the British most of what they wanted without having to fight for it.

During the war de Valera used radio to tell the people about his policies

De Valera's secret pro-British policies

- He allowed Irish people to work in Britain and to join the British forces. He also sold large quantities of food to Britain.
- He arranged secret talks between the Irish and British armies about what to do if the Germans invaded.
- The Irish sent any information they found out about German plans to Britain.

Irish people did not know any of this. Outwardly, de Valera remained strictly neutral. Only long after the war did historians discover what he had been doing.

How the war changed Ireland

World War II brought death and destruction to millions. Compared with them, Irish people had an easy time.

Staying neutral showed that Ireland was fully independent of Britain. This ended the old debate about whether the Treaty gave the country enough independence. After the war people were able to turn to other problems. The biggest of them was how to run the economy.

Questions

1. What does 'neutral' mean? Give two reasons why Ireland was neutral in World War II.
2. How did the country plan to defend itself in case it was attacked? Was it likely to be successful?
3. What was the main threat to Irish neutrality?
4. Why were supplies of food and fuel short during the war? Who was responsible for dealing with this problem? Describe some of the steps he took.
5. Explain why neither Germany nor Britain invaded Ireland during the war.

Write an essay on life in Ireland in World War II. *(Junior Certificate, 2002)*

Chapter 4

Ireland Changing, 1945–66

A new kind of government

When the war ended in 1945, people thought life would get better but it did not. Unemployment was high and food was still rationed. Then in 1946–47 came the worst winter of the twentieth century. With little coal or oil, people were cold as well as hungry.

Unfairly, they blamed de Valera and Fianna Fáil, who had ruled the country since 1932. When there was a general election in 1948, Fianna Fáil lost seats.

Other political parties saw a chance to get rid of de Valera after sixteen years in power. Fine Gael, the Labour party and a new party called **Clann na Poblachta** joined together to form a coalition government. **John A. Costello** of Fine Gael was the Taoiseach. Everyone thought the Coalition would soon break apart but in fact it lasted from 1948 to 1951.

John A. Costello became Taoiseach in 1948. He led Ireland's first coalition government.

What is a coalition?

It is a government formed when two or more parties join together. Up to 1948, all Irish governments had only one party. In 1948 a coalition seemed an odd, foreign idea, so the people who formed the first coalition did not use the word. They called it **'The Inter-Party Government'**. Since then we have had many coalitions and the idea no longer seems strange.

The policies of the Inter-Party government

The Coalition made several important decisions.

- They cut all ties with Britain and declared a **Republic**.
- When the Cold War began, they refused to join the **North Atlantic Treaty Organisation (NATO)**, which the Americans set up to oppose Stalin. This continued Ireland's policy of neutrality.
- They got the ESB to provide electricity to all farmers. This was called **rural electrification**. It made a great difference to the lives of farmers and their families.

Noel Browne and public health

Noel Browne was the Minister for Health. He was a doctor and several members of his family had died of tuberculosis (TB). This disease killed about 3,000 young Irish people every year. To wipe it out, Browne built hospitals, organised mass X-rays and paid for newly discovered drugs.

Noel Browne, Minister for Health, was concerned about the death rate from TB (tuberculosis). He built new hospitals and paid for new drugs to wipe it out.

Browne also wanted to improve the health of mothers and babies. In 1951 he proposed giving free medical care to all of them **(the Mother and Child Scheme)**. The doctors and Catholic bishops objected. They said this was too like communism. Other members of the Coalition supported the bishops. Browne resigned in protest. The Coalition collapsed soon after and de Valera won the next election.

Questions

1. What was different about the government formed in 1948? Name two of the leaders of that government.
2. Describe the main achievements of the Inter-Party government of 1948–51. Why did it fall?

Seán Lemass and New Policies in the 1960s

A failing economic policy in the 1950s

By the 1950s the Fianna Fáil economic policy, which had worked in the 1930s, was out of date. The main problems were:

Parked

This cartoon appeared when de Valera retired as Taoiseach and became President. After fourteen years in that job he finally retired at the age of ninety-one!

- High taxes kept out imports.
- Irish-owned companies made many of the things people needed but they were too small and inefficient to export to other countries.
- The only exports were agricultural produce like beef and butter. These did not earn enough to buy the imports the country needed like fuel, tea or the raw materials used by the factories.

After 1951, this caused an economic crisis. Jobs disappeared and between 1951 and 1961 almost 500,000 people left the country to find work. This crisis forced the government to look for new economic policies.

Seán Lemass as Taoiseach, 1956–66

In 1959 de Valera, who was seventy-two years old, at last retired. He handed over the job of Taoiseach to **Seán Lemass**, who had been his deputy for many years. De Valera was then elected President.

Seán Lemass was Taoiseach from 1956–66

Lemass understood that the country needed to change. He promoted younger men with new ideas like Jack Lynch and Charles Haughey. In other parties too new leaders appeared at the start of the 1960s.

A Programme for Economic Development

In 1958 a civil servant called **T.K. Whitaker** drew up a plan to deal with the economic crisis. Called ***A Programme for Economic Development***, it suggested that the government must:

- Give grants to Irish firms to help them to become more efficient so that they could export their goods.
- Give grants and tax relief to foreign companies to encourage them to set up in Ireland. They would export the goods they produced and also show Irish people how to run a modern business.

Lemass and the new economic policy

Lemass liked Whitaker's ideas. When he became Taoiseach he put them into effect. They were very successful. In the 1960s American, German and Japanese firms came to Ireland. They created jobs and exports. For the next ten years the economy grew steadily and emigration slowed down.

Donogh O'Malley

Encouraging better education

The new industries needed well-educated workers. But at the start of the 1960s only 30 per cent of pupils went to secondary school, where many studied Latin and Greek rather than science or French. Lemass thought this would make it hard to develop industry.

He encouraged his Minister for Education, **Donogh O'Malley**, to bring in free secondary education for all. New schools were built and buses were hired to carry pupils from the country to school in nearby towns. The number of students at secondary schools grew very quickly after that. Grants and scholarships also helped many more students to go on to further study after leaving school.

Gay Byrne, presenter of *The Late Late Show* for thirty-seven years

The impact of RTÉ

In the 1960s old attitudes began to change in Ireland. Better education encouraged people to think for themselves, but the biggest cause of change was television. In the 1950s people on the east coast could watch British TV programmes. This created a demand for an Irish station, which Lemass encouraged. On 1 January 1961 **Radio Telefís Éireann (RTE)** sent out its first pictures.

By 1970 over half of Irish homes had a TV set. People watched programmes from Britain and the US that showed a very different society from their own. On Irish programmes like *The Late Late Show* they heard debates about issues like poverty, contraception and violence.

TV influenced the books people read, the songs they sang and the way they furnished their homes. It made Irish people more like the British, Americans or Europeans who watched the same programmes.

The power of the Catholic Church

Changes in the Roman Catholic Church also encouraged new ideas. In the Republic over 90 per cent of people were Catholics and so were almost all the political leaders. They listened carefully to the advice of Catholic priests and bishops. As a result

- Contraception, which the Catholic Church condemned, was against the law. Irish Catholic families were usually big.
- De Valera put a ban on divorce into his 1937 Constitution.
- Books and films that discussed sex frankly were censored. Many books by Irish writers were not allowed into the country.
- When the bishops opposed Noel Browne's Mother and Child Scheme in 1951, it was dropped.

Changes in the Catholic Church

In 1958 a new pope, **John XXIII**, was elected. He hated the old divisions between Christians that went back to the Reformation. He encouraged the **Ecumenical Movement**. Its aim was to encourage Catholics and Protestants to be friendly to each other. This movement was successful in the Republic but less so in Northern Ireland.

Pope John summoned a Council of Catholic bishops to modernise the Church. Called the **Vatican Council**, it changed many things in the Church. Listening to the bishops argue about change encouraged Catholics to question the Church's ideas. In the 1960s censorship of books and films almost disappeared and divorce and contraception began to be discussed openly.

Making friends with the North

One very important change was in relations between the Republic and Northern Ireland. Ever since 1922, leaders in the South had made speeches attacking partition. Lemass disapproved of this. He thought that the best way to re-unite Ireland was to make the Republic so prosperous that the unionists would want to join it. When he became Taoiseach he stopped the attacks.

In 1963 a new prime minister called **Terence O'Neill** was elected in Northern Ireland. He responded to Lemass by inviting him to go to Belfast. Later O'Neill visited Lemass in Dublin. The two leaders encouraged their governments to work together on tourism and other common issues. But this development was ended when a crisis developed in the North in 1968. We will look in more detail at this in Topic 2C.

Seán Lemass and Terence O'Neill

Questions

1. What was the Irish economy like in the 1950s? What happened as a result?
2. Who drew up the first Programme for Economic Development? What changes did he propose?
3. Who was Taoiseach from 1959 to 1966? List three of his achievements and write a paragraph on one of them.
4. Ireland changed greatly in the 1960s. List two of the changes and write a paragraph on one of them.

Review the chapter

1. Write an account of the first Inter-Party government. *(Junior Certificate, 1999)*
2. Write a sentence about the main achievement of each of the following: T. K. Whitaker, Donogh O'Malley, Gay Byrne.
3. What do the words 'Ecumenical Movement' mean? Explain why the Ecumenical Movement was important in Ireland in the 1960s.

4 Copy out this paragraph and fill in the missing words.

In 1959, at the age of seventy-two, Eamon —— ———————— resigned as Taoiseach. He was replaced by Seán ———————— who remained in office until ———––. During this time Ireland changed greatly. A new economic policy encouraged —————————— firms to set up in Ireland. Donogh O'Malley introduced free ————————————— ————————————— for all. After the Vatican —————————— Catholics and ———————————————— became more friendly. RTE, which began to broadcast in ———––, encouraged people to discuss issues like divorce. Lemass visited Belfast and met the Prime Minister of Northern Ireland, Terence ————————. This encouraged co-operation between Northern Ireland and the ———————————.

5 Match the items on the left with the corresponding items on the right.

Column 1	Column 2
1 Seán Lemass	**A** Leader of the Blueshirts
2 Terence O'Neill	**B** Cumann na nGaedheal minister
3 Eoin O'Duffy	**C** Health minister who dealt with TB
4 Kevin O'Higgins	**D** Prime minister of Northern Ireland
5 Noel Browne	**E** One of the founders of Fianna Fáil

6 Are the following statements true or false? If false, write down the correct statement.

(i) De Valera retired in 1945.
(ii) Seán Lemass was a member of Cumann na nGaedheal.
(iii) Ireland was neutral in World War II.
(iv) De Valera declared a Republic in 1937.
(v) Terence O'Neill met John A. Costello in 1964.
(vi) Noel Browne wrote the Programme for Economic Development.

The Republic's Leaders, 1966–2000

In 1966, Seán Lemass retired. Since then the Republic has had many leaders:

Jack Lynch became Taoiseach when Lemass retired. He negotiated Ireland's entry into the European Economic Community in 1973. In 1977 he won the largest victory in Fianna Fáil's history but was forced to retire in 1979.

Liam Cosgrave led a coalition of Fine Gael and Labour from 1973 to 1977. To try to bring peace in Northern Ireland he negotiated the Sunningdale Agreement in 1973. It failed because of IRA violence and unionist opposition.

Garret FitzGerald led Fine Gael in two coalitions in the 1980s. He set up the New Ireland Forum that helped reshape the Republic's view of Northern Ireland. In 1985 he and the British prime minister Margaret Thatcher signed the Anglo-Irish Agreement to improve co-operation between Britain and the Republic. He failed in his campaign to remove the ban on divorce in the Constitution.

Charles Haughey replaced Lynch as leader of Fianna Fáil in 1979. Suspicion about his financial dealings led to a split in the party. He was Taoiseach several times in the 1980s and led Fianna Fáil into its first coalition in 1989. He signed the Maastricht Treaty, which expanded the European Union.

Albert Reynolds replaced Haughey as leader of Fianna Fáil and Taoiseach in 1992. He helped to negotiate the IRA ceasefire that began the Northern Ireland peace process in 1994.

John Bruton, the leader of Fine Gael, led a coalition with Labour from 1994 to 1997. He continued to work on the peace process.

Bertie Ahern became leader of Fianna Fáil in 1994 and Taoiseach in 1997. He signed the **'Good Friday Agreement'** in 1998, which brought peace to Northern Ireland. After this a referendum in the Republic removed Articles 2 and 3 (which claimed power over Northern Ireland) from the Constitution.

Questions

Name three men who held the office of Taoiseach after 1966. In each case mention one of his achievements.

A Changing Economy

Between the 1960s and 2000 the Irish economy changed greatly, as this table shows.

The economy in the 1960s	The economy in 2000
The main exports were cattle and other agricultural produce.	While Ireland still exports a lot of agricultural produce, it also sells large quantities of computers, machines and chemicals.
Over 80 per cent of these exports went to Britain.	Only a quarter of exports go to Britain.
Most firms were small, Irish owned and exported little	Many huge multinational companies have set up in Ireland. They export enormous quantities.
Half of Irish workers lived in the country and worked on farms. Unemployment was still high and many Irish people emigrated to get work.	Most Irish workers live in towns or cities and work in industry. Unemployment is low and many foreigners come here to get work.

There were many reasons for the changes in the Irish economy:

- The **Industrial Development Authority (IDA)** encouraged foreign firms to set up factories here and develop new industries.
- The government helped with grants and tax concessions.
- An educated young workforce was attractive to foreign firms.
- The most important reason was membership of the European Union, which turned the Republic from a small, isolated island into part of a great economic unit.

What is it called?
At first the European Union was mainly about trade, so it was called the European Economic Community **(EEC)** or the Common Market. Then political unity became important, so the name changed to the European Community **(EC)** and later to the European Union **(EU)**, which is now its official name.

Joining the European Economic Community (EEC)

In 1957 six European countries signed the **Treaty of Rome** and set up the **European Economic Community (EEC)**. (You can read more about this in Topic 1C). At first the British refused to join but as the EEC prospered, they applied for membership in 1961.

Lemass decided the Republic must apply too, because over 80 per cent of our trade was with Britain. However, the French leader, General de Gaulle, disliked the British and blocked their application. It was only in 1972, after de Gaulle retired, that the British tried again.

Jack Lynch led the Irish negotiations. When they were completed he held a referendum on joining the EEC. Over 70 per cent of the people voted to accept and on 1 January 1973 Ireland signed the Treaty of Rome.

"You go first, Macmillan, and see how deep it is."

This cartoon appeared in 1961. The man on the left is Harold Macmillan, the British Prime Minister and the other is Taoiseach Sean Lemass. **Which of them is speaking and what is he saying? What does the 'swiming pool' represent? According to the cartoonist, did Lemass have any choice about whether he dived in or not? Do you think the cartoonist was correct about that? Explain your answer.**

The impact of membership

The European Community poured resources into Ireland.

- As an agricultural country, Ireland gained greatly from the **Common Agricultural Policy (CAP)**. It guaranteed farmers high prices for their produce. Although grants were reduced in the 1980s, the CAP still helped farmers to have a decent standard of living.
- As a poor country, Ireland gained from the **Structural Fund**, which gave money to bring poor regions up to the level of rich ones. The Fund helped improve roads, telecommunications and education.
- Ireland did less well in fishing. EU rules require that the rich fishing grounds off Ireland's shores be open to all EU fishing fleets, and Spanish fishing fleets have been better than Irish fishermen at exploiting this opportunity.
- The EU has a charter of human rights. This allows citizens of the EU who think their human rights have been abused to take a case against their governments. As a result of court cases, Irish governments had to change the law on contraception, give equal pay to women and equal rights to gay people.

From the 1920s Ireland had its own notes and coins, even though their value was the same as the British currency. The designs of the notes changed over time. This was the Irish £5 note and £20 note when the euro replaced it in 2002.

Changing the pound for the euro

Even after Ireland became independent in 1922, the Irish currency was linked to Britain. The Irish pound had the same value as the pound sterling. But in 1979 the EU decided to link the members' currencies together. The British stayed out but Ireland went in. That broke the link with sterling.

This development went further in 1999 when EU members decided to abolish local currencies and replace them with a new one called the **euro**. Unlike Britain, Ireland joined the euro zone. On 1 January 2002 euro notes and coins replaced Irish notes and coins.

Ireland in the United Nations

In 1955, Ireland joined another international organisation, the United Nations. Through it, Irish soldiers, police and diplomats have played a part in keeping the peace in various troubled parts of the world.

The first peace-keeping effort took place in the Congo in 1960. The UN intervened to try to stop a civil war and Ireland was asked to send troops. One battalion was caught in an ambush and ten men were killed. Although this was the worst single episode, other Irish soldiers have died while helping with UN peace-keeping efforts in Cyprus, the Lebanon and other places.

Irish soldiers marching past the GPO before they set out for UN service in the Congo

The last years of the twentieth century

In the last decade of the twentieth century the Republic changed very fast. After a period of economic weakness in the 1980s, the Irish economy grew faster than any other economy in Europe. People called Ireland the **'Celtic Tiger'**. These changes affected the country in various ways:

- There was full employment. This reduced the levels of poverty and gave many people money to spend on luxury items such as second homes and foreign holidays.
- From being a nation of emigrants, sending its young people abroad to work in other countries, Ireland became a magnet for people from Europe, Asia and Africa seeking jobs here.
- The population, which had hardly grown at all for over a century, suddenly expanded, as this graph shows:

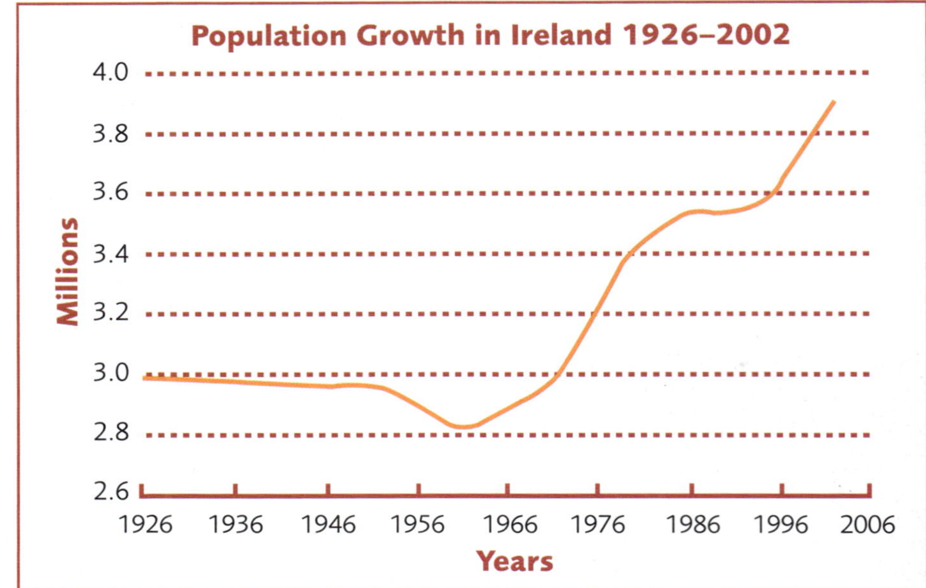

- To house the extra people, many new houses were built but the price of houses went up very fast, making it difficult for many people to find accommodation.

How the Troubles in Northern Ireland affected the Republic

Another important change in the 1990s was the end of the conflict in Northern Ireland (see Topic 2C). Although violence seldom spread to the Republic, the conflict in the North had damaged the economy. Foreign firms were reluctant to set up in any part of a troubled island. The Irish government also had to spend a lot of money on the army and police to patrol the border and search for IRA arms.

The Financial Services Centre in Dublin attracted many foreign banks. Their steel and glass buildings symbolised the new Ireland of the twenty-first century.

Nationalists' attitudes to unionists

Nationalists had always turned a blind eye to unionist concerns. They did not try to understand that unionists felt very strongly that they were British or that they feared the power of Catholic priests in a Catholic country.

After partition, nationalists refused to recognise Northern Ireland and insisted on the reunification of the island. Before Seán Lemass in the 1960s no Southern leader would talk to a unionist leader. When the civil rights campaign began in the 1960s, most people in the South were firmly on the side of the nationalists.

However, as IRA violence grew, these views began to change. People in the South became more interested in the unionist point of view. They asked:

- Were unionists right in their belief that the Catholic Church had too much power in the Republic?
- Should the Republic change its laws on contraception and divorce, which were seen by many as unjust to Protestants?
- Was it right that Articles 2 and 3 of the Constitution should claim power over Northern Ireland?
- Could the Republic really force one million hostile unionists to join the South against their will?

Margaret Thatcher was prime minister of Britain from 1979 to 1992

In 1983, Garret FitzGerald set up the **New Ireland Forum**, where issues like these were discussed. The discussions helped people to accept the need to change the Republic's laws on contraception and divorce. It also made nationalists accept that the unionists had a right to exist.

One result of this was the **Anglo-Irish Agreement**, which FitzGerald made with the British prime minister Margaret Thatcher in 1985. In this, the British accepted that the Republic could act as guarantor for nationalists in Northern Ireland. This produced closer links between the London and Dublin governments and paved the way for the IRA truces and the 1998 Belfast Agreement, which finally brought the conflict to an end.

Questions

1. List three ways in which the Irish economy has changed since the 1960s and give three reasons for the change.
2. Write a paragraph describing how Ireland joined the EU. List three important ways in which EU membership has changed Ireland. Which do you think is the most important? Explain your choice.
3. Describe Ireland's involvement in the United Nations.
4. How have the Troubles in Northern Ireland affected the Republic? Describe how Southern attitudes to the North have changed since the 1960s.

Topic 2C

Northern Ireland, 1920–2000

The Foundation of Northern Ireland, 1920–45

Northern Ireland

The Government of Ireland Act partitions Ireland

On page 125 you read about the different things nationalists and unionists wanted in the early 1900s. To give each side what it wanted, the British passed the **Government of Ireland Act** in 1920.

The Act partitioned (divided) Ireland into two parts. One part, with twenty-six counties, was for nationalists and we have studied it in Topic 2A. The remaining six counties went to the unionists and became Northern Ireland.

Why unionists welcomed partition

About 1,500,000 people lived in Northern Ireland in 1920. One million of them were Protestant unionists. They welcomed partition because:

- It left Northern Ireland in the United Kingdom. The British king was still their king and the London parliament decided on things like trade, war and most taxes. Northern Ireland elected twelve MPs to the London parliament.
- But in Belfast unionists had a parliament of their own to run local affairs like education and health.
- And because they were two-thirds of the population, they would always win elections to the Belfast parliament. This protected them against the Catholic nationalists.

Why Northern nationalists opposed it

The remaining 500,000 people in Northern Ireland were Catholic nationalists. When Northern Ireland was set up they felt betrayed.

- They wanted to be with other nationalists in the rest of Ireland.
- They did not want to be trapped within Northern Ireland where they would always be out-voted by the unionist majority.

Sir James Craig defeats the IRA

The first Northern Ireland election was held in 1921. Unionists won 40 of the 52 seats in the Belfast parliament. They chose **Sir James Craig** as their first prime minister. He faced many problems:

- The IRA went on fighting the Northern Ireland police, the **Royal Ulster Constabulary (RUC)** and the British army, even after it made peace in the South.
- In Belfast, there were riots between Catholics and Protestants, and thousands of Catholics were driven from their homes and jobs.

Craig was determined to defeat the IRA.

- He enrolled many former Ulster Volunteers (see page 132) as **Special Constables** to fight them.
- He got parliament to pass the **Special Powers Act**. It allowed the RUC and Special Constables to search people's houses and imprison anyone without trial (internment).
- Thousands were arrested and imprisoned. Some were executed.

These measures worked. By 1923 Northern Ireland was at peace. But it was a sullen peace. The events of these years made the two communities, Protestant unionists and Catholic nationalists, deeply suspicious of each other.

ULSTER
IS IN SAFE HANDS
ULSTER
HER FATE IS IN
YOUR HANDS
VOTE LOYALIST

Sir James Craig led the unionists in Northern Ireland from 1921 until his death in 1940

The nationalist attitude to Northern Ireland

Angry and resentful nationalists refused to accept Northern Ireland. They knew they would always be in a minority and that the unionists would not pay any attention to them. But they were divided.

- Some nationalists wanted nothing to do with the unionist state. They still supported the IRA, which was prepared to use violence to end partition.
- Most nationalists were moderates. They voted for the Nationalist Party, which wanted to work peacefully for the reunification of Ireland.

At first they expected that the Boundary Commission (see page 158) would put many of them back into the South. After the Commission failed in 1925, nationalist MPs went into the Northern Ireland parliament. But they found they could achieve nothing. The Unionist Party always won elections and paid no attention to nationalists' problems.

The Unionist Government built itself a huge new parliament house at Stormont Castle. It opened in 1931. The Northern Ireland parliament is often referred to as 'Stormont'.

How unionists viewed the nationalists

Unionists resented the nationalist attitude to Northern Ireland. They were also afraid. In the whole of Ireland, Catholic nationalists were in a majority (3 million against 1 million). Unionists always feared that some day nationalists, North and South, would force them under the control of a Catholic-dominated Dublin parliament.

Orange Order parade

The Orange Order

To protect themselves, unionists felt it was important to stay united. The Orange Order helped with that. It was set up in 1796 to defend Protestantism. After 1920 it became very powerful in Northern Ireland. All leaders of the Unionist Party belonged to it. Every year it organised marches to foster a sense of Protestant unity and power. Many marches went through Catholic areas and were intended to show which community was on top.

Note

Ways of Voting

In **Proportional Representation (PR)** parties get seats in proportion to the number of people voting for them. In 'first past the post' voting, the party with the most votes gets all the seats. The British brought in PR in the 1920 Government of Ireland Act. The South kept it; Craig got rid of it because he feared it would weaken the Unionist Party.

Two separate communities

The distrust between the two communities kept them apart. Catholics and Protestants prayed in different churches and went to different schools. They shopped in different shops, read different newspapers, played different games. This separation meant that neither side understood the other's point of view and no one made any attempt to reconcile their differences.

Sir James Craig (Lord Craigavon) as prime minister

Craig (whom the king made **Lord Craigavon** in 1927) remained Prime Minister of Northern Ireland until his death in 1940. Although he said he wanted to be fair to Catholics, he did nothing to correct injustices against them. In fact, some of his policies made things worse:

- To ensure unionists had power, he got rid of **Proportional Representation (PR)** in voting for local councils in 1922. As a result, unionists controlled local councils even in areas where Catholics were in a majority.
- Later he got rid of PR voting for the Northern Ireland parliament. This made it harder for small parties like the Nationalists and Labour to win seats there.

Craigavon and the Northern Ireland economy

Northern Ireland also had big economic problems, which Craigavon did little to solve.

Before World War I the area around Belfast was the most prosperous in Ireland. It had two big industries: linen and ships.

- Linen mills provided many jobs for women.
- Shipbuilding employed many men. In 1912 the biggest ship in the world, the *Titanic*, was built in Belfast and hundreds of ships were built there during World War I.

But in the 1920s and 1930s demand for linen and ships fell and these industries declined. This put many people out of work. Craigavon's government gave little help to the unemployed and people were often hungry. In 1932 Protestants and Catholics joined together to demand better conditions.

This alarmed the Unionist Party. If Catholic and Protestant workers joined together, it could mean the end of Unionist rule. They were determined to prevent this happening.

They organised public works where unemployed workers could earn money but made sure few Catholics got jobs in these works. One unionist minister even advised Protestant employers to employ only Protestant workers. These tactics worked. The brief unity between Catholic and Protestant workers ended in sectarian riots in 1935.

Questions

1. What was the Government of Ireland Act and when was it passed?
2. What was a unionist (see page 125) and why did unionists welcome partition in 1920?
3. What was a nationalist (see page 125) and why did Northern nationalists oppose partition in 1920?
4. Who was the first prime minister of Northern Ireland and what did he do to repress opposition to Northern Ireland in 1920–22?
5. What was the Orange Order and why was it important for unionists?
6. Write a short essay on Sir James Craig as prime minister of Northern Ireland.

Northern Ireland in World War II

The war begins

In 1939 Britain declared war on Germany. This drew Northern Ireland into the war because it was part of the United Kingdom. Northern Ireland was very useful to the British war effort.

- Ships and aircraft were built in Belfast.
- Linen for parachutes, uniforms and tents was produced in Northern Ireland.
- From bases in Derry, British ships and aircraft patrolled the Atlantic, looking for German warships and submarines.
- After America entered the war in 1941, American troops trained throughout the North.

Although there were shortages and rationing, the war also brought prosperity to Northern Ireland. Busy factories offered well-paid jobs to many people. But there was a high price to be paid.

A corner in Belfast after a German bombing raid in 1941

Bombs in Belfast

On a moonlit night in April 1941, 150 German bombers flew in over Belfast. There were no anti-aircraft guns to stop them because the government thought Northern Ireland was too far from Germany to be hit.

The Germans were probably aiming at the shipyards but they hit houses, churches, schools and hospitals. The bombs set buildings blazing, killing 747 people and injuring about 1,500. From Dublin, de Valera sent fire brigades to help fight the fires.

In May the Germans came again but they did less damage this time. After that they never returned.

A new Prime Minister, Lord Brookeborough

Craigavon died in 1940. The next prime minister was J.M. Andrews. When the German bombers attacked Belfast, the city had few defences. Unionists blamed Andrews for incompetence. In 1943 he had to resign and Lord Brookeborough was elected in his place.

Lord Brookeborough was Prime Minister of Northern Ireland from 1943 to 1963

Note

During World War II 31,000 men and 7,000 women from Northern Ireland served in the British forces. James Magennis, a Catholic from Belfast, was awarded the North's only Victoria Cross – Britain's highest award for bravery.

Questions

1. Why was Northern Ireland involved in the war from the start?
2. How did Northern Ireland help Britain's war effort?
3. Describe the bombing of Belfast.

Review the chapter

1. Write an essay about the establishment of Northern Ireland. *(Junior Certificate, 1996)*

2. Write an account of the war years in Ireland, North and South (1939–45). (You will need to look back to pages 165–167 to do this.) *(Junior Certificate, 2000)*

3. Write a brief account of two of the following:
   (i) The Government of Ireland Act.
   (ii) The Boundary Commission.
   (iii) The Orange Order.
   (iv) The Bombing of Belfast in 1941.

4. Copy out this paragraph and fill in the missing words.
   When Northern Ireland was set up in 1920, ——————— welcomed it. They felt it protected them from the Catholic ——————— in the rest of Ireland. Sir James ———— became the first ———— ——————— of Northern Ireland. Later the king made him Lord ————————. To fight the IRA he formed the —————— Constables and got the Northern Ireland parliament to pass the Special —————— Act. Later he got rid of the P————————— R——————————— system of voting. In the 1930s, the linen and ——————————— industries declined and unemployment ————.

Chapter 2 How the Welfare State Changed Northern Ireland

Northern Ireland and the welfare state

In 1945 World War II ended. In Britain there was a general election. The Labour Party promised to improve living conditions for people and it won. In the next few years, Labour set up the **welfare state**. This gave

- free medical care to all
- better old age pensions
- better unemployment pay
- free secondary education to all children and good grants to able students to allow them to go to university.

In Northern Ireland, Lord Brookeborough and the Unionist Party did not want the welfare state at first. They only agreed to set it up when the British promised to pay most of the cost.

John Hume, later leader of the SDLP, was one of the many young boys and girls who got a good education because of the welfare state.

How the welfare state affected Northern Ireland

The welfare state made a huge difference to the lives of poor people, both Catholic and Protestant. They got decent housing and health care, even if they were old, ill or unemployed.

But young people from poor families gained the most. If they passed an exam at eleven (known as the 'eleven-plus'), they got a free place in a grammar school and a chance to go to university.

The eleven-plus helped thousands of boys and girls to get a good education in the 1950s and 1960s. The exam was open to all, regardless of religion, so Catholics benefited as much as Protestants. One of the boys who gained from this was **John Hume**, who later became the leader of the nationalists. His poor family could not have afforded a good education but he got it free once he passed the eleven-plus.

Catholic views on Northern Ireland change

British tax-payers paid for the welfare state. In the 1950s and 1960s that meant people in Northern Ireland had a much higher standard of living than the Republic could afford for its people. This made many Catholics in Northern Ireland reconsider their view of Northern Ireland. They looked at the Republic where there was no free education or free medical care. They asked: do we really want a united Ireland?

Nationalists reject the IRA border campaign

In 1956 the IRA began a new campaign to win a united Ireland. They attacked police barracks and customs posts along the border. But very few nationalists in Northern Ireland supported them. By 1962 they realised their campaign had failed and called it off.

Terrence O'Neill became Prime Minister of Northern Ireland in 1963. He wanted to modernise it by moving away from sectarian politics.

Lord Brookeborough is replaced by Terence O'Neill

But the unionists did not appreciate that Catholics had changed. Lord Brookeborough, who was prime minister from 1943 to 1963, did nothing to win them over. His main worry was the economy. The old industries of linen and shipbuilding declined again after the war and he could not find replacements for them. In the end he was forced to retire. The man who succeeded him was **Terence O'Neill**. He hoped to modernise Northern Ireland.

Questions

1. Explain what is meant by the 'welfare state'. Which British party brought it in? Who paid for welfare in Northern Ireland?
2. How did the welfare state help young people in Northern Ireland?
3. Explain why Catholic attitudes towards Northern Ireland began to change when the welfare state came in.
4. Can you refer to one event that supports the opinion that Northern Catholics were less interested in a united Ireland after the welfare state started?

How Discrimination Against Catholics Led to the Civil Rights Campaign

Why unionists discriminated against Catholics

The welfare state made young Northern Catholics less interested in a united Ireland than their parents had been. But unionist discrimination against Catholics made it difficult for them to play any part in the life of Northern Ireland. There were several reasons for this discrimination.

Note

Sectarian politics = political parties based on religion.

Unionists felt outnumbered in Ireland

- Even though unionists had their own state since 1920, they never felt secure. The map opposite shows why. On the island as a whole, Catholics outnumbered Protestants by three to one.
- Unionists believed that Catholics throughout Ireland were plotting to force them into a united Ireland.

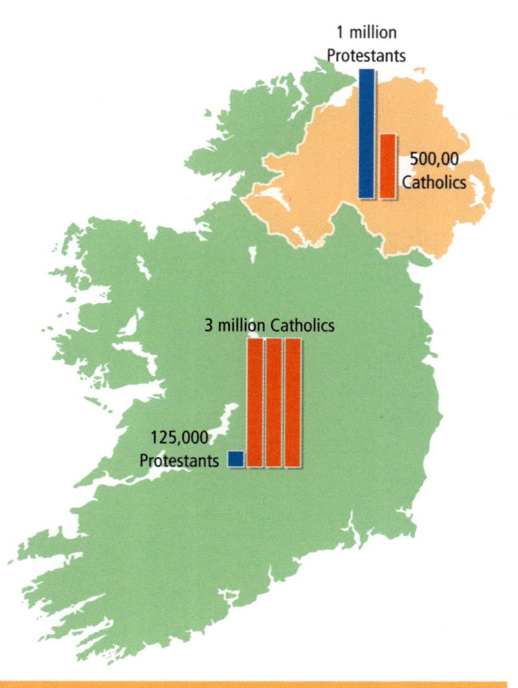

The numbers of Catholics and Protestants North and South

- They could point to Articles 2 and 3 in the 1937 Constitution as proof that this was true. These Articles said that the Constitution applied to the whole island, not just to the South.
- Unionists also pointed to the many speeches by de Valera and other leaders in which they called for partition to end.

Why unionists feared a united Ireland

Unionists feared that in a united Ireland the Catholic majority would deprive them of their freedom. They could point to developments in the South that supported their fears.

- Books and films were heavily censored. This interfered with freedom of speech, which Protestants valued highly.
- In his 1937 Constitution, de Valera gave the Catholic Church a special position. The Constitution also outlawed divorce, whereas Protestants accepted divorce.
- Contraception, which the Catholic Church condemned, was outlawed in the Republic, even though Protestants thought it was all right.
- In 1951, when the Catholic bishops opposed Noel Browne's Mother and Child scheme, Browne had to resign. To unionists this was proof that Catholic bishops had too much power in the Republic.

Unionist fears lead to discrimination

In 1921 when Craig became prime minister, he had promised to be fair to Catholics, but unionist fears meant this never happened. Between 1920 and 1972 unionists made sure that Catholics were kept out of jobs in the government, the police and the civil service.

The worst discrimination against Catholics was in local government. County and city councils had a lot of power. They employed many people and they built and distributed council houses. Unionists tried to stop nationalists gaining control of local councils. They did this in two ways:

- Each local area was divided into districts called wards. Each ward elected some local councillors. The lines between the wards were carefully drawn to ensure that more unionist councillors were elected than nationalists. This is called **gerrymandering**. Gerrymandering ensured that unionists controlled areas like Derry City or County Fermanagh, even though nationalists were in the majority there.
- Only people with property were allowed to vote for local councils. That kept many poor people, Protestant as well as Catholic, from voting. But people like businessmen who owned several buildings had several votes. By and large, Protestants owned more property than Catholics and this meant they had more votes.

The unionist-controlled councils elected in this way made sure that Catholics got fewer council houses and fewer jobs than Protestants.

Evidence of discrimination

Nationalists had complained for years about discrimination but no one listened. Then in the 1960s evidence to support them emerged. Here are some examples:

- Of the top 319 jobs in the civil service, Catholics held only 23.
- The shipbuilder Harland and Wolff employed only 400 Catholics in a workforce of 10,000.
- Only 12 per cent of the RUC and none of the Special Constables who policed Northern Ireland were Catholics.
- In Derry City, 8,781 Protestant voters elected 12 councillors while 14,229 Catholic voters elected 8 councillors.
- In County Fermanagh, where a majority of the people were Catholic, the unionist-controlled council employed 338 Protestants and only 32 Catholics.

Prime Minister Terence O'Neill makes gestures

In the 1960s, better educated young Catholics grew frustrated at the discrimination that kept them out of many jobs. Their hopes rose when **Terence O'Neill** became prime minister in 1963. He said he wanted better relations with Catholics in the North and also with the Republic. He invited the Taoiseach, Seán Lemass, to visit Belfast and went to Dublin himself. He also visited a Catholic school and made a few speeches that expressed friendly feelings towards Catholics.

The civil rights campaign

But O'Neill only made gestures. He did nothing to end the actual discrimination. To encourage him, some people set up the **Northern Ireland Civil Rights Association (NICRA)** in 1967. NICRA organised peaceful marches demanding:

- 'one man, one vote' in local elections
- an end to discrimination in housing and jobs.

A civil rights march blocked by the RUC. The police often tried to stop the marches and this led to violence. **Can you see what the marchers want?**

Ian Paisley

Ian Paisley

While many unionists sympathised with the civil rights campaign, others were horrified. Ian Paisley became their leader. He was a clergyman who founded his own Free Presbyterian Church. Paisley began a campaign demanding that 'O'Neill must go'. Whenever NICRA organised a march, he held a rival one. This caused riots in which the RUC (police) often intervened on the side of the Paisleyites.

TV pictures embarrass the British government

Riots between Catholics and Protestants were not new in Northern Ireland but this time there were TV cameras present. They got pictures of RUC men beating peaceful protestors and the pictures flashed around the world. Reporters flocked to the North to see what was going on. They dug up stories of discrimination and injustice and published them.

This seriously embarrassed the British government. It was supposed to be in charge of Northern Ireland but for fifty years it had ignored Catholic complaints about discrimination. Now they forced O'Neill to end gerrymandering and bring in 'one man, one vote' in local elections.

The reforms divided unionists. Ian Paisley set up a new political party, the **Democratic Unionist Party (DUP)** to oppose any change. He won seats in the Stormont parliament and O'Neill was forced to resign in 1969.

Growing violence brings in the British army

In August 1969 fierce fighting broke out between Protestants and Catholics in Derry and Belfast. In Belfast Protestant mobs attacked Catholics and burned their houses. Many fled to the South. The British government sent in the army to keep the two sides apart and Catholics welcomed them as protectors.

The formation of the SDLP

Moderate nationalists felt they needed a party to express their point of view. In 1970 the old Nationalist Party and the Labour Party united with some of the members of the civil rights campaign to form the **Social Democratic and Labour Party (SDLP)**. It was led by **Gerry Fitt** and **John Hume**.

The emergence of the Provisional IRA

The IRA played little part in these developments. After its border campaign ended in failure in 1962, its leaders had given up violence. They backed the civil rights campaign and hoped for a peaceful socialist revolution. When Catholics in Belfast were attacked, the IRA could not defend them. People wrote 'IRA= I ran away' on the walls.
This caused a split in the IRA in 1970.

- The **Official IRA** still favoured peace and socialism
- The **Provisional IRA** wanted to use violence to achieve a united Ireland.

Violence increases

The Provisionals (soon nicknamed **the 'Provos'**) got guns and began shooting at British soldiers. The soldiers then searched Catholic homes for arms. Often they tore up floorboards and damaged furniture. This turned the Catholics against them, especially in the poorer districts of Derry and Belfast. Many young people saw the Provisionals as protectors and joined them.

Throughout 1971 violence increased. As well as IRA attacks, a unionist terror group, the Ulster Volunteer Force (UVF), killed Catholics. Riots became common, with the police using CS gas and rubber bullets.

After internment, nationalists in the Bogside district of Derry proclaimed their area was 'Free Derry' and refused to allow Northern Ireland officials to enter

Brian Faulkner

Brian Faulkner introduces internment

In 1971 **Brian Faulkner** was prime minister of Northern Ireland. He decided to round up trouble-makers and imprison them without trial **(internment)**. Early on 9 August 1971 the British army and RUC rounded up 337 people.

But Catholics noted bitterly that most of those picked up were Catholics, even though a lot of the violence had come from the Protestant side. This injustice won new recruits to the IRA. Far from ending the violence, internment actually increased it, as these figures show.

	People killed
1969	13
1970	25
1971 (before internment)	30
1971 (after internment)	143

Bloody Sunday ends the Stormont government

Nationalists organised marches to protest against internment. On Sunday 30 January 1972 British soldiers opened fire on a march in Derry. Thirteen unarmed men were killed.

In response, violence flared up in Belfast and Derry. This convinced the British government to suspend the Stormont government and rule Northern Ireland directly from London. On 1 April **William Whitelaw** was appointed as the first **Secretary of State for Northern Ireland**.

Questions

1 Why did unionists not feel secure in Northern Ireland?
2 Why did unionists believe that Catholics were plotting to force them into a united Ireland?
3 List three things that made unionists fear a united Ireland.
4 Why was the Northern Ireland Civil Rights Association set up and what did it do?
5 Who was Ian Paisley and what did he do?
6 Why did the British intervene in 1969?
7 Who were the Provisionals? List two things they did.
8 What was 'internment'? Who brought it in? What effect did it have?
9 What happened in Derry on Bloody Sunday? What did the British do after that?

Review the chapter

1 Supply the missing words in the following sentences.
   (i) Sir James ——————— was the first prime minister of Northern Ireland.
   (ii) The ————————— Party was the largest party in Northern Ireland in the 1920s.
   (iii) ——————————————————— was the practice of dividing electoral districts in order to give some party an electoral advantage.
   (iv) The prime minister of Northern Ireland from 1963 to 1969 was Sir Terence ————————.
   (v) The Civil Rights Movement was set up to campaign for better conditions for the ————————— minority.
   (vi) ——————————— or imprisonment without trial was introduced by the Northern Ireland government in 1971.

(Junior Certificate, 2002)

2 In relation to Northern Ireland after 1939, write about one of the following:
   (i) The war years.
   (ii) Political parties.
   (iii) The experience of the nationalist minority. *(Junior Certificate, 1998)*

3 Explain the following words:
   (i) Discrimination.
   (ii) Gerrymandering.
   (iii) Internment.

Chapter 3 Looking for Peace, 1972–2000

Sunningdale: an experiment that failed

The British never wanted to rule Northern Ireland directly. They hoped the leaders of the two communities there would quickly find a way of working together. Soon after Stormont was suspended, talks began and in 1973 the SDLP and a section of the Unionists led by Brian Faulkner signed the **Sunningdale Agreement**.

Brian Faulkner, the Unionist leader, with Gerry Fitt and John Hume, leaders of the SDLP, at the time of the Sunningdale Agreement

It set up a 'power-sharing' government. Faulkner was the prime minister and Gerry Fitt, the SDLP leader, was his deputy. For the first time since 1921, unionists and nationalists came together to govern Northern Ireland.

But many people opposed this experiment. The IRA continued to plant bombs and Ian Paisley persuaded Protestant workers to go on strike against the power-sharing government. They closed down the electricity system and Northern Ireland ground to a halt. The Sunningdale experiment collapsed and the British resumed direct rule.

UNITED ULSTER
UNIONIST COUNCIL
THE BIG PEACE LIE
EXPOSED
REJECT THE
COUNCIL OF IRELAND
and
S.D.L.P. – I.R.A. RULE
SIGN THE
SAVE ULSTER PETITION
SAT. 26th JAN. & SAT. 2nd FEB.

A unionist poster opposing the Sunningdale 'power-sharing' agreement

Violence grows worse

Meanwhile the violence got worse. The fall of Stormont had convinced the Provisionals that they were winning and they stepped up their terror campaign. They planted car bombs in towns and villages, killing people at random. On 21 July 1972 they set off twenty bombs in Belfast. Eleven people died and 130 were injured on what became known as 'Bloody Friday'. They continued to bomb during the Sunningdale period, which made it harder for unionists to accept the compromise.

Hunger strikes

IRA violence dismayed many nationalists, but in the early 1980s the IRA won back support when IRA prisoners went on hunger strike to win political status. The strike attracted worldwide attention, especially after one of the strikers, Bobby Sands, was elected to parliament. But the British government refused to negotiate until after Sands and nine others had died.

The aftermath of an IRA bombing

The impact on the republic

Violence and hunger strikes made people in the Republic re-examine their attitudes to the North. At first they sympathised with the nationalists but as IRA violence grew, this changed.

In 1983 Garret FitzGerald's government set up the **New Ireland Forum** to examine Southern attitudes to the North. All political parties were invited, though most Unionists refused to come. The discussions at the Forum made people in the South think critically about the things in the Republic that the unionists feared, like the influence of the Catholic Church.

The 1985 Anglo-Irish Agreement

Irish governments worked hard to persuade the British that co-operation between them on the North was the best way to bring peace. This led in 1985 to the Anglo-Irish Agreement, signed by Garret FitzGerald and Margaret Thatcher, the British prime minister. In it:

- The Irish government promised to respect the unionist right to remain in the United Kingdom.
- The British promised to consult the Irish government about developments in the North.

Unionists were bitter about the Agreement because they were not consulted and because it gave the Republic a voice in Northern affairs. Ian Paisley tried to repeat his success against the Sunningdale Agreement but the British stood firm. The Agreement led to regular meetings between Irish and British officials, which helped each side to understand the other's problems better.

Moving to a ceasefire

All through the years, attempts to find a solution went on in secret. In the early 1990s these began to produce results. In spite of IRA violence, John Hume, the leader of the moderate nationalist SDLP, had secret talks with Gerry Adams, leader of Sinn Féin, the political wing of the IRA. Hume wanted to convince Adams that violence was leading nowhere.

Many people attacked Hume for talking to the IRA but he won the backing of the Taoiseach, Albert Reynolds. Reynolds also persuaded the British government to issue the **Downing Street Declaration**. It promised 'parity of esteem' (i.e. equal respect) to nationalists in Northern Ireland. The British government also said that if the people in Northern Ireland could work something out for themselves, the British would not stand in their way.

The 'Good Friday Agreement', April 1998

These moves prompted the IRA to declare a ceasefire in 1994. Between 1969 and 1994 over three thousand people lost their lives. More than half the casualties were caused by the IRA. Loss of loved ones deepened the distrust between the two communities and made it more difficult to reach an agreement between them.

Mutual distrust meant the talks that followed took much longer than expected. In 1997 an election in Britain produced a new prime minister, **Tony Blair**, who was committed to achieving peace. The Unionist Party also had a new leader, **David Trimble**, who was willing to talk to republicans.

These men, together with Hume, Adams, and Taoiseach Bertie Ahern, finally made the Belfast Agreement. It was signed on Good Friday, 10 April 1998, and for that reason was also known as the 'Good Friday Agreement'. Under it:

- The Republic agreed to remove Articles 2 and 3 from its Constitution and replace them with a form of words that recognised the unionist identity.
- A Northern Ireland Assembly would be elected and a **Power-Sharing Executive** (government) would be set up containing ministers from all parties, even Sinn Féin.

The Agreement is voted in

A referendum on the Agreement was held in Northern Ireland and the Republic on the same day. Ian Paisley and the DUP opposed it but 70 per cent of voters in the North voted for it. In the South an amazing 90 per cent voted for it.

Taoiseach Bertie Ahern, George Mitchell and the British prime minister, Tony Blair, at the signing of the Belfast Agreement in 1997. George Mitchell, an American, acted as mediator during the attempts to end the violence, and his patient diplomacy played a large part in the Agreement.

But mutual suspicions remained. Unionists demanded that the IRA decommission (destroy) their arms, something the IRA were reluctant to do. The Power-Sharing Executive came into existence briefly but was soon suspended. Violence continued but on a much lower scale than before, and Northern Ireland began to recover from the economic damage caused by thirty years of violence.

Questions

1. What was the Sunningdale Agreement? Why did it fail?
2. How many people died in Northern Ireland during the thirty years of violence? What was the effect of the violence?
3. How did the violence change attitudes in the Republic?
4. What was the Anglo-Irish Agreement of 1985? How did it change the Republic's relationship with Northern Ireland?
5. What moves led to the Good Friday Agreement? What did it say?
6. List two things that held up its implementation.

Review the chapter

1 Write a short account of one of the following:
- Terence O'Neill
- Ian Paisley
- John Hume

2 What was the Sunningdale Agreement? Why did it fail?

3 Write a paragraph about the Good Friday Agreement.

www Political Developments in Ireland on the Internet

Political Developments in Ireland, 1900–1921

There are not many internet sites about this period in Irish history. Here are some of the more useful ones.

www.bbc.co.uk/history/war/easterrising/index.shtml This is the first of a number of entries from the BBC history website. It gives a detailed account of the 1916 Rising and its aftermath, including the war of independence.

www.ucc.ie/ucc/depts/history/multitext/1916.html This website contains primary documents such as newspaper articles relating to the 1916 Rising.

http://islandireland.com/Pages/history/archives/easter.html At this address you will find a collection of postcards showing events and personalities from the Rising.

www.dungarvanmuseum.org Find out about the war of independence in Waterford at the Dungarvan Museum website.

www.geocities.com/heathcliffiam/mcopening.htm This is a privately run website dedicated to Michael Collins.

Independent Ireland, 1921–2000

www.rte.ie/culture/millennia/history/1900.html Explore the history of independent Ireland at the RTE history website.

www.clarelibrary.ie/eolas/coclare/people/eamon.htm Information on Eamon de Valera from the website of *The Clare People* newspaper.

Northern Ireland, 1920–2000

Northern Ireland is well covered on the web, especially the Troubles.

www.bbc.co.uk/history/timelines/ni/troubles.shtml These pages from the BBC website look at the history of Northern Ireland from the early 1920s until today.

www.bbc.co.uk/northernireland/belfastblitz/index.shtml Find out about the terrible suffering of the people of Belfast when the city was bombed in 1941.

http://cain.ulst.ac.uk/bibdbs/newlinks.html#2 This page from the website called 'Conflict Archive on the Internet' contains links to politics and history in Northern Ireland.

Getting to Know the Junior Certificate

The following is what the syllabus recommends you should know about Political Developments in Ireland, 1900-2000.

Topic	Description	Approach
Political developments in Ireland in the twentieth century	Overview of the main political events which influenced contemporary Ireland.	Chronological overview

Political Developments in Ireland is a very popular topic on the Junior Certificate. It often appears in Questions 1, 2, 3 and 4 on both Higher and Ordinary level papers. On Higher Level papers it usually also comes up as part of Question 6.

For **Higher Level** you need to know the main points (five or six) about each of the topics below.

1. Home Rule and the Unionist opposition to it
2. The 1916 Rising
3. The war of independence
4. Why people supported or opposed the Treaty
5. The achievements of Cumann na nGaedheal, 1922–32
6. Relations with the United Kingdom up to the Anglo-Irish Agreement of 1938
7. Life in Ireland, North and South, during World War II
8. The First Inter-Party government, 1948–51
9. Seán Lemass as Taoiseach, 1959–66
10. Terence O'Neill, Prime Minister of Northern Ireland, 1963–69
11. Discrimination against Catholics in Northern Ireland
12. Developments in Northern Ireland up to the Good Friday Agreement

For **Ordinary Level** you can choose to study Political Developments in Ireland, 1900–2000 or Ireland: Social History. If you choose Political Developments, you should be able to write down the main events and leaders during the following periods of Irish history. Seven or eight points of information are required:

1. Events and leaders in Ireland, 1910 to 1922
2. Main developments in Ireland, North and South, 1922 to 1945
3. Main political developments in Ireland, North and South, 1945–2000

Section 3

Ireland: Social History

Chapter 1

How Did Life in Rural Ireland Change in the Twentieth Century?

1900–2000: A century of change

The twentieth century was a time of huge and rapid change. The lifestyles of ordinary Irish people were very different in 2000 from the lifestyles of their grandparents one hundred years before. The houses they lived in, the clothes they wore, how they earned their living, how they travelled and what they did in their spare time – all these have changed greatly. In this section we will look at:

- how life in rural Ireland changed
- how life in urban Ireland changed
- how women's lives changed
- how transport changed
- how communications changed
- how work and leisure changed

How rural houses have changed

The houses country people live in have changed hugely since 1900.

1 Photo A shows a typical farmhouse from 1900. **Describe it, listing what the roof is made of, the colour of the walls, the size of the windows.**

2 Look at photo B. **List five ways in which it is different from the 1900 house.**

A

This photograph was taken around 1900. The photographer called this house a 'typical Irish farmhouse'. He got the family to pose outside with their activities and their animals. **Can you see the side-car in which the photographer travelled? Side-cars were the taxis of the time. List the animals and forms of transport that you can see.**

B

This is a typical rural house from 2000.

A farming community

In 1900, over 60 per cent of people in Ireland lived on farms or in small towns and villages. Farming families produced most of the things they ate, e.g. potatoes, vegetables and eggs. Women baked bread every day and made butter with milk from the family's cows. They went to the local small town to shop for a few groceries like meat, flour, tea and sugar. But they would never have heard of most of the fruit and vegetables we can buy any day in our local supermarkets.

A farm kitchen in 1900

In both 1900 and 2000 the kitchen was the heart of a house. But over the twentieth century, the kitchen has changed more than any other room.

This is a photograph of a kitchen around 1900. Most kitchens at the time had the following items. **Can you find them in the picture?**

- **A stone floor**
- **An open fire**
- **A crane over the fire with a kettle hanging from it**
- **A three-legged pot for baking bread or making stews**
- **A churn for making butter**
- **A water barrel**
- **A *súgán* chair**

Where do you think people got most of these items? List six things you would see in a modern kitchen that are not in this picture.

In 1900 the kitchen was where the woman of the house spent most of her time. It was dark, with only one small window. The door was divided into two parts. The top half was usually left open to let in light and allow the woman to see anyone who was passing. The bottom half was kept closed to keep farmyard animals out and young children in.

By modern standards, these houses had very little furniture. In the kitchen there were simple wooden stools or benches. The woman prepared food on a big table where the family later ate its meals. There were also *súgán* chairs, made from straw ropes, and perhaps a dresser with a few pieces of good china. In the bedroom there were beds and perhaps a simple wardrobe made by a local carpenter.

A hard life for women

Farm women never stopped working.

- They had to tend the turf fire that always burned on the open hearth. (the family cut its own turf on the local bog).
- They had to bake bread and cook meals for their families on the open fire.
- There was no running water and no toilets. Women and children carried all the water needed for cooking and cleaning from a nearby pump or well. The water was stored in a barrel in the kitchen.
- There was no electricity, so women had to wash and iron all clothes by hand.

How people entertained themselves

There were no radios or TVs, so people had to make their own entertainment. In many country areas, neighbours visited each other and sat in the kitchen gossiping and telling stories. Sometimes a musician came along and they had a dance in the kitchen.

Going to bed in the dark

There was no electricity in rural houses in 1900. That meant people used candles and oil lamps for light. These made only a faint impression on the surrounding darkness. Read this poem. What kind of light did the poet have? Would you prefer it to electric light?

'All around the house is the jet-black night.
It stares through the window-pane
It crawls in the corners, hiding from the light,
And it moves with the moving flame!'

Robert Louis Stevenson

Oil lamp

Questions

1. Select five facts about the appearance of a farmhouse in 1900. Now use these facts to write a paragraph about rural houses in Ireland at the start of the twentieth century.
2. From your own knowledge of a modern house, list six ways in which it is different from a house in 1900.
3. Write a paragraph about a woman's life on a farm in 1900. Include at least five facts from this chapter.

Farming in 1900

At the start of the twentieth century, over 60 per cent of Irish people worked on the land. Farming was hard work because there were very few machines.

Most farms were small and the whole family had to work together to raise animals and grow crops.

- As well as doing all the housework, women milked cows, made butter and raised chickens, ducks, geese and turkeys. The money they earned from the eggs and chickens was an important part of the family's income.
- Men used horses to plough the land, to sow crops and to reap them. Neighbours helped each other at harvest time when crops had to be saved quickly. In parts of Ireland this was called the ***meitheal***.
- Children also helped with farm work, especially at busy times like harvesting. This often meant that they had to miss days at school.

Men and women doing the harvesting

Milking cows was women's work. Milk was sold to the local creamery, where it was made into butter.

Leaving the farm

These farming families were very poor. Life was hard, especially in the 1920s and 1930s and again after the war. Prices were low and although they all worked terribly hard, they earned very little.

Many farmers' children decided that farming was too hard a life. They emigrated to Britain or the United States where they got well-paid jobs on building sites or in factories. Every year from 1920 until 1960, between 20,000 and 40,000 young people left Ireland!

From the 1960s huge combine harvesters were used to gather grain. In a combine, one man could do the work previously done by many. This made the farmer's life a lonelier one than it had been before.

New machines change the way farmers work

Farming began to change dramatically in the 1950s. Tractors and other machines became common, and horses almost disappeared. With machines a farmer could do much more work by himself. Farms became much bigger and the old *meitheal* system of neighbours helping each other died out.

Changes caused by rural electrification

Another reason for the change was the government's decision to link every farm to the electricity grid. Called 'rural electrification' this began at the end of the 1940s and within ten years most farms had electric power. This made life easier, especially for women.

- Electric milking machines did away with the need to milk cows by hand.
- In the 1960s and 1970s electric pumps brought running water, bathrooms and indoor toilets to farm houses.
- Electric washing machines, irons and vacuum cleaners reduced the amount of housework women had to do.
- These changes made it possible for some women to get paid work off the farm. This provided another source of income for the family.

How EU membership changed farming

The biggest change in farming came after Ireland joined the European Economic Community (now the European Union) in 1973. The EEC had two policies that helped country areas:

- The **Common Agricultural Policy (CAP)** guaranteed good prices for farm produce.
- The **Social Policy** gave grants to improve living standards in poor areas.

These two policies made a huge difference to farmers. Because they got better prices for their produce, they were able to build new houses and buy cars and new machinery.

But being in the EU also brought problems. It meant that farm produce from other member states could now be sold in Irish shops. Spanish onions or Dutch potatoes appeared on supermarket shelves to compete with Irish produce.

The CAP also encouraged farmers all over the EU to produce too much. Mountains of surplus butter, beef and wine appeared. This forced a change in policy. Irish farmers had to accept **quotas** (limits) on the amount they could produce. By the 1990s the CAP grants had fallen but they still helped to keep farm incomes up.

The main changes in rural life

This chart shows how life in rural Ireland changed between 1900 and 2000.

	1900–1930	1930–1970	1970–2000
Population	Over 60 per cent of people lived in rural areas and worked on the land.	Low prices for farm produce. Many farmers' children emigrated.	Only 35 per cent now live in rural areas. Many farmers work in towns and only farm part-time.
Houses and standard of living	Most houses were small thatched cottages with no running water or electricity. Most had only three rooms and no bathroom.	Rural electrification in the 1940s brought light, pumps, washing machines and other electrical goods into homes. People began to add bathrooms to houses.	In 1973 Ireland joined the EEC. The CAP gave better prices. Farmers could build modern houses. Three or four-bed bungalows became common in rural areas. Since the 1980s dormer bungalows have become very popular.
Work	Most farm work was done with horses and human labour. All the family helped out.	Tractors and other machines reduced the need for labour.	Large milking parlours and combine harvesters reduced the need for farm labour further.
Food	Farmers grew much of the food they ate and bought the rest locally.	The food in the shops was still mainly Irish-produced.	Food produced in Ireland had to compete in supermarkets with food from other parts of the EU and elsewhere.
Entertainment	Farming families provided their own entertainment.	Radios and TVs became common.	Computers and the Internet gave another source of entertainment.

Questions

1 Name three main types of food that people ate in rural Ireland in 1900. Where did these foods come from?
2 List five features of a typical Irish cottage in 1900.
3 How were houses lighted in 1900? When did this change?
4 List four ways in which farming has changed since 1900.
5 Give two examples of how the EU has changed farming in Ireland.

Review the chapter

1 **Picture Source**
Look at this cartoon. Explain the point the artist was making.

American Visitor: "I suppose you rear those calves for export?"
Farmer: "Yes, indeed, Sir. Same as the children!"

2 Write an account of how rural life has changed since 1900 under the following headings: houses, food, farming, rural electrification, the EU.

Chapter 2 How Did Life in Urban Ireland Change in the Twentieth Century?

Not many townspeople

In 1900 only 35 per cent of Irish people lived in cities or big towns. Irish cities were small. Belfast was the biggest with about 400,000 people. Dublin was next with 350,000. Cork, Limerick and Galway had under 100,000 people each.

Since then, Irish towns and cities have grown very rapidly. Big housing estates sprawl out on to land where farmers once worked. By 2000 over 70 per cent of Irish people lived in towns or suburbs.

	Population in 1901
Dublin	350,000
Cork	76,000
Limerick	38,000
Belfast	400,000
Derry	41,000
Galway	13,000

Then and now

Towns changed greatly in the twentieth century. These photographs illustrate some of the changes. The picture on the left shows a street in Castlebar in 1900; the picture on the right shows the same street in 2000. Can you find at least three differences between them?

This picture shows a street in Castlebar in 1900 and the same street in 2000. **List four differences you can see between the two periods. Can you find two pieces of evidence to show that Castlebar was more prosperous in 2000 than in 1900?**

What was money worth?
£1 in 1900 would buy about as much as €400 today.

The life of the rich

In 1900, differences in lifestyle between the rich and the poor were greater than they are today. Wealthy people such as businessmen, lawyers or top government officials earned up to £2,000 a year. They were able to own a house like the one below, with gardens around it.

Their houses were in the suburbs. Usually wives stayed at home and husbands travelled to work by tram or bus. Some of the trams were horse-drawn; others were electric.

A big house built around 1900 for a wealthy family

Wealthy people had many servants to wait on them. There were maids to do the housework and a cook to prepare the meals. Maids who lived in were paid about £10 a year; a good cook earned £18. There were usually nannies to look after the children.

The family would also have a horse and carriage and employ a coachman to look after them. If they were really modern they might have bought one of the new motor cars that were beginning to appear. Cars were very expensive, costing up to £1,000. Most car-owners employed a chauffeur to drive the car and repair it when it broke down.

Dinner in a rich man's house. Most people in 1900 could not dream of living like this.

Middle-income people

People who earned £300 to £500 a year were considered well-off. They could usually afford at least one maid who helped the housewife with the heavy work of washing, ironing, cleaning and cooking. The man would walk to work or take the tram. People like this rented their houses, rather than owning them.

Questions

1. Write a paragraph containing four points about the life of a wealthy family in 1900.
2. How much did a middle-income person earn in a year?
3. Describe three ways in which a middle-income person's life was different from the life of a similar person today.

The life of the poor: skilled workers

The vast majority of people did not earn good wages. A man with a skilled job, e.g. a carpenter or a bricklayer, might get up to £3 a week.

Belfast was the only place in Ireland where there were many jobs for skilled workers. The shipyards and engineering works employed most of them. Many women worked in the linen factories. That brought two incomes into a family, which gave them a better standard of living than workers had in the rest of Ireland.

Houses like these were for skilled workers with regular jobs

Skilled workers could afford to rent a house in a street like this.

These houses were called 'two-up, two-down' because there were two bedrooms upstairs and a living room and kitchen downstairs. There was a small yard outside with a toilet and a water tap in it. Two-up, two-down houses were very common in Belfast and there were a few in other towns and cities.

There was not much furniture in these houses – just beds, chairs and tables. The floor would be covered with linoleum. This was a recent invention. It was warmer and easier to keep clean than stone floors or bare boards.

The life of the poor: unskilled workers

In other Irish cities there were very few jobs for skilled workers. In Dublin there were only 10,000 skilled workers out of a total male workforce of 40,000. The rest had no skills. They worked as carters, labourers and dockers.

The average wage of an unskilled worker was about £1 a week or £52 a year. From that a family had to pay for food, clothes and rent. Because they could not afford tram fares, most workers lived in the city centre where most jobs were. The only places they could afford to rent were a room in a **tenement** or a tiny one- or two-roomed cottage.

Note

How 'old money' worked

In 1900, people in the United Kingdom (which included Ireland) used pounds, shillings and pence. £1 contained 20 shillings and each shilling contained 12 pence. It was written like this: £1.12s.5d. That means one pound, twelve shillings and five pence.

Life in a tenement

In 1900 about a third of the people in Irish cities lived in tenements. These were large old houses near the centre of the city. At one time wealthy families lived in them but they moved out to the suburbs and the poor moved in.

In 1900 there was a family in every room of these old houses. Some families had ten or twelve people in them. Their rent was sixpence for a basement or one shilling for a bigger, brighter room upstairs.

Here is one woman's memory of her Dublin tenement.

> *'All tenements was poor. I think our street, Queen's Terrace, was the poorest 'cause there was so many families living in it. Eight families living in my tenement. I had four sisters and three brothers. Me mother's sister had twenty-one children! We grew up in one little room and six of us slept in one bed. And we had no bedclothes; we mostly slept with me daddy's overcoats over us. Sure the bed was loaded with bugs and hoppers and you'd be scratching yourself…'*
>
> (Maggie Murray, born 1913)

It was difficult to keep clean in the tenements. The only toilet was a shed in the yard, shared by all the people in the house. All water for washing and cooking came from a tap near it. It had to be carried up several flights of stairs to the family's room.

These people lived in the stables behind them or in the tall tenement houses in the background. Each room in these houses held one family – imagine how many people altogether lived in one of these houses!

Poor people could only afford to buy small quantities of food at a time. That made it expensive. It was cooked over a small open fire but, as coal was dear, many people did not cook. They lived most of the time on bread with cheese or jam. This caused malnutrition.

Overcrowding, dirt and malnutrition led to disease. Measles, TB and other diseases were common. Half of all babies died in their first year, and few people from the tenements lived beyond forty.

Helping one another

But tenements could also be friendly places. Communities were close. Everyone in the street knew everyone else, and they often helped each other in time of need.

Because rooms were so crowded, people lived more of their lives on the street. Cars were rare, so children could play there safely. There were lots of small shops and less crime than today. The doors of all the tenement houses could be left open all night! There was no drug problem, although street fighting, alcohol abuse and prostitution were common.

When in the 1930s and 1940s the local councils moved people from the tenements to housing estates like the one below, not everyone was pleased. Read what this woman said. Do you understand her feeling?

> *'When they started tearing the old tenements down it was like tearing us apart. It tore me apart. It broke me heart. We were all one family, all close. We all helped one another. If I had a tenement house now I'd go back and live in it... Yes, I would.'*
>
> (Elizabeth Murphy, formerly of Corporation Street, Dublin)

From the 1930s, councils built housing estates like this to replace the tenements. At first people rented their houses from the council, but from the 1970s they were able to buy them. **Give two advantages of living in an estate like this and two disadvantages.**

How urban life has changed

Life in Irish towns and cities changed little until the 1930s. Since then the pace of change has been very fast. This chart shows some of the changes.

	1900–1930	1930–1970	1970–2000
Size of towns and cities	Cities were small and compact. Most people lived in the centre and walked to work. Only the well-off lived in suburbs.	Cities began to expand. New estates were built on the outskirts. Buses and cheaper cars made commuting possible.	Cities continued to sprawl out into the countryside. Many families could afford cars and many people now drive a long way to work.
Shops	People bought most of the things they needed in small local shops.	Supermarkets began in the 1950s. They offered a wider choice of goods, often at a lower cost.	Big shopping centres appeared on the outskirts of towns. People drove long distances to them.
Work	Outside Belfast, few Irish towns or cities had industries. Most jobs were in transport and services such as shops, banks and offices.	From the 1930s small new industries developed on the outskirts of some towns. The first industrial estates were built. From the 1950s the **Industrial Development Authority (IDA)** gave government grants to Irish industries to help them get a start. The IDA also encouraged foreign companies to set up in Irish towns.	Many multinational companies set up in Ireland. They got large grants and tax reductions from the government. In the 1990s they gave thousands of people work in computing and chemical industries. More jobs in services like shops or call centres appeared. Immigrants came to Ireland for the first time.
Houses	Only the rich could own their own homes. Middle-income people rented houses. Unskilled workers lived in one room in a tenement house.	More middle-income people began to buy their houses in new housing estates in the suburbs. Councils built houses with three bedrooms, a bathroom and a garden to house people who had lived in the tenements. These were in the suburbs of cities, for example Finglas in Dublin or Turners Cross in Cork.	Councils sold their houses to the occupiers. By 2000 over 80 per cent of families owned their own homes.

Questions

1 What was a 'two-up, two-down'? Who lived in them?
2 What was a tenement? Why did some people live in tenements?
3 Describe the life of people in a typical tenement in 1900. Refer to work and wages, living conditions, food they ate, and street life.
4 Read the quote from Elizabeth Murphy on page 216. Why did she regret the end of the old tenements?
5 Name two council or corporation estates that were built in the 1930s.
6 From the table on the previous page explain briefly how (i) urban work and (ii) urban housing have changed since 1900.

Review the chapter

1 Make a table showing how much (i) rich, (ii) comfortable and (iii) poor people earned in 1900. Using the figures on page 213, work out whether people were better or worse off in 1900 than they are now. Give reasons for your answer.

2 Look at the chart below.

Percentage of workers in each sector in Ireland

	Agriculture	Industry	Services
1926	53%	13%	34%
1971	26%	31%	43%
1996	10%	27%	63%

(i) What kind of work do most people in towns do now?
(ii) What kind of work did most people do in Ireland in 1926?
(iii) Give two reasons why this change has come about.

3 Imagine you are an eighty-year-old man or woman. Write an account for a newspaper of the changes you'd have seen in your local area during your lifetime. You could interview an older person to see what changes they have noticed.

4 Would you prefer to live in the 2000s or the 1900s? Give three reasons for your answer.

In this section we will look at how women's lives changed between 1900 and 2000 under the headings: Dress and Leisure; Education; Work and Politics.

What women wore

These pictures show how women dressed at different times in the twentieth century.

1900

1920s

Give three differences between the dresses women wore in 1900 and those worn in the 1920s and1950s.

What other changes do you see in women's clothes between 1900 and 2000? List five.

List three things women do now that would have been difficult to do in the 1900 dress.

1950s

2004

In 1900 all women wore long skirts. A woman was supposed to keep her head covered when she was out. Better-off women wore hats but many poor women wore shawls.

Fashions began to change during World War I. With so many men fighting, women began to work in areas where they had not worked before. That and the shortage of cloth encouraged them to wear shorter skirts.

A revolution occurred in women's dress in the 1920s. Skirts became much shorter – up to knee level. Since then, even though fashions have changed, skirts for daytime wear have never become really long again. In the 1930s a few fashionable women wore trousers and since the 1960s they have become acceptable for everyone.

Hair and make-up

All women wore their hair long in 1900. A woman would boast that her hair was so long that she could sit on it. Young girls wore their hair loose but once a woman was grown up, she always wore it up in a bun or in plaits around her head.

In the 1920s short hairstyles became fashionable and many young women cut their hair. Since then both long and short hair have been equally acceptable.

In 1900 it was considered 'fast' for a woman to wear make-up. This changed in the 1920s when younger women shocked their parents by wearing lipstick and rouge. Some even dyed their hair. Since then make-up has never gone out of fashion.

Leisure

In 1900 richer girls played 'ladylike' games like tennis and croquet. Some working women could afford to buy bicycles but most women had no time for sports. After World War I shorter skirts made it easier to take part in sports. This sometimes met with opposition from groups like the clergy who thought it was 'unladylike'.

When the Olympic Games began there were no contests for women, but that changed in the 1920s. At the same time, women began to engage in international competitions in tennis and golf. Playing team sports like football took longer to be accepted, but this was common by the 1980s.

Up to World War II it was not considered nice for a woman to smoke in public or to go into a public house. Some bars had special areas called 'snugs' where 'respectable' women could get a drink. These attitudes changed in the 1960s, and now women smoke and drink almost as much as men.

Questions

1 Look at the fashion pictures on page 219. Describe how women's clothes have changed since 1900.
2 What do these clothes tell us about the change in women's lifestyles in the twentieth century?
3 How have hairstyles and make-up changed since 1900?
4 Describe how women's sports have changed between 1900 and 2000.

Women and education

Girls had been getting a free primary education in Ireland since the 1840s – more or less the same as boys. But in many poor families, both boys and girls were expected to earn money from the age of ten or twelve, so parents usually did not let them stay in school any longer than that.

Better-off parents paid for their children to go to secondary schools. Co-education was thought to be dangerous, so all schools were either for boys or girls. In the 1880s the government set up the Intermediate Examination system, and from the start the girls did as well as the boys. But many girls' schools did not teach science or higher maths, which made it difficult for girls to get work in these areas.

A classroom in 1913. **How does this classroom differ from a classroom today?**

By the 1880s Irish women could also do exams and get university degrees, although they could not actually attend a university. But most parents assumed that their daughters would get married and have husbands to look after them, so they did not need to train for a career. For that reason few parents sent their daughters to university even when it was allowed in the early 1900s.

The few women who did go to university became doctors or teachers or joined the civil service. But once they married most had to give up paid work. This was known as the 'marriage bar' and remained in place until the 1970s. The only exception was primary school teaching because there was a shortage of male teachers.

Changes in education

Since about 1970 there have been several important changes in education which have affected both boys and girls.

- In 1967 the government brought in free education at both primary and secondary levels.
- Free places and more schools meant that now most girls and boys finish secondary school rather than leaving at twelve.
- Many children go to mixed-sex schools.
- Subjects like science and metalwork are open to both boys and girls.
- Parents now realise that girls need a career just as much as boys, so girls are encouraged to go on to third-level education.

Students in a modern classroom. **Is it an advantage for girls to be educated with boys?**

Questions

1. How long did most girls stay at school in 1900?
2. Why did few girls go to university before the 1960s?
3. Give three ways in which women's education has changed since the 1960s.

Women's work in the 1901 Census

This is part of the report from the Census taken in 1901. It lists the occupations of women at that time. Look at the figures and then answer the questions.

Professional	32,675
Domestic servants	193,331
Commercial	5,026
Agricultural workers	85,587
Industrial workers	233,256
Indefinitive and non-productive	1,708, 861

1. How many women were there altogether in the 1901 Census?
2. What percentage of women had a professional qualification (nurse, doctor, teacher, etc.)?
3. How many women worked in offices (commercial)?
4. What percentage worked as domestic servants?
5. What percentage were industrial workers? What part of Ireland do you think most of them lived in?
6. Which was the biggest group of women? What job description is given to them? What do you think the people who gave them this description meant by that?

Women's work in the home

What answer did you give for Question 6? In fact, 'indefinite and non-productive' covers all the women who worked at home or in a family business from home without wages. If you took this at its face value, you would think those women did nothing.

Yet most of them worked very hard indeed. As well as minding children, they cooked and cleaned without any of the labour-saving machines we have today. Many also worked on the family farm or in the family shop. But because their work was not waged, men saw it as 'indefinite and non-productive'. Do you think attitudes have changed today?

Between 1900 and 1970 women's position in the workplace changed little.

- The 'marriage bar' meant that most women had to give up work after they married. That made it difficult for a well-qualified woman to get to the top of her profession.
- Certain low-paid jobs were considered 'women's work' and higher status jobs were kept for men.
- Women got paid less than men for doing the same job.

Winning equality

Things began to change in the 1970s. Here are some of the reasons.

- 'Labour-saving devices' like washing machines and vacuum cleaners freed women from the worst drudgery of housework and gave them time to seek paid employment outside the home.
- Women became better educated and began to demand equal treatment.
- A new women's movement won an end to the marriage bar and got laws passed ending discrimination in jobs on grounds of gender. The **Employment Equality Act of 1977** meant that men and women doing the same job would get the same pay.
- Better educated women were able to compete on terms of equality with men.

This 1920s advertisement for electricity illustrates how electricity changed women's lives. Without the electrical machines which reduced the labour of housework, few married women could get paid work outside the home.

Are women more equal in 2000?

Although the law changed, employers were slower to adopt new attitudes. Read the sources below and reach your own conclusion.

Source 1

In 2000 women's average wage was 75 per cent of men's.

Source 2

In 1995 a representative of the Law Society said on the radio:

'Fifty per cent of people entering the profession are women. Twenty-five to thirty per cent of people practising as solicitors are women. Yet in a big city law firm, with hundreds of partners, only half a dozen will be women. Women tend to get pushed into doing matrimonial work (divorce, etc.). Women are assumed just to be doing the job to fill time in before they have a family.'

Questions

1. List in order the three jobs most commonly done by women in 1900. (i) Which of these would top the list today? (ii) Which would not appear?
2. Work in the home was the most common job women did in 1900. Was it valued by men? Explain your answer.
3. What was the 'marriage bar' and how did it affect women? When was it removed?
4. Give three reasons why women's status at work has improved since 1970.
5. Look at the two sources above. Were women fully equal with men in 2000? Explain your answer.

Women and politics in 1900

In 1900 women had some political rights, but not as many as men. They could stand for election in local councils and vote in local elections. But they could not vote for members of parliament or become members of parliament themselves.

Hanna Sheehy Skeffington, a university graduate, wrote in 1900. *'I was amazed and disgusted to learn that I was classed among criminals, infants and lunatics – in fact my status as a woman was worse than any of these.'* These were the people who could not vote. **Is it any wonder she became a feminist?**

Demanding 'votes for women'

The right to vote was known as the **suffrage**. Since the 1860s a few women like **Isabella Tod** had been campaigning for it. They felt that women could not make governments pay attention to their problems if they did not have the right to vote.

But by 1900 they had not made much headway. One reason was that many women did not support this campaign. They did not see why they needed to vote when their husbands did it for them!

This began to change in the twentieth century. Younger women like **Hanna Sheehy** were able to go to university. They were angry when they realised that they were not allowed vote, even though men who could neither read nor write were.

This cartoon appeared in 1912. **What was Mary? What had she done? Did the cartoonist sympathise with her? Explain your answer.**

Hanna Sheehy married Francis Skeffington who also supported women's rights. To show this they joined their surnames. They set up the **Irish Women's Franchise League** to campaign for the vote.

Hanna Sheehy Skeffington and her friends were more active than the earlier campaigners. They heckled politicians and threw bricks through windows. When they were arrested, they went on hunger strike. The press tried to belittle them by labelling them the **'suffragettes'**.

The 'votes for women' campaign was interrupted by World War I (1914–18) and by the struggle for Irish independence (1916–22).

Questions

1 What political rights did women have in 1900?
2 What rights did they not have?
3 Name two women who campaigned for the right to vote.
4 Who set up the Irish Women's Franchise League? Give two examples of its activities.

The crisis over Home Rule divides women

After 1912 Ireland was deeply divided over the question of Home Rule (see page 126). Unionists wanted Ireland to remain in the United Kingdom. Nationalists wanted Ireland to have its own parliament. This division affected women too.

Unionist women had their own organisation – the **Ulster Unionist Women's Council**. It had about 200,000 members and they were very active in opposing Home Rule.

Most nationalist women supported the Home Rule party, but a small group founded a republican movement called **Cumann na mBan** in 1914. Cumann na mBan women were active in the Easter Rising of 1916. One woman, **Constance Markievicz**, was sentenced to death for her part in the rising, though because she was a woman the British never intended to execute her.

Getting the vote

In 1918 the British government changed the law and gave the vote to women over thirty. In the election that year, Sinn Féin put up two women candidates and one of them, Markievicz, was elected. She was the first woman ever elected to the British parliament, although, like the rest of the Sinn Féin party, she did not take her seat there. Instead, when Sinn Féin set up an Irish government, she was appointed a Cabinet minister. She was only the second woman to become a minister in Europe.

After the Treaty with Britain in 1921, the Irish Free State was set up. In its 1922 constitution it gave the vote to all women over twenty-one, on exactly the same terms as men. This did not happen in Britain and Northern Ireland until 1928.

Constance Markievicz in 1922. She was the first woman elected to the British parliament after women were given the vote in 1918 but her party, Sinn Féin, boycotted it, so she never took her seat. De Valera appointed her Minister for Labour in 1919.

Máire Geoghegan-Quinn. After Markievicz, no woman became a Cabinet minister until 1979, when Máire Geoghegan-Quinn was appointed.

Women and politics after 1922

But although women were free to get involved in politics from 1922, few of them did. There were not many women TDs in the Dáil before the 1970s, and no more female ministers until 1979, when Máire Geoghegan-Quinn was appointed.

In the 1970s a new women's movement appeared. Younger women began to demand equal representation in the Dáil. The number of female TDs rose, though by 2000 it was still only 1 in 8. In 1990 Mary Robinson became the first woman to be President of Ireland; in 1997 she was followed by Mary McAleese.

Mary Robinson was Ireland's first female president

Mary McAleese succeeded Mary Robinson as President of Ireland

Questions

1. Name (i) a unionist women's organisation and (ii) a nationalist women's organisation in the early 1900s.
2. When did women first get the right to vote in Ireland? Name the first woman elected to the British parliament and the first female minister in Ireland.
3. Who was the first female president of Ireland?
4. What percentage of TDs in the Dáil were women in 2000?

This table shows the main changes in women's lives between 1900 and 2000.

	1900–1930	1930–1970	1970–2000
Dress	Long dresses, hats, shawls, no make-up, long hair.	Short dresses, shorter hairstyles until 1960s. Trousers become common in 1960s.	Fashions become more casual. Extreme styles like punk more acceptable.
Leisure	Not much sports, except cycling and tennis. No women's competitions.	Women in Olympics and competitive sport.	Women's sports get more media attention. More women interested in fitness.
Education	Limited access to universities until 1904. Equal access to schools with boys but parents often did not want to spend money on girls.	**1960s:** Free secondary education from 1967 helped more girls to go to school and university.	Co-ed schools meant a wider range of subjects open to girls. More women than men graduating in many areas.
Work	Many girls from middle-income families did not work before marriage. Poor girls worked as servants or in farms and factories.	More women working before marriage but **marriage bar** kept most from reaching top of their profession. Women's work less well paid.	Removal of marriage bar and equal pay for equal work improved women's wages. Most women work after marriage.
Political rights	Women could vote for local councils but not for MPs. **Woman's Franchise League** campaigned for vote. **1918:** Women over 30 got vote. **Markievicz** elected MP and Minister.	**1922:** In Irish Free State women had same voting rights as men. But few were elected to Dáil Éireann.	New women's movement encouraged women to seek election. **1979:** Second woman minister. **1990:** First woman president.

Review the chapter

1 A Catholic priest who was against giving women the right to vote wrote this. Read it and then answer the questions below.

> *'When a wife forgets her place… and does not defer to the authority of her husband in the home, peace is destroyed, children are disedified* [shocked] *and the solidarity of the domestic kingdom is threatened. But how much would these evils be intensified if the bickering and contention became public…? Is it probable that a husband and wife that were in rival political camps during the day would call a truce in the evening, and unite in training their children, and cherishing them, and each other?'*

(i) What, according to the priest, destroys peace in the home?
(ii) List two reasons the priest gives for opposing votes for women.

2 **Class Survey**
Try out the following survey in your class. Get each class member to ask both
(i) a grandparent or someone of that age group, and
(ii) a parent or someone of that age group about:
- the kind of work the female members of the family did
- what women did in their free time
- what level of education most women in the family received when the grandparent or parent was young.

3 Write about a woman born at the start of the twentieth century. Talk about the changes in her life under the following headings: early life; education; changing work practices; changing lifestyles.

Chapter 4 How Did Transport Change During the Twentieth Century?

The term 'transport' means the ways in which people or goods are carried from one place to another. In this chapter we will look at the changes that took place in transport between 1900 and 2000.

This picture shows Patrick Street, Cork, around 1900. **Can you find three different means of transport? What source of power do you think the tram used?**

Walking around

The most common way to get around in 1900 was on foot. People walked to work, to the shops, to school and to visit friends. There were other forms of transport: horses, trams, bicycles, trains and motor cars. But they were too expensive for most people to use every day.

Horse-drawn cabs and side-cars provided the taxi service in most cities and towns. The women in this picture are sight-seeing in Dublin from a side-car.

Horses

For thousands of years people had used horses to carry goods and people. In 1900 they were still the most common form of transport. They were everywhere and city streets smelled strongly of their dung. They drew the carts that carried most goods, and the cabs and side-cars that acted as taxis. But only farmers or rich people could afford a horse for private use.

Trams

In the cities, trams ran on tracks through the streets. The first trams were pulled by horses, but around 1900 many began to use electricity. Dublin was one of the first cities to have electric trams and in 1910 it had one of the best transport systems in Europe. But it cost one penny a mile to travel on trams and that was too dear for most working people.

Trains

In 1900, anyone who wanted to go a long distance used the trains. They were numerous, efficient and cheap. Ireland had over 3,400 miles of railways. You can see them on the map on the next page. Trains went between the main cities and towns. A horse-drawn bus service linked towns that were not on the railway.

A day at the seaside was the only holiday most people could afford until the 1960s. This photograph shows holiday-makers arriving at Youghal from Cork city.

There were three classes on the train – first, second and third class. First class had beautiful carpets on the floor, cushioned seats and curtains on the windows. Third class had hard wooden benches, which were often shared with hens or sheep. On bank holidays train companies offered cheap outings to the seaside. This was the only time when poor people could travel for pleasure.

Fast express trains linked the main cities, but other trains were slow, stopping at every town and village. A journey from Bantry in Cork to Dublin took about eleven hours. Country people used these local trains to go to towns to shop and to sell produce like eggs and poultry.

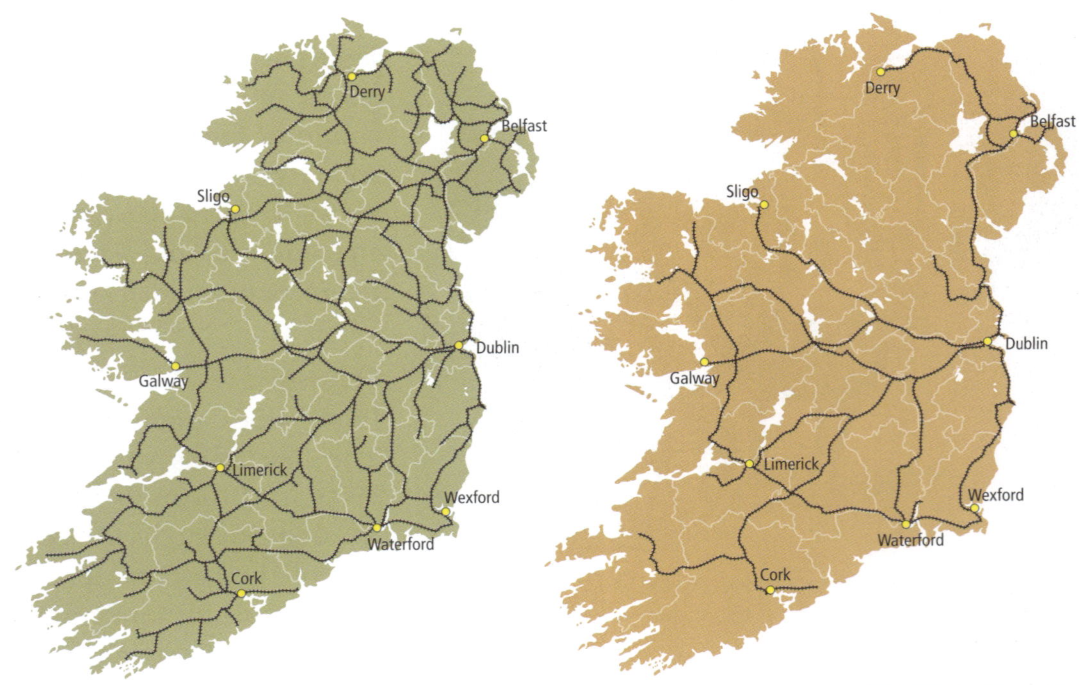

In 1900 most places in Ireland were near a railway station. But as cars and lorries became more common, fewer people travelled by train. By the 1960s many railway lines were uneconomical and were closed down, as the second map shows.

Bicycles

Shortly before 1900 modern bicycles appeared. They were the first kind of private transport that middle-income people could afford to buy. Cycling became very popular with young people. Both women and men cycled and that was one reason why women's skirts began to get a little shorter after 1900.

People thought nothing of cycling thirty or forty miles in a day to attend a match or visit friends. The roads they used were empty but in poor condition. They had been neglected after trains became widespread in the 1860s because only local horse transport used them.

Racing cyclist around 1905

Motor cars

In 1900 a new motor car cost up to £1,000. Do you remember what people earned at that time? As you can see, this made cars far too expensive for most people.

John Brown of Dunmurray, Belfast, imported the first motor car into Ireland in March 1896. The car was a Serpollett Steamer, which came from France. It took more than an hour to start up! In 1903 only 250 motor cars were registered in Ireland.

Apart from cost, motor cars were difficult to maintain. There were few garages and petrol was hard to find: only a few chemists sold it! The bad roads led to frequent punctures and breakdowns. Most car owners employed a chauffeur who also acted as a mechanic.

Model T Ford

In 1809, the 'drive on the left' rule had been introduced. Up to 1896, the speed limit for motor vehicles in the United Kingdom was 4 mph and a man had to walk in front with a red flag. In 1896, this rule was abolished and the speed limit was raised to 12 mph. Apart from that there were no rules of the road and no road markings or road signs.

This began to change after World War I. Cars became cheaper. Henry Ford introduced his Model T, which cost about £125. Other makers followed his example. That allowed many middle-income people to afford a car. Roads improved after the government taxed cars and used the money to tarmac roads. By the 1960s cars had ceased to be a luxury that only the rich could afford.

Questions

1. List six ways in which people could get around in 1900.
   (i) Which one was fairly new and enjoyed by young people?
   (ii) Which one could only the rich afford?
   (iii) Which one was used to carry goods (i) in towns and (ii) across the country?
2. Why were roads in such bad condition in 1900?
3. Which is dearer: a car in 2000 at €20,000 or a car in 1900 at £500? Give reasons for your answer. (Hint: Look at what people earned in 1900 and what they earn today – see page 213.)
4. Explain why cars became more common after World War I.

The *Titanic* embarking on its ill-fated maiden voyage

Leaving Ireland

All the forms of transport mentioned so far were for travel inside Ireland. In 1900 the only way of leaving Ireland was on a ship.

There were more ferry routes between Britain and Ireland than there are now. For example, you could travel by boat from Limerick to Glasgow. Ships also called at Queenstown (Cobh) to pick up people going to the United States. Some of these ships were huge luxury liners like the Belfast-built *Titanic*, which called at Queenstown on its first and fatal voyage.

These great liners crossed the Atlantic in as little as five days. They carried wealthy people in great luxury. Poorer people, most of them emigrating to a new life in America, travelled in 'steerage', where conditions were much less luxurious.

Luxury liners continued to cross the Atlantic until the 1960s. Then airplanes replaced them. Today liners are only used for holiday cruises.

Airplanes

In 1903 the Wright Brothers made the first heavier-than-air flight in North Carolina in the United States. The first flight in Ireland took place in County Down in 1909.

World War I speeded up the development of airplanes. They became bigger and more reliable. Regular passenger-carrying flights began in the 1930s. The Irish Government set up **Aer Lingus** in 1936. Its first regular flights were between Dublin and Bristol. The plane, which was called the *Iolar*, carried five passengers!

The first plane to fly non-stop across the Atlantic leaves Newfoundland on its record-breaking flight in 1919. It landed near Clifden in County Galway.

Flying the Atlantic

Because of its location, Ireland played an important part in the development of transatlantic air transport. It was the first point in Europe that planes from America could reach. This was important in the early days of aviation when planes were small and could carry only small amounts of fuel.

- The first plane to fly across the Atlantic from America to Europe crash-landed near Clifden in 1919.
- It was much more difficult to fly the other way, because it was against the prevailing winds. In 1928, the first successful Europe-to-America flight started from Baldonnel. One of the pilots was an Irish airman, James Fitzmaurice.
- The first regular transatlantic passenger route was set up at Foynes on the Shannon in 1938. The planes were flying boats that could land on water.

Note

One of the first women to fly (and build her own plane) was an Irish woman, Lilian Bland. Lilian described one of the problems she encountered while building the plane: *'There was no petrol tank, so we used a whiskey bottle and fed fuel into the engine with my aunt's large ear trumpet.'*

A flying boat

A modern jet

- After the war, the invention of jet engines meant that planes could now fly directly to Europe and did not need to land in Ireland.
- Since the 1950s most people have crossed the Atlantic by plane.
- Flying became cheaper in the 1980s and by 2000 it was not uncommon for people to spend a weekend in New York or a holiday in Florida.

Questions

1. How did people travel outside of Ireland in 1900?
2. Where did the first flight in Ireland take place?
3. Describe the first Aer Lingus plane.
4. What were flying boats? Why do you think they were used?
5. Why did Ireland play such an important part in the history of transatlantic flights? List two important events in this history.

This table shows the main changes in transport in the twentieth century.

	1900–1930	1930–1970	1970–2000
Getting around in cities and towns	Most people walked everywhere or took horse-drawn cabs or electric trams.	Petrol-driven buses replaced trams. Horse transport becoming rare.	Fewer people walked. Most families got cars. Roads became crowded and dangerous.
Roads	Roads were made with stone and gravel. They were untarred with no signs or markings. In 1909 motor cars were taxed. The money was used to improve roads.	Tarmacadam and concrete gave roads a smooth surface along which cars and lorries could travel quickly. Road signs and traffic lights became common.	Motorways were built. The first motorway was opened in Northern Ireland in the 1960s.
Carrying goods	Most goods were carried in trains or locally in horse-drawn carts.	Trains still carried goods over long distances but lorries replaced horses for local transport.	Huge container lorries carried goods across continents. Horses were no longer used for transport.
Bicycles and cars	Bicycles were newly invented. They were the first cheap transport. Cars were expensive and not reliable. Roads were bad and petrol was hard to find.	Cars became cheaper. Many middle-income people owned a car. Roads improved. The number of garages grew.	Cars became so common that roads became congested and dangerous for cyclists and pedestrians.
Long-distance travel	Trains within Ireland, ships to go abroad. **1903:** First airplane flight. **1919:** First transatlantic flight.	Trains and ships still used but regular passenger-carrying flights began. From the 1950s jet engines made planes faster.	Planes replaced ships for most long journeys. Plane travel became cheap and quick, allowing people to take long-distance holidays.

Review the chapter

1 Picture Source

(i) Look at this photo of Dame Street in Dublin. On which of these dates do you think it was taken?

- ☐ 1900
- ☐ 1930
- ☐ 1970

Tick the right answer.

(ii) Write down the reasons why you chose this date.

2 Why has the number of railway lines been reduced in Ireland in the twentieth century?

3 List six ways in which horses were used in transport and travel in 1900. Why had horse transport almost disappeared by 1970?

4 Write an account of changes in transport in twentieth-century Ireland under these headings: horses, bicycles, roads, cars, trains and planes.

Chapter 5

How Did Communication Change During the Twentieth Century?

The term 'communication' means the way in which people keep in touch with one another. In this chapter we will look at how communication changed between 1900 and 2000.

An early telephone

A telephone around 1950

A modern telephone

Writing letters

The most common way of getting a message to someone in 1900 was to write a letter. A penny stamp on the letter would take it to any part of the United Kingdom. The post was regular and fast. A letter posted anywhere in Ireland reached its destination the next day.

Telegrams

In an emergency, people sent telegrams. These were short messages, tapped out in Morse Code and sent along the telegraph wires to your local post office. From there a 'telegraph boy' carried it to your house. During the two World Wars, news of a soldier's death was sent to his family by telegram. Telegrams were expensive so people kept them short, rather like text messages today. Telegrams stopped being sent when phones became more common in the 1970s.

Telephones

The telephone was invented by Alexander Graham Bell in 1876. The first telephone exchange was opened in Ireland in 1880. In 1900 there were fifty-six exchanges in Ireland but most telephones were in offices. Only rich people had them in their homes.

To make a call, you turned a handle and told the operator what number you wanted. The operator could eavesdrop on your call. The first automatic exchange opened in Dublin in 1927, but manual exchanges survived in places up to the 1980s.

From the 1960s telephones became common in private houses. In the 1990s mobile phones, which could be carried around in your pocket, were invented. In 2000 one person in three had one in Ireland. They also allowed people to send short text-messages to each other.

Radio

Radio was invented by Marconi, whose mother was Irish. In 1902 he set up a radio station in Clifden to transmit signals across the Atlantic. Because radio sent its messages through the air rather than along wires like the telegraph, it was called 'wireless telegraphy'.

Marconi with his first 'wireless telegraphy' machine in 1896

At first it was mainly used to send messages between ships, and between a ship and the shore. Later, 'broadcasting' developed. That meant sending out signals to anyone who happened to be listening.

In Ireland, the first radio station began broadcasting in 1926. It was called 2RN, and changed its name to Radio Éireann in 1937. It broadcast music, news, sports and talks. The government controlled it tightly and gave it very little money. Radios were expensive and many families could not afford one. By 1947 Radio Éireann had only 260,000 listeners.

This 1938 advertisement for radios shows what an important place the radio occupied in people's houses before the TV replaced it in the 1950s.

An early television set. **Do you see how small the screen is?**

Television

Television was invented in Britain. Just before World War II, the BBC began broadcasting TV signals but then suspended it until after the war. In the 1950s Irish people living along the east coast and the border bought TV sets to watch the BBC, and the demand for an Irish TV service grew.

In December 1961 Radio Telefís Éireann (RTE) began. It was an instant success. By 1963 one-third of houses had a television set, and by the 1980s that had risen to 90 per cent. Television changed the way people saw and understood the world.

New ways of communicating

In the 1990s two new forms of communication came into widespread use. One was the fax machine, which sent images over the telephone line. The other was the Internet. Using it people could send and receive messages and images from anywhere in the world.

Internet connection on a laptop through a mobile phone

The first computer, known as the ENIAC, in 1946. It had less computing power then the laptop on the left.

Conclusion

Better communications have brought people all over the world much closer together. In 2000 we know much more about other countries by watching them on TV and in films. This has helped us to understand other people's culture more easily. The world is now often referred to as the 'global village' because of these developments.

Questions

1 List two of the ways in which people could send messages to each other in 1900.
2 What were telegrams? What were they used for?
3 How did the early telephones work?
4 Who invented the radio? What was it first used for?
5 Explain 'broadcasting'. When did broadcasting begin in Ireland ? What was the first station called?
6 When did television come to Ireland?
7 Name three new types of communication that began in the 1990s.

This table shows the main changes in communications in the twentieth century.

	1900–1930	1930–1970	1970–2000
Personal communication	People mostly communicated by letter. Post was fast and reliable. Telegrams were used in emergencies. Phones were rare and mainly in offices.	Letters and telegrams were still popular. Phones were becoming more common.	Phones could be used without going through an operator. There was one in most homes. Faxes, mobile phones, text-messaging and email were invented. Letters became less common.
Mass communication	Radio was newly invented and used for direct communication.	Radio broadcasting spread. **1926:** 2RN opened **1930s:** TV began. **1961:** RTE began. In 1970 most homes had a black and white TV.	Colour TV was invented. More radio stations appeared.

Review the chapter

Name four new means of communication that have developed in the twentieth century.
Which of these have had the biggest impact on people's lives? Give reasons for your answer.

Chapter 6 How Did Work and Leisure Change in the Twentieth Century?

In this chapter we will look at the main changes that have taken place in work and leisure in the twentieth century.

Alexandra Park, Belfast. Parks were a very popular place to visit in the early 1900s. **Why do you think this was so? Why are there not more poor people?**

Less free time

In 1900, working people had much less free time than they have today. People worked very long hours. It was common for shop assistants, for example, to work from 9am until 8pm.

People who worked in factories and shops were entitled to Sunday and one half-day off each week, but they did not get an annual holiday. The only official times off were the Monday bank holidays, which had been introduced in the nineteenth century. In Ireland the biggest group of workers were farmers, and they had no official holidays at all.

Entertainment in the home

Unskilled workers earned so little they could barely afford food and rent and had nothing left over for entertainment. But even middle-income people could not afford to go out much. As a result, most people provided their own entertainment, usually with their neighbours.

- The most common entertainment was visiting a neighbour's house. People sat chatting by the fire, gossiping and exchanging news. Sometimes they played music and sang or played cards or games.
- Wakes and weddings were very important social occasions and in country areas they usually lasted for days.

- Wealthy people held formal balls to which the guests came in evening dress. Usually there would be an orchestra to play for the dances, which went on until dawn. Then the servants cleared up.

A formal ball

Music halls and theatres

Some public entertainments were available in 1900. In the cities many people went to the music halls. The usual entertainment was a 'variety show' that involved many different acts, one after another. They usually included comics, jugglers, acrobats and singers.

From around 1900 music halls began to include a short 'moving picture' with the other acts. Moving pictures (called kinematography) had been invented by two French brothers in 1896. At first, people were satisfied to watch images of trains moving or people walking. But very quickly the moving pictures began to tell short stories.

There were also theatres which put on plays. In Dublin the Abbey Theatre was set up in 1904 to put on Irish plays. Outside the cities, small companies of travelling actors visited towns and villages and put on plays. They were known as 'fit-ups' because they had to fit up a stage at each place they visited.

Sports

Organised sports began in the nineteenth century. Cricket, soccer and rugby were first, but in the 1880s an Irish sporting organisation, the Gaelic Athletic Association (GAA), emerged. It organised inter-parish and inter-county competitions. But the number of people who had time to go to these matches or who could afford the price of a ticket remained small. In 1911, only 10,000 people attended the All-Ireland hurling final.

A Gaelic football match in Carlow in 1941

Questions

1. Why did people have so little leisure time in 1900? Give two reasons.
2. What was the most common form of entertainment?
3. 'People went to music halls around 1900.' True or False?
4. When were 'moving pictures' invented and where were they first shown?
5. What did travelling players do?
6. List the main games played in Ireland around 1900. Why were audiences so small?

A middle-income family gathered around their new household appliance – a gramophone – in 1908. The white rolls on the right were the records. Each played for about three minutes.

How leisure changed

The way people spend their leisure time changed totally over the twentieth century. Here are some of the main changes.

Less home entertainment

Entertainment in the home has changed most of all.

- In the 1920s the 'wireless' became common. People listened to news, sports reports, talks and music. This reduced the opportunity for neighbours to drop in for a nightly gossip.
- In the 1960s televisions became popular. They dominated most living rooms. At first most people had access to only one channel, but in the 1980s multi-channel TV became common.
- In the 1990s computers and the Internet began to appear in homes. People played computer games, surfed the net or 'chatted' with distant people in chat rooms.
- These changes mean that in 2000, people visited neighbours much less than they did in 1900. They do far less to provide their own entertainment. They rely mainly on the electronic media to keep them occupied.

King Kong movie poster from 1933

Films

The first full-time cinema opened in Dublin in 1909. By 1916 there were 149 cinemas around the country. They showed dramatic and romantic stories that thrilled the viewers. Up to 1927 the films were silent. A local pianist played accompanying music as the drama unfolded on the screen. Film stars like Charlie Chaplin and Mary Pickford became household names.

In the 1930s talking pictures arrived. They attracted huge audiences. Many people went to the cinema several times a week. Admission prices were low, and even children could go to the Saturday matinee. Huge cinemas, seating hundreds of people, were built in the cities.

This enthusiasm for films lasted until the 1960s, when competition from TV reduced the size of audiences. In the 1980s the arrival of videos meant that people could watch films in their own homes. Many big cinemas closed down. Others were divided into several smaller cinemas.

Dance halls and popular music

In 1900, people often organised dances in their houses or at crossroads in country areas. In the 1920s dance halls began to appear.

Some Catholic bishops opposed public dancing. Zealous priests smashed dancing platforms or tried to limit the hours they operated. But other priests encouraged the building of parish halls because they gave local people a centre where they could entertain themselves.

Dance halls were most popular between the 1940s and the 1960s. As cars became more common, people could travel long distances to dance to a good band. Showbands like The Dixies and The Bachelors were very popular and attracted big followings. They played the popular tunes that people heard on the radio. **Jazz** and **swing** were popular in the 1940s, and **rock and roll** in the 1950s and 1960s. In the 1970s **discos** began to replace dance halls.

Jazz

Ballroom

Jive

Going on holidays

In 1900 only well-off people went away for a holiday, and only the seriously rich went abroad. For everyone else, a day at the seaside was the best they could hope for. Railway companies provided cheap fares on bank holidays.

This had changed totally by 2000.

- People had far more free time. Most had at least three weeks' paid holidays each year.
- Wages were better. There was money left over after the basic necessities were bought, so people could spend it on leisure.
- In the 1960s airplanes became more common and flying became cheaper. That put foreign holidays within reach of more people than ever before. Others took their cars abroad to tour Europe.
- Some people had the time and money to travel to exotic parts of the world for their annual holidays.

Sports

Sports are more popular now. Up to the 1930s few people were interested, but radio and television broadcasts changed that. Now people can watch their favourite team play at venues on the other side of the world.

As cars became more common, people took less exercise. This increased their interest in sport as a leisure activity. People became members of sports clubs or leisure centres or jog for fun.

The Republic of Ireland soccer team at the 2002 World Cup in Japan

Questions

1. List four ways in which home entertainment has changed since 1900. Do you think this is a good thing or not? Explain your answer.
2. When did the first cinema open in Ireland? What kind of films did it show?
3. Name three styles of popular music in the twentieth century. Say when they were popular.
4. Give three reasons why more people took foreign holidays in 2000 than in 1900.
5. Give one reason why sports have become more popular.

This table shows the main changes in work and leisure in the twentieth century.

	1900–1930	1930–1970	1970–2000
Work	Long working hours and no annual holidays. A twelve-hour working day was common. Low wages left little money to spend on leisure.	After World War II, hours reduced, holiday entitlements extended and wages improved.	An eight-hour working day became the norm. Ireland has become a richer country so there is more time and money for leisure activity.
Entertainment	People made their own entertainments at home – they visited neighbours, played music and games, talked and danced. Occasional visits were made to music halls or travelling shows.	Radio replaced visits. There were cinemas in every town. People went several times a week. Dance halls appeared in many places. Bands played the latest pop music – jazz (1930s), rock 'n roll (1950s), disco (1960s). From the 1960s there was a TV in every house.	Discos replaced dance halls. Many cinemas closed. **1990s**: computer games and Internet.
Holidays	Only the rich could afford foreign holidays.	Better wages and more leisure let more people take holidays, which were mostly spent in Ireland.	Cheap flights allowed most people to go on foreign holidays.
Sports	Team games were common but not many could afford a ticket to go to a match.	Radio and TV broadcasts of matches made sports more popular.	More people watched sports on TV. More people became involved in sports to stay fit.

Review the chapter

1 Make two columns in your copybook. Call one 'Entertainments in 1900'; call the other 'Entertainments not available in 1900'.
Now put the items in this list into the proper column.

1 Cycling	**10** Playing snakes and ladders
2 Going to the theatre	**11** Going on a picnic
3 Playing 'Trivial Pursuit'	**12** Texting friends
4 Going to the cinema	**13** Playing marbles
5 Reading	**14** Listening to the radio
6 Watching TV	**15** Playing football
7 Playing cards	**16** Going for a drive in a car
8 Playing computer games	**17** Doing crossword puzzles
9 Going to the seaside	

2 Write four paragraphs comparing your life today with the life of a person growing up in the 1930s and 1940s. Include:
- the main differences between then and now
- which things you would have enjoyed
- which things you would have found it difficult to live with.

3 Would you say people had more or less time for leisure activities near the start of the twentieth century? Give a reason for your answer.

4 Write an account of the changes that have taken place in leisure-time activities in the twentieth century. Use the summary of changes above as a guideline for your answer.

5 Here are four sources on leisure in the twentieth century. Look at them and then answer the questions below.

Source A

Extract from *Christian Politeness*, a book on etiquette for boys attending Christian Brothers schools in the 1930s.

'Nothing contributes more to exterior dignity and propriety of manners than exactness in preserving the natural position and motions of the body...while standing in the hall, it is exceedingly improper to hum a tune, speak loudly, finger the furniture, or gaze through the windows.'

Source B

Source C

Source D

(i) What do you think the author of Source A would have felt about the young people in Source B?
(ii) What does Source C tell us about seaside fashions in 1900?
(iii) Describe two ways in which people behave differently at the seaside now.
(iv) Use the above sources and anything else you have read in this chapter to describe two ways in which people's behaviour in public has changed since 1900.

Solution to Question 1: Only 1, 2, 4, 5, 7, 9, 10, 11, 13, 15 were possible in 1900.
(Note: The first known crossword puzzle was made up by Arthur Wynne in England in 1913.)

Index